General Prison Board

# Fifth Report of the General Prisons Board, Ireland: 1882-83

with appendices

General Prison Board

**Fifth Report of the General Prisons Board, Ireland: 1882-83**
*with appendices*

ISBN/EAN: 9783741105814

Manufactured in Europe, USA, Canada, Australia, Japa

Cover: Foto ©Suzi / pixelio.de

Manufactured and distributed by brebook publishing software
(www.brebook.com)

General Prison Board

**Fifth Report of the General Prisons Board, Ireland: 1882-83**

# FIFTH REPORT

OF THE

# GENERAL PRISONS BOARD, IRELAND,

## 1882–83;

## WITH APPENDICES.

Presented to both Houses of Parliament by Command of Her Majesty.

DUBLIN:
PRINTED BY ALEX. THOM & CO., 87, 88, & 89, ABBEY-STREET.
THE QUEEN'S PRINTING OFFICE.

To be purchased, either directly or through any Bookseller, from any of the following Agents, viz.:
Messrs. Hansard, 13, Great Queen-street, W.C., and 32, Abingdon-street, Westminster;
Messrs. Eyre and Spottiswoode, East Harding-street, Fleet-street, and Sale Office, House of Lords;
Messrs. Adam and Charles Black, of Edinburgh;
Messrs. Alexander Thom and Co., or Messrs. Hodges, Figgis, and Co., of Dublin.

1883.

[C.—3757.] *Price 9d.*

# CONTENTS.



A 2

# FIFTH REPORT

OF THE

# GENERAL PRISONS BOARD, IRELAND.

---

TO HIS EXCELLENCY JOHN POYNTZ, EARL SPENCER, K.P., K.G.

LORD LIEUTENANT GENERAL AND GENERAL GOVERNOR OF IRELAND.

Dublin Castle, July, 1883.

MAY IT PLEASE YOUR EXCELLENCY,

1. We have the honour to submit, pursuant to statute, this our Fifth Report on the condition of the prisons and prisoners within our jurisdiction, and with respect to the registration of criminals, during the year ending March 31st, 1883. 40 & 41 Vic., cap. 49, sec. 15.

## I.—LOCAL PRISONS.

2. In our last report we had occasion to describe in detail the nature of the various arrangements we had been called upon to make in carrying out the provisions of the Act for "The better Protection of Person and Property in Ireland."

This Act, which came into operation on the 2nd March, 1881, having expired on the 30th September last, we were enabled at that date to restore to their normal condition the several prisons, twelve in number, which it had been found necessary to appropriate, either wholly or partly, to the custody of the prisoners committed under its provisions, as well as to discontinue the services of the large extra staff with which, as already explained, it had been found necessary to supplement the number of officers required to meet the ordinary exigencies of the service. 44 Vic., cap. 4.

3. We were enabled last year to announce the then approaching completion of the works which had been for a considerable time in progress at Maryborough for the conversion, by convict labour, of a part of the local prison there into an "invalid convict prison," for the reception of such convicts as were found to be unfitted by reason of constitutional delicacy, or mental or physical infirmity to bear the restraints and more rigid discipline of ordinary prison life. Maryborough Invalid Convict Prison.

We have on the present occasion the satisfaction of reporting, for your Excellency's information, that this arrangement has been since carried into practical effect, and with, so far as our present experience enables us to speak, the very best results in every way.

We stated that the intended accommodation for this class was estimated for fifty, and the number at the present time found eligible for the purpose is, we may observe, forty-three, or seven less than the maximum number provided for.

It has been found perfectly practicable, under the arrangements at Maryborough, to employ a large number of this class at certain descriptions of light, out-door daily labour, and this has been, we are glad to know, attended, besides other advantages, with the most beneficial effects as regards the health and general conduct of the convicts concerned.

**Execution of works of reconstruction and repair, &c. &c.**

4. In Table XVIII. will be found the usual detail of the numerous works and repairs undertaken during the past year, under the supervision of our architect, in connexion with the several prisons.

**Proposed additional buildings, &c., &c.**

These several works, though exceedingly valuable in themselves were none of them, taken singly, it will be observed, of a large or comprehensive character, but it is proposed during the ensuing year to proceed in the erection of some very important additions and other structural works in connexion with the Convict Prison of Mountjoy, and also at the Local Prisons of Cork, Galway, and Tralee respectively, to each of which a party of convicts has been recently transferred from Spike Island Prison, with a view to this object.

**Drogheda Prison.**

5. In our Second Report, par. 19, we explained that the Local Prison at Drogheda had been then converted by us, as a tentative measure, into an exclusively Female Prison, and in our Third Report, par. 12, we expressed the hope that, owing to the small number of female prisoners committed to it, we should soon be in a position to recommend its discontinuance.

This purpose we have during the past year felt ourselves enabled to carry out, and accordingly Drogheda has been since the 30th December last added to the number of our "Minor Prisons"—that is of prisons having only the same status as "Certified Bridewells"—and to which only prisoners on remand or convicted prisoners whose sentences do not exceed a term of seven days, are committed.

**Bridewells.**

6. At the date of our last Report the number of Bridewells then remaining in existence, out of a total of 93 originally transferred to the Board, had been reduced to 34, and during the present year this has been further reduced to 33, consequent on the closing of that of Baltinglass, county Wicklow.

**Prison punishments.**

7. We were enabled in our last Report to refer to Table X. as indicating a diminution in the number of prison punishments, as compared with the return for the previous year, and as affecting male and female prisoners both alike.

This year it will be observed with satisfaction that a still larger diminution is exhibited—the number for each of the last three years respectively being:—

| Year. | Number Punished. | | |
|---|---|---|---|
| | Males. | Females. | Total. |
| 1882–83, | [illegible] | [illegible] | [illegible] |
| 1881–82, | [illegible] | [illegible] | [illegible] |
| 1880–81, | [illegible] | [illegible] | [illegible] |

8. In the Appendix A, Tables IX. and X., will be found the usual educational statistics in regard to the commitments to the larger prisons, and which do not this year appear to present any features calling for special observation. **Educational Statistics.**

The number of "wholly illiterate" prisoners, as shown in last year's report, was 13,833, out of a total of 33,968 commitments, as against this year 12,377, out of 33,440—and the number that received school instruction during the past year was 1,776, as against 1,870 for the year preceding.

9. In referring to par. 15 in our Third Report, and par. 19 in our Report of last year, dealing with the subject of the various industries pursued in the different local prisons, and the particulars of which will be found detailed as usual in Appendix A, we have the honour to here submit a comparative statement showing the actual profits realised during each of the years ended 31st March, 1883 and 1882 respectively, and from which it will be seen that though, owing to special causes, some falling off is exhibited in this, as compared with the previous year's return, the amount yielded is still very satisfactory, showing as it does the substantial net profit of £5,085 5s. 7d. on the operations of the year, viz:— **Industrial Labour.**

| | Year 1882–83. | | | Year 1881–82. | | |
|---|---|---|---|---|---|---|
| | £ | s. | d. | £ | s. | d. |
| Profit realised on Manufactures, | [illegible] | 5 | 11 | [illegible] | [illegible] | [illegible] |
| Do. Farm and Garden, | 1,111 | 5 | 10 | [illegible] | 5 | 6 |
| Total profit on productive services, | [illegible] | 11 | 9 | [illegible] | 5 | [illegible] |
| Extra receipts, | [illegible] | 18 | 10 | [illegible] | 4 | 10 |
| Total payable to the Exchequer, | 5,085 | 5 | 7 | [illegible] | [illegible] | [illegible] |

10. In Appendix A, Table XI., will be found the usual particulars relating to the offences and commitments of prisoners not exceeding sixteen years of age. **Juvenile Offenders.**

It will be observed that the number of convictions under this head shows an increase of more than thirty over the returns for the previous year; this increase being, however, confined to the classes of male juveniles—the females showing on the contrary a tendency in the opposite direction.

The following are the figures bearing on this point, viz.:—

| Year. | Number of Commitments. | | |
|---|---|---|---|
| | Males. | Females. | Total. |
| 1882–83, | [illegible] | [illegible] | [illegible] |
| 1881–82, | [illegible] | [illegible] | [illegible] |

11. In our Third Report, par. 17, we took occasion, as a matter for congratulation, to observe on the gradual decline which, even under adverse circumstances, the statistics indicated, in the yearly **Number of commitments to Prison.**

number of commitments to the Local Prisons, which we considered might fairly be in a great measure attributed to the influence of the stricter and more uniform system of penal discipline to which the criminal classes were now, under existing arrangements, everywhere subject to while undergoing imprisonment.

The following are the figures as to this for each of the last five years, viz. :—

| Year. | No. of Commitments. | Year. | No. of Commitments. |
|---|---|---|---|
| 1882–83, . . . | 35,471 | 1879–80, . . . | 44,[illegible] |
| 1881–82, . . . | 41,[illegible] | 1878–79, . . . | 44,[illegible] |
| 1880–81, . . . | 40,197 | | |

From this return it will be seen that the commitments for last year fall below those for the year immediately preceding it by 5,054—while, as compared with the first year of the series, viz., that of 1876–79, the reduction is still more striking, amounting to no less than 9,864, or considerably more than one-fifth of the total number of commitments for that year.

Abstracts.

12. Following up the practice pursued by us in our four previous reports, we here submit three abstracts, the two first dealing with the numbers in custody at certain recurring dates in all the local prisons of Ireland from 1851 to 1883, and the third showing the number of commitments and the daily average number in custody during each year from 1854 to 1883, viz. :—

Numbers in custody on the 1st January in each of the last 33 years.

No. 1.—Number of Prisoners (of all Classes) in County and Borough Gaols on the 1st January in each year at unlock.

| | | | | | | | |
|---|---|---|---|---|---|---|---|
| On 1st January, | 1851, | . | 10,084 | On 1st January, | 1868, | . | 2,463 |
| Do. do. | 1852, | . | 8,603 | Do. do. | 1869, | . | [illegible] |
| Do. do. | 1853, | . | 7,404 | Do. do. | 1870, | . | [illegible] |
| Do. do. | 1854, | . | 5,755 | Do. do. | 1871, | . | 3,161 |
| Do. do. | 1855, | . | 5,080 | Do. do. | 1872, | . | [illegible] |
| Do. do. | 1856, | . | 3,601 | Do. do. | 1873, | . | [illegible] |
| Do. do. | 1857, | . | 3,419 | Do. do. | 1874, | . | [illegible] |
| Do. do. | 1858, | . | 3,285 | Do. do. | 1875, | . | [illegible] |
| Do. do. | 1859, | . | 2,844 | Do. do. | 1876, | . | [illegible] |
| Do. do. | 1860, | . | 2,838 | Do. do. | 1877, | . | [illegible] |
| Do. do. | 1861, | . | [illegible] | Do. do. | 1878, | . | [illegible] |
| Do. do. | 1862, | . | 2,916 | Do. do. | 1879, | . | 3,407 |
| Do. do. | 1863, | . | 3,088 | Do. do. | 1880, | . | [illegible] |
| Do. do. | 1864, | . | 3,023 | Do. do. | 1881, | . | [illegible] |
| Do. do. | 1865, | . | 2,747 | Do. do. | 1882, | . | [illegible] |
| Do. do. | 1866, | . | 2,663 | Do. do. | 1883, | . | [illegible] |
| Do. do. | 1867, | | 2,333 | | | | |

[No. 2.

No. 2.—Return of the Numbers (of ordinary Prisoners, all Classes) in Gaols on the 1st day of each Month in the Years as under:— Monthly return of prisoners in custody last 33 years.

| Year | Jan. | Feb. | March | April | May | June | July | August | Sept. | Oct. | Nov. | Dec. |
|---|---|---|---|---|---|---|---|---|---|---|---|---|
| 1851, | [illegible] | [illegible] | [illegible] | [illegible] | [illegible] | [illegible] | [illegible] | [illegible] | [illegible] | [illegible] | [illegible] | [illegible] |
| 1852, | [illegible] | [illegible] | [illegible] | [illegible] | [illegible] | [illegible] | [illegible] | [illegible] | [illegible] | [illegible] | [illegible] | [illegible] |
| 1853, | [illegible] | [illegible] | [illegible] | [illegible] | [illegible] | [illegible] | [illegible] | [illegible] | [illegible] | [illegible] | [illegible] | [illegible] |
| 1854, | [illegible] | [illegible] | [illegible] | [illegible] | [illegible] | [illegible] | [illegible] | [illegible] | [illegible] | [illegible] | [illegible] | [illegible] |
| 1855, | [illegible] | [illegible] | [illegible] | [illegible] | [illegible] | [illegible] | [illegible] | [illegible] | [illegible] | [illegible] | [illegible] | [illegible] |
| 1856, | [illegible] | [illegible] | [illegible] | [illegible] | [illegible] | [illegible] | [illegible] | [illegible] | [illegible] | [illegible] | [illegible] | [illegible] |
| 1857, | [illegible] | [illegible] | [illegible] | [illegible] | [illegible] | [illegible] | [illegible] | [illegible] | [illegible] | [illegible] | [illegible] | [illegible] |
| 1858, | [illegible] | [illegible] | [illegible] | [illegible] | [illegible] | [illegible] | [illegible] | [illegible] | [illegible] | [illegible] | [illegible] | [illegible] |
| 1859, | [illegible] | [illegible] | [illegible] | [illegible] | [illegible] | [illegible] | [illegible] | [illegible] | [illegible] | [illegible] | [illegible] | [illegible] |
| 1860, | [illegible] | [illegible] | [illegible] | [illegible] | [illegible] | [illegible] | [illegible] | [illegible] | [illegible] | [illegible] | [illegible] | [illegible] |
| 1861, | [illegible] | [illegible] | [illegible] | [illegible] | [illegible] | [illegible] | [illegible] | [illegible] | [illegible] | [illegible] | [illegible] | [illegible] |
| 1862, | [illegible] | [illegible] | [illegible] | [illegible] | [illegible] | [illegible] | [illegible] | [illegible] | [illegible] | [illegible] | [illegible] | [illegible] |
| 1863, | [illegible] | [illegible] | [illegible] | [illegible] | [illegible] | [illegible] | [illegible] | [illegible] | [illegible] | [illegible] | [illegible] | [illegible] |
| 1864, | [illegible] | [illegible] | [illegible] | [illegible] | [illegible] | [illegible] | [illegible] | [illegible] | [illegible] | [illegible] | [illegible] | [illegible] |
| 1865, | [illegible] | [illegible] | [illegible] | [illegible] | [illegible] | [illegible] | [illegible] | [illegible] | [illegible] | [illegible] | [illegible] | [illegible] |
| 1866, | [illegible] | [illegible] | [illegible] | [illegible] | [illegible] | [illegible] | [illegible] | [illegible] | [illegible] | [illegible] | [illegible] | [illegible] |
| 1867, | [illegible] | [illegible] | [illegible] | [illegible] | [illegible] | [illegible] | [illegible] | [illegible] | [illegible] | [illegible] | [illegible] | [illegible] |
| 1868, | [illegible] | [illegible] | [illegible] | [illegible] | [illegible] | [illegible] | [illegible] | [illegible] | [illegible] | [illegible] | [illegible] | [illegible] |
| 1869, | [illegible] | [illegible] | [illegible] | [illegible] | [illegible] | [illegible] | [illegible] | [illegible] | [illegible] | [illegible] | [illegible] | [illegible] |
| 1870, | [illegible] | [illegible] | [illegible] | [illegible] | [illegible] | [illegible] | [illegible] | [illegible] | [illegible] | [illegible] | [illegible] | [illegible] |
| 1871, | [illegible] | [illegible] | [illegible] | [illegible] | [illegible] | [illegible] | [illegible] | [illegible] | [illegible] | [illegible] | [illegible] | [illegible] |
| 1872, | [illegible] | [illegible] | [illegible] | [illegible] | [illegible] | [illegible] | [illegible] | [illegible] | [illegible] | [illegible] | [illegible] | [illegible] |
| 1873, | [illegible] | [illegible] | [illegible] | [illegible] | [illegible] | [illegible] | [illegible] | [illegible] | [illegible] | [illegible] | [illegible] | [illegible] |
| 1874, | [illegible] | [illegible] | [illegible] | [illegible] | [illegible] | [illegible] | [illegible] | [illegible] | [illegible] | [illegible] | [illegible] | [illegible] |
| 1875, | [illegible] | [illegible] | [illegible] | [illegible] | [illegible] | [illegible] | [illegible] | [illegible] | [illegible] | [illegible] | [illegible] | [illegible] |
| 1876, | [illegible] | [illegible] | [illegible] | [illegible] | [illegible] | [illegible] | [illegible] | [illegible] | [illegible] | [illegible] | [illegible] | [illegible] |
| 1877, | [illegible] | [illegible] | [illegible] | [illegible] | [illegible] | [illegible] | [illegible] | [illegible] | [illegible] | [illegible] | [illegible] | [illegible] |
| 1878, | [illegible] | [illegible] | [illegible] | [illegible] | [illegible] | [illegible] | [illegible] | [illegible] | [illegible] | [illegible] | [illegible] | [illegible] |
| 1879, | [illegible] | [illegible] | [illegible] | [illegible] | [illegible] | [illegible] | [illegible] | [illegible] | [illegible] | [illegible] | [illegible] | [illegible] |
| 1880, | [illegible] | [illegible] | [illegible] | [illegible] | [illegible] | [illegible] | [illegible] | [illegible] | [illegible] | [illegible] | [illegible] | [illegible] |
| 1881,* | [illegible] | [illegible] | [illegible] | [illegible] | [illegible] | [illegible] | [illegible] | [illegible] | [illegible] | [illegible] | [illegible] | [illegible] |
| 1882,* | [illegible] | [illegible] | [illegible] | [illegible] | [illegible] | [illegible] | [illegible] | [illegible] | [illegible] | [illegible] | [illegible] | [illegible] |
| 1883, | [illegible] | [illegible] | [illegible] | .. | .. | .. | .. | .. | .. | .. | .. | .. |

No. 3.—Committals (exclusive of Debtors) in the Twenty-nine Years ended 31st March, 1883. Number of committals, daily average, &c.

| Years. | Number of Committals. | Daily Average No. of Prisoners. | Years. | Number of Committals. | Daily Average No. of Prisoners. |
|---|---|---|---|---|---|
| 1854, | 52,445 | 4,700·9 | 1869, | 30,878 | 3,183·8 |
| 1855, | 46,481 | 4,410·3 | 1870, | 32,272 | 3,271·1 |
| 1856, | 40,712 | 3,387·7 | 1871, | 35,139 | 3,234·9 |
| 1857, | 34,686 | 2,953·4 | 1872, | 36,259 | 3,238 |
| 1858, | 33,298 | 2,694·8 | 1873, | 32,804 | 3,070 |
| 1859, | 32,343 | 2,500·1 | 1874, | 38,483 | 2,770 |
| 1860, | 31,712 | 2,623·1 | 1875, | 36,383 | 2,741 |
| 1861, | 32,567 | 2,491·8 | 1876, | 43,917 | 2,896 |
| 1862, | 33,530 | 2,583·8 | 1877, | 46,411 | 2,996 |
| 1863, | 33,348 | [illegible] | 1878-79* | 46,287 | 3,025 |
| 1864, | 33,070 | 2,313·7 | 1879-80* | 44,758 | 2,812 |
| 1865, | 32,731 | 2,218·8 | 1880-81* | 40,182 | 2,690 |
| 1866, | 29,097 | 2,358·5 | 1881-82* | 41,366 | 3,111 |
| 1867, | 30,067 | 2,540·5 | 1882-83* | 45,454 | 3,025 |
| 1868, | 33,591 | 2,180·5 | | | |

* To 31st March.

18. The following Table, which exhibits the number confined in the Bridewells from 1850 to 1883, will shew that the progressive Bridewell statistics.

* Exclusive of Prisoners committed under P. P. P. Act, 44 Vic., cap. 4.

reduction in numbers observed in the returns of previous years has been this year not quite maintained, though the fluctuation is inconsiderable.

No. Confined in Bridewells.

| Years. | | Years. | |
|---|---|---|---|
| 1850 | 62,[illegible] | 1867 | 16,6[illegible] |
| 1851 | 55,080 | 1868 | 14,137 |
| 1852 | 53,[illegible] | 1869 | 16,610 |
| 1853 | 56,[illegible] | 1870 | 13,601 |
| 1854 | 48,356 | 1871 | 10,[illegible] |
| 1855 | 38,003 | 1872 | 7,622 |
| 1856 | 33,584 | 1873 | 5,789 |
| 1857 | 31,004 | 1874 | 6,704 |
| 1858 | 27,424 | 1875 | 6,368 |
| 1859 | 25,196 | 1876 | 4,669 |
| 1860 | 22,421 | 1877 | 5,578 |
| 1861 | 20,156 | 1878–79* | 4,256 |
| 1862 | 22,064 | 1879–80* | 4,247 |
| 1863 | 21,053 | 1880–81* | 3,658 |
| 1864 | 20,563 | 1881–82* | 3,510 |
| 1865 | 20,556 | 1882–83* | 3,913 |
| 1866 | 18,417 | | |

14. We beg to refer to the Appendix A for the detailed reports furnished by the respective governors as to the several local prisons, and which show, in regard to each separately, the daily average number of prisoners, employed and unemployed, the description of their employments, the net profit realised on the work done, and the estimated value of the work done for the prisons.

## II.—Convict Prisons.

15. The accommodation afforded for convicts by the four Convict Prisons on the 1st of January, 1883, may be still estimated, as last year, at 1,070, and the number in custody at that date was:—

| | Male. | Female. | Total. |
|---|---|---|---|
| In Convict Prisons, | 763 | 104 | 867 |
| In Local Prisons, | 31 | – | 31 |
| Gross total of Convicts in Custody on 1st January, | 794 | 104 | 898 |

16. The number of Convicts sentenced to Penal Servitude during the year ending 31st March, 1883, was:—

| | Males. | Females. | Total. |
|---|---|---|---|
| 5 years, | 173 | 19 | 192 |
| 7 " | 33 | 8 | 41 |
| 8 " | 1 | – | 1 |
| 10 " | 21 | – | 21 |
| 15 " | 4 | – | 4 |
| 20 " | 4 | – | 4 |
| 30 " | 1 | – | 1 |
| Life, | 14 | 2 | 16 |
| Gross Total sentenced during year, | 251 | 29 | *280 |

* Fifty-five of these were military convicts.

Disposal of Convicts during the year ending 31st March, 1863.

I.—No. discharged from Prisons:—

| | M. | F. | Total. |
|---|---|---|---|
| On Orders of Licence to be at large, | 98 | 19 | 117 |
| On Commutation of Sentence, | 3 | – | 3 |
| On Completion of Sentences, | 20 | 5 | 25 |
| | 121 | 24 | 145 |

II.—No. of Females discharged from Refuges:—

| | M. | F. | Total. |
|---|---|---|---|
| On Orders of Licence to be at large, | – | 38 | 38 |
| No. discharged from Prisons and Refuges during the year, | 121 | 62 | 183 |

Of the above number discharged during the year 8 males and 3 females had previously been released on licence under the same sentences, but had forfeited their licence and been recommitted to Prison.

Sixteen female convicts were transferred from Prison to Refuges during the year.

The number of female convicts in Refuges during the year ending 31st March, 1863, was 56. Of these 15 had undergone previous sentences of penal servitude, and 8 of them had been previously in Refuges.

17. The Revocations and Forfeitures of Licences in Ireland during the year ended 31st March, 1863, were as follow:—

| | Males. | Females. | Total. |
|---|---|---|---|
| Forfeited or revoked for breach of conditions of Licence, | 1 | – | 1 |
| Forfeited or revoked in consequence of a conviction for other offences, | 16 | 8 | 24* |
| Gross Total, | 17 | 8 | 25* |

18. Subjoined is a table showing the number of Convicts respectively in "Custody," "Convicted," and "Discharged," since the year 1854.

* Three of them were English Licence Holders.

[TABLE.

TABLE showing the number of Convicts in "Custody," "Convicted," and "Discharged," since the year 1854, inclusive.

| In custody in Convict Prisons, January 1st. | Year. | Convicted. | No. Discharged. |
|---|---|---|---|
| *3,933 | 1854 | 710 | 656 |
| 3,427 | 1855 | 818 | 820 |
| 3,209 | 1856 | 389 | 1,107 |
| 2,614 | 1857 | 425 | 910 |
| 2,277 | 1858 | 258 | 946 |
| 1,778 | 1859 | 323 | 505 |
| 1,631 | 1860 | 331 | 594 |
| 1,492 | 1861 | 358 | 561 |
| 1,314 | 1862 | 502 | 517 |
| 1,375 | 1863 | 511 | 526 |
| 1,703 | 1864 | 407 | 391 |
| 1,770 | 1865 | 399 | 410 |
| 1,637 | 1866 | 285 | 430 |
| 1,481 | 1867 | 290 | 330 |
| 1,338 | 1868 | 346 | 345 |
| 1,325 | 1869 | 191 | 291 |
| 1,230 | 1870 | 248 | 253 |
| 1,276 | 1871 | 219 | 253 |
| 1,120 | 1872 | 201 | 255 |
| 1,143 | 1873 | 236 | 250 |
| 1,122 | 1874 | 271 | 270 |
| 1,103 | 1875 | 241 | 254 |
| 1,128 | 1876 | 182 | 195 |
| 1,125 | 1877 | 188 | 243 |
| 1,114 | 1878 | 184 | 280 |
| †969 | 1879-80 | 154 | 274 |
| †911 | 1880-81 | 183 | 236 |
| †739 | 1881-82 | 209 | 242 |
| †757 | 1882-83 | ‡320 | 169 |
| †696 | 1883 | | |

Condition and working of Prisons.

19. To the Appendix B, we beg to refer for the usual reports and returns relating to the four Convict Prisons of Mountjoy, male, Mountjoy, female, Spike Island, and Lusk, and which will be found to furnish very full information as to the condition and general working of each.

Insubordination at Spike Island.

20. Towards the close of January last, we regret to report, it became our duty to deal with a most unusual occurrence, and what, for a short time, threatened to prove a serious outbreak of insubordination and violence on the part of some of the convict prisoners then undergoing sentence at Spike Island.

The circumstances, however, having been promptly inquired into on the spot by Captain Barlow, who at once proceeded to

* In addition to this number there were 343 convicts under detention in the county prisons, and several hundreds in Bermuda and Gibraltar, who were subsequently discharged in Ireland.

† In addition to these numbers, 44, 30, 90, 47 and 31 convicts were in Local Prisons on 1st January, '79, '80, '81, '82, and '83 respectively.

‡ Fifty-five of these were military convicts.

the Island for that purpose, and the Board, acting on the results of Captain Barlow's investigation, having awarded to the several principal offenders such punishment as the circumstances of each case appeared to call for, the spirit of disorder which had so unexpectedly manifested itself amongst them was speedily and effectually quelled, and has not been since followed by any attempt to revive it.

Spike Island Prison.

21. In each of our three last reports we had occasion to urge, as strongly as we could, the importance of discontinuing this prison, the entire unsuitability of which for its purpose, in several essential particulars, had been long conceded upon all hands; the difficulty experienced in dealing with the question being, in fact, confined to agreeing on a proper substitute for it elsewhere.

Since the date of our last report, however, this difficulty has, we are most happy to say, been solved by the "interim report," made on the 15th February, by the Royal Commission recently appointed by your Excellency to inquire generally into the Irish Prison system.

Surrender to Military.

In conformity with their recommendation, we are now at length in a position to report the total disuse of Spike Island for convict purposes, and the final surrender of it to the military authorities.

Difficulties experienced.

22. The difficulties encountered by us in at once carrying out the necessary arrangements have, however, been very formidable; nor can we even now venture to think that they have been by any means as yet surmounted; as it is obvious that, without any Public Works Prison at our command, continuous and suitable outdoor employment for the large body of convicts now concentrated at Mountjoy will not be at all times easily insured by any arrangement open to us to adopt.

Neither, we would observe, in addition to the foregoing consideration, can we disguise from ourselves the further fact that the bringing together of so large a number of convicts on the limited space available at Mountjoy, must be always attended with more or less risk of leading to combinations unfavourable to discipline on the part of the prisoners.

Royal Commission.

The Royal Commission, however—recognising, no doubt, the paramount importance of discontinuing Spike Island, at all hazards—having strenuously urged that some means of even temporarily absorbing the convicts located there, should be at once devised by us, we have, to the utmost of our power, endeavoured to second their wishes on this head, and we trust that for some time to come at least, the several arrangements made, if not in all respects everything that could be desired, will still sufficiently meet the more pressing exigencies of the case.

23. At the date when the discontinuance of Spike Island Prison was finally agreed upon the number of Convicts confined there, and for whom some other provision had then to be immediately devised, was 445—a number since entirely absorbed, in part by the transfer of the invalid class to Maryborough, and the working parties sent, as already described, to certain Local Prisons, but chiefly by the conversion of Mountjoy Female Prison, which

Par. 4.

contains 364 cells, into a Male Prison, and the removal of the Female Convicts to Grangegorman Local Prison—which has now been constituted an exclusively Female Prison—one side being appropriated to the Convict Class, and the other being still made use of as a Local Prison, for the Female commitments from the county and city of Dublin, &c.

New Public Works Prison.

We cannot, however, too strongly urge that these arrangements cannot at best be regarded as supplying more than a temporary palliative, and that the selection of some suitable site for a properly constructed public works prison in substitution for that of Spike Island, still remains to be dealt with, as a necessity of the Irish prison system.

Select Class.

24. The Report of 1879 of the Commissioners appointed to inquire into the working of the Penal Servitude Acts, amongst the several other important conclusions arrived at by them, recommended, it will be observed, as follows, viz.:—

"That in order to prevent contamination of the less hardened convicts by old and habitual offenders, a separate class should be formed (subject to the exceptions we have mentioned) of convicts against whom no previous conviction of any kind is known to have been recorded."

And in a preceding part of their Report—par. 78, p. 29—the exceptions referred to in this extract are thus described:—

"Besides those whose removal might be necessary on account of their misconduct in prison, or who were found to be actually exercising a pernicious influence on their companions, prisoners who have committed certain crimes, although not known to have been previously convicted, would be obviously unfit to be placed in such a class. For example, a receiver of stolen goods who had escaped conviction during a long career of crime, when at length made amenable to justice, would be the last man whom it would be desirable to place in contact with the younger and less hardened offenders. Men guilty of unnatural crimes and indecency should also, of course, not be admitted into this class."

25. Fully appreciating the great practical value of such a classification as that referred to in the extracts we have quoted, we took the necessary steps for giving effect to the recommendation of the Commissioners at the earliest possible period. A Select Class, taken from the Prisoners not previously convicted, was accordingly, before the close of 1880, established in the Mountjoy Male and Female Prisons respectively—and at Spike Island a similar arrangement was completed in 1882.

There are at the present time 32 Male, and 17 Female Prisoners included in these Selected Classes, and no doubt can be entertained that the change has proved in every way a most valuable improvement.

## III.—Registration of Criminals.

Alphabetical Register.

26. To the Appendix C to this Report we beg to refer Your Excellency for the usual statistical tables relating to the registration of criminals.

In our two last reports we took occasion to explain fully the circumstances under which the preparation of a complete "Alphabetical Register of Habitual Criminals" had been undertaken and concluded under our direction, and we at the same time described the steps we had taken for the purpose of practically utilising the compilation by the extensive circulation of it amongst the proper authorities, both in Ireland and Great Britain.

27. We have referred in previous reports to the great reduction in the number of habitual criminals annually registered and photographed, which had been effected since 1876, by the operation of the "Prevention of Crimes Act Amendment Act" of that year—39 & 40 V., c. 23,—and it will be seen from the subjoined table that a still further tendency in this direction is indicated by the return for the last year, viz.:— Number Annually Registered.

RETURN showing the Number of Habitual Criminals registered in:—

| Year. | No. | Year. | No. |
|---|---|---|---|
| 1870, . . . | 861 | 1878, . . | 179 |
| 1871, . . . | 1,0[illegible] | 1879, . . | 185 |
| 1872, . . . | 840 | 1880, . . . | 174 |
| 1873, . . . | 1,116 | From 1st April, 1880, to 31st March, 1881, . | [illegible] |
| 1874, . . . | 1,[illegible] | Year ended 31/3/82, . | 794 |
| 1875, . . . | [illegible] | " 31/3/83, . | 154 |
| 1876, . . . | [illegible] | | |
| 1877, . . . | [illegible] | | |

## IV.—DEPARTMENTAL ARRANGEMENTS.

28. We have no departmental changes to report during the past year.

The services of our architect, referred to in our last report, have been temporarily continued to us. The question of his permanent retention, as recommended by us, as well as several kindred questions affecting the staff arrangements of some of our local prisons, have been deferred by the Government pending the result of the Inquiry of the Royal Commissioners. Architect. Local Prison Staff.

29. But though, as just stated, we have this year no change to record in the ordinary arrangements of our Head Office, several very important reductions and transfers, &c., have recently been effected by us amongst the staff both of our Convict and Local Prison Officers, following on the discontinuance of the establishment at Spike Island, and the consequent redistribution of the prison population which that proceeding necessarily and in several directions involved. Reduction of Convict and Local Prison Staff, &c., &c.

30. These changes have been now, we are glad to be in a position to report, finally completed. They were only decided upon by us after the fullest and most careful consideration, and were made, in every instance, in the strictest conformity with what a due regard for the interest of the public service seemed to us to suggest.

V.—Appendix.

31. We refer to the Appendices hereto,—A B C D and E, for the usual statistical and other information which it has been our practice to submit with each annual report.

We have the honour to be

Your Excellency's obedient, faithful servants,

CHARLES F. BOURKE, *Chairman.*
J. BARLOW, *Vice-Chairman.*
W. P. O'BRIEN.

JOHN LENTAIGNE, *Hon. Member.*

# APPENDICES

TO

## FIFTH REPORT OF GENERAL PRISONS BOARD IRELAND, FOR THE YEAR 1882–83.

---

Circular No. 330.

General Prisons Board, Dublin Castle,
5th April, 1882.

The Governors, H. M. Prisons.

The General Prisons Board desire that in future when replying to references from this office, you will write your report on a separate sheet of paper, and in no case are such reports to be written on the original file which should accompany report.

By Order,

Richard Clegg, Chief Clerk.

---

### Military Prisoners.

Circular No. 331.
9116/82.

General Prisons Board, Dublin Castle,
13th April, 1882.

To Bridewell Keepers,

You are hereby informed that it will be your duty from time to time to receive into your custody any Military Offenders, whether tried or untried, that may be committed to the Bridewell under your charge by the Commanding Officer in the district.

Should any difficulty arise from the commitment of such class of Offenders you will, at once, report the circumstance for the information of the Prisons Board, if necessary, by telegram.

By order,

Richard Clegg, Chief Clerk.

---

Circular No. 332.
7407/82.

General Prisons Board, Dublin Castle,
14th April, 1882.

The Governors, H. M. Local Prisons.

During the summer months visits to prisoners of all classes are to be permitted on every week-day between the hours of 10 a.m. and 3 p.m., and in the winter months between the hours of 10 a.m. and 2.30 p.m.—the dinner hour excepted in both cases.

By order,

Richard Clegg, Chief Clerk.

**9398.**

General Prisons Board, Dublin Castle,
CIRCULAR MEMO. 14th April, 1882.

I am directed by the General Prisons Board to request that when submitting applications for leave of absence to this office for approval you will forward therewith a detailed statement, signed by you, showing the leave of absence granted to the person applying during the preceding twelve months.

RICHARD CLEGG, Chief Clerk.

The Governors, H. M. Prisons.

---

Circular No. 233.
9,229.

General Prisons Board, Dublin Castle,
18th April, 1882.

SIR,—I am directed by the General Prisons Board to apprise you that they consider that Medical Officers of Prisons should attend at the Gaols not later than twelve noon.

Please inform the Medical Officer accordingly.

I am, sir, your obedient servant,

RICHARD CLEGG, Chief Clerk.

The Governors, H. M. Prisons.

---

**AMENDED RULES as to DISCIPLINE and DIETARY of PRISONERS in CUSTODY under sentences for consecutive terms of IMPRISONMENT.**

Circular No. 234.

General Prisons Board, Dublin Castle,
2nd May, 1882.

SIR,—I am directed by the General Prisons Board to send you for your information and guidance a copy of the above Rules, and to inform you that His Excellency the Lord Lieutenant has approved of their being put into operation at once.

Please inform the Medical Officer as to these Rules and as to His Excellency's sanction for their immediate adoption.

I am, Sir, your obedient servant,

RICHARD CLEGG, Chief Clerk.

To the Governors, H. M. Prisons.

---

BY THE GENERAL PRISONS BOARD FOR IRELAND.

In pursuance of the General Prisons (Ireland) Act, 1877, the General Prisons Board hereby make the following Amended Rules for the government of Prisons:—

I. Addendum to Rule 24 (General Rules for the government of Prisons):

For the purposes of this rule, a prisoner in custody under sentences for consecutive terms of imprisonment which in the aggregate exceed one month shall be considered as a prisoner whose sentence exceeds one month.

II. Addendum to Rule 33:

The word "sentence" in this rule includes the period, or the aggregate of the periods, during which a male prisoner above 16 years of age sentenced to hard labour is to be retained in custody, whether under one, or more than one, committal.

III. Dietaries for Local Prisons:

The word "term" in schedule to "Rules for the Dietaries of Local Prisons in Ireland" shall include the period, or aggregate of the periods, during which a convicted prisoner is to be retained in custody, whether under one, or more than one, committal.

The foregoing rules shall apply to the prisoners confined in every ordinary prison, and shall come into operation upon the expiration of forty days after the same, having been settled and approved by the Lord Lieutenant, or Lords Justices and Privy Council, shall have been laid before Parliament.

Made and executed this 6th day of April, 1882, by "The General Prisons Board for Ireland."

J. Barlow, Vice-Chairman.

[Seal.

---

By the Lord Lieutenant and Privy Council of Ireland.

Cowper.

In pursuance of the General Prisons (Ireland) Act, 1877, We, Francis Thomas De Grey, Earl Cowper, Lord Lieutenant-General and General Governor of Ireland, with the approval, advice, and consent of the Privy Council of Ireland, have settled and hereby approve of the foregoing rules made by the General Prisons Board for Ireland.

Given at the Council Chamber, Dublin Castle, this 20th day of April, 1882.

H. Law, C. Belmore.
Leinster. Henry Ormsby.

---

General Prisons Board, Dublin Castle,
4th May, 1882.

Circular Memorandum.

Referring to Circular No. 170, I am directed by the General Prisons Board to inform you that in cases where application for an officer's increment is not submitted a month before the time for such becoming due, the Board will consider the propriety of refusing to consider such case for that year, unless a very full and satisfactory explanation is made as to the cause of delay.

You will apprise the several officers concerned as to this order.

By order,
Richard Clego, Chief Clerk.

---

Circular No. 235.
11,862/82.

General Prisons Board, Dublin Castle,
30th May, 1882.

Sir,

I am directed by the General Prisons Board to inform you that the following rules for Military Prisoners desiring to memorial for remission or mitigation of sentences are to be strictly adhered to in future:—

(1.) Military Prisoners under sentence of imprisonment only, may address applications for remission or mitigation of such sentences direct to the Commanding Officer who confirmed such sentences, such applications to be written on plain paper, and not on the forms used for Memorials to the Lord Lieutenant or to the Commander of the Forces in Ireland.

(2.) Military Prisoners under sentence of penal servitude will not be permitted to memorial the Lord Lieutenant or the Commander-in-Chief for remission of sentence until they shall have completed three years of their sentence, and then only in case of continuous good conduct.

The foregoing rules will not apply to cases where the *health* of a Military Prisoner is affected.

I am, sir, your obedient servant,

RICHARD CLEGG, Chief Clerk.

The Governors of H. M. Prisons.

See Circular No. 248.

---

Circular No. 236.
13510.

Office of General Prisons Board, Dublin Castle,
26th May, 1882.

Sir,

With reference to Circular No. 79, dated 22nd January, 1878, I am directed by the General Prisons Board to inform you that when forwarding reports against Prison Officers for having been under the influence of drink, it will be necessary to state clearly whether the officer complained of was unfit for duty.

I am, sir, your obedient servant,

RICHARD CLEGG, Chief Clerk.

The Governors of H. M. Prisons.

---

General Prisons Board, Dublin Castle,
6th June, 1882.

To the GOVERNORS of PRISONS.

I am directed by the General Prisons Board to forward you for transmission to the keepers of Bridewells attached to your Prison, for their future guidance, the subjoined copy of a Memo., dated 18th July, 1881.

A. NEWTON BRADY, pro Chief Clerk.

---

10463/81.
MEMO.

General Prisons Board, Dublin Castle,
18th July, 1881.

The General Prisons Board have to acquaint you that in the event of a female prisoner with an infant being committed to the Prison under your charge, you are authorized to issue one quart of milk, and half a pound of white bread—or a portion of the above allowance—daily for the use of such child in case the mother is unable to maintain it.

CHARLES F. BOURKE, Chairman.

The Governors of Prisons.

## Prevention of Crime (Ireland) Act, 1882.

Circular No. 238.

General Prisons Board, Dublin Castle,
20th July, 1882.

Sir,

I am directed by the General Prisons Board to transmit to you the attached copy of the Supplement to the *Dublin Gazette*, dated 19th July, 1882, and to draw your special attention to sections 4, 5, 8, and 13 in the order therein.

I am, sir, your obedient servant,

Richard Clego, Chief Clerk.

The Governors H. M. Prisons.

## Prevention of Crime (Ireland) Act, 1882.

### By the Lord Lieutenant and Privy Council in Ireland.

Spencer.

We, the Lord Lieutenant-General and General Governor of Ireland, by and with the advice of the Privy Council in Ireland, in pursuance and by virtue of "The Prevention of Crime (Ireland) Act, 1882," and of every other power and authority in this behalf, do hereby make and prescribe the following rules:—

### Section 4.

*Governors of Prisons to transmit Prisoners.*

In every case in which an Order is made under The Act, clause 4, on the application of the Attorney-General, directing the trial in the county named in such Order of a prisoner who is in custody in a prison other than the prison of or for the county in which the trial is to take place, the Governor of the first-mentioned prison shall, three days before the day on which the Assizes at which the prisoner is to be tried are appointed to be held, send without any writ of Habeas Corpus, such prisoner to the prison of or for the county in which the trial is to take place, for the purposes of his trial, and shall take all proper steps for his transmission to the last-mentioned prison and his maintenance by the way; and such prisoner while so being conveyed by the Governor or his assistants to the secondly-mentioned prison shall be in the proper and legal custody of such Governor, and the Governor of the secondly-mentioned prison shall receive the prisoner into his charge and custody on arrival, and shall keep and maintain him in that prison until he is either ordered to be discharged or remanded by proper authority, or until he shall have been tried and sentenced, and proper arrangements have been made for his being sent back to the prison to which he would have been remitted had he been tried at the Assizes in the county where but for the aforesaid Order under the Act, he would have been tried; and if such prisoner is ordered to be conveyed back to the first-mentioned prison, the Governor of that prison, or one or more of his assistants, shall attend and receive and convey the prisoner, and while so being conveyed, the prisoner shall be in the proper and legal custody of the Governor of the prison to which he is so being conveyed.

### Section 5.

*Payment of Expenses of removal of Accused, &c.*

In every case in which an Order is made under The Act, clause 5, on the application of the Attorney-General, directing a trial of any prisoner in the county named in such Order, the expenses of and incidental to the removal of the prisoner from a prison in which, when the Order is made, he is confined to any other prison, for the purpose of his trial, and of his maintenance in the last-mentioned prison, and of his removal after trial from that to any other prison, shall be paid by the Grand Jury of the county in which the first-mentioned prison is situated, and charged upon the county in which that prison is situated, as if the same were expenses duly incurred and certified within the meaning of the 4th section of an Act passed in the Session of Parliament held in the 14th and 15th years of the reign of Her present Majesty, chapter 55, as amended by "The General Prisons (Ireland) Act, 1877," and any difference between the prison authorities as to the liability to or amount of such expenses shall be determined by the Chief Secretary of the Lord Lieutenant for the time being, and his decision shall be final.

SECTION 8.

*Duties of Officers, &c.*

Every Justice of the Peace, Coroner, Clerk of the Crown, Clerk of the Peace, Clerk of Petty Sessions, Bailiff, Governor of any of Her Majesty's Prisons, Constable, Officer, and person having authority and being under an obligation to attend the assizes to be held in any county other than the county in which the trial shall, under *The Act*, clause 6, on the application of the Attorney-General be ordered to take place, or to certify, transmit, or deliver to the Court of Assize, or the proper officer thereof, any indictment, inquisition, recognizance, examination, deposition or document, shall have the same authority and be under the same obligation to attend at the place where the trial is, under *The Act*, ordered to take place as aforesaid, and to certify, transmit, and deliver to the Clerk of the Crown for the county in which the trial is ordered to take place as aforesaid, every such indictment, inquisition, recognizance, examination, deposition, or document.

SECTION 13.

*Execution of Sentence.*

Every sentence and punishment of a prisoner convicted in a county in which, on the application of the Attorney-General, a trial is ordered under *The Act*, clause 6, to take place, shall be carried into effect by the Sheriff, officers, and persons of the county, in which the trial would, but for such order, have taken place, in the same manner in all respects as if the prisoner had been tried and convicted in the last-mentioned county.

---

CIRCULAR MEMO.
13,312.

General Prisons Board, Dublin Castle,
31st July, 1882.

In accordance with the request of the Secretary of State for War, the General Prisons Board have to desire that the following arrangements to enable men of the 1st Class Army Reserve, relegated to the Reserve on discharge from Civil Prisons in Ireland after improper enlistment, to reach the District in which they intend to reside, may be carefully carried out in the cases of such men:—

1. When a man of the 1st Class Army Reserve is committed to Civil Prison to undergo a sentence of imprisonment, and ordered, at the expiration of his sentence, to be relegated to the Reserve, the Officer commanding the Corps in which the man is serving at the time, will inform the Governor of the Prison of the Corps in which the man served previously to transfer to the Reserve, and the District from which he deserted.

2. On the termination of the man's period of imprisonment, the Governor will advance to him, for Subsistence and Travelling Expenses, such sum, in cash, not exceeding £1, as may be necessary to enable him to reach the District in which he intends to reside.

3. A suit of plain clothes will, if necessary, be issued to the man by the Governor of the Prison. This suit may be purchased locally by the Governor of the Prison, at a cost (repayable) not exceeding 12s., or can be obtained from the Director of Clothing, Royal Army Clothing Depot, Pimlico, London. Demands for suits of plain clothes upon the Director of Clothing should be made one month before the Prisoner's discharge, and should show the articles required, and the date of discharge of each soldier, and be accompanied by size rolls.

4. The amount advanced in cash, together with the value (repayable) of the clothing purchased locally, is to be immediately reported to the Under-Secretary of State for War, War Office, Pall Mall, London, together with the following particulars:—

(*a.*) The Corps in which the man was serving when committed to Prison, and the name under which he was serving.

(*b.*) The Corps in which he served previously to transfer to the Reserve, and the name under which he served in that Corps.

(*c.*) The District from which he deserted.

(*d.*) The District to which he intends to proceed.

Steps will then be taken by the War Office to recover, by stoppages from the man's Reserve pay, the amount which has been advanced to him. If no clothing is supplied to the man, or if the suit supplied is obtained from the Director of Clothing, a statement to that effect should be made on the report.

5. The amount advanced to the man, and the value (not exceeding 12s.) of the suit of plain clothes purchased locally, will be repaid to the Governor of the Prison by the District Paymaster at either Dublin, Cork, or Belfast, according to the District in which the Prison is situated, on production of the man's receipt (on Form 14) for the advance, and the receipted bill for the clothing purchased. The receipt of the man should be dated, and should state the District to which he intends to proceed.

The amount advanced in cash for Subsistence and Travelling Expenses, and the cost (not exceeding 12s.) of the clothing, if any, purchased locally, will be included by the Governor in the Prison Accounts as payments under the sub-head "Advances for War Department," copies of the man's receipt for the advance, and of the receipted bill for the clothing purchased being furnished with the Accounts to the Office of the General Prisons Board.

When repayment is made by the District Paymaster to the Governor, it will be included in the Prison Accounts as received, under the sub-head "Refund of Advances for War Department," and a voucher (on Form 4) for the repayment will be furnished with the Accounts to the Office of the General Prisons Board.

If the man desires to obtain a suit of clothing of a better description than can be purchased for the sum of 12s. allowed by the War Department, and if he has gratuity or private money due to him by the Prison, the General Prisons Board will permit the excess in cost over 12s. of the suit purchased locally for him to be paid out of his gratuity or private money.

In this case the Governor when paying him on release will take care to obtain from him a receipt (on the usual Form 28) for the full amount of his gratuity and private money, including the portion paid in excess in cost of the clothing. In the Report to the War Office and the demand made on the District Paymaster for repayment the charge for the clothing must not exceed 15s.

<div align="right">CHARLES F. BOURKE, Chairman.</div>

The Governors of the several Prisons for Males.

---

CIRCULAR MEMO.

16,013.

<div align="right">General Prisons Board,
21st August, 1882.</div>

I am directed by the General Prisons Board to issue the following instructions with reference to the Uniform of Officers when leaving the Service.

(I.) If any article of Uniform Clothing has been in wear more than half the period allowed by the regulations for each, the article may remain with the officer when leaving.

(II.) The following articles must in all cases be taken from Officers, viz., cap, belt, whistle and chain, these articles should be returned to store for re-issue when necessary.

(III.) The brass uniform buttons must in all cases be taken off any article of uniform allowed to remain with officers when leaving the service.

<div align="right">GEO. SPROULE, Superintendent of Stores.</div>

To Governors of the several Prisons.

---

Circular No. 239.

16,737.

<div align="right">General Prisons Board, Dublin Castle,
26th August, 1882.</div>

SIR,

I am directed by the General Prisons Board to send you the accompanying Jacket and Splint, sanctioned by His Excellency the Lord Lieutenant, for restraining violent prisoners.

### DIRECTIONS FOR USE.

The long sleeves of the jacket are to fold the arms in front of the chest, and then to be tied in a knot at the back.

The board or splint is to be used to control in the sitting posture, the leg placed on the splint, and then the tapes tied round the limb prevent all movement.

The cord at end of splint is to be passed round the chair or seat on which the person sits, to prevent him slipping off.

I am, sir, your obedient servant,

<div align="right">RICHARD GANE, Chief Clerk.</div>

CIRCULAR MEMO.

General Prisons Board, Dublin Castle,
6th September, 1882.

THE GOVERNORS, H. M. Prisons,

Please state (I.), the names and dates of appointment of the present Chaplains and Medical Officers of the Prison, and (if appointed since 1st January, 1880), date of confirmation of appointment; (II.), names of any gentlemen other than the present holders of the offices who may have filled these offices for any period since the 1st January, 1880.

You are requested to be careful in future to note all such appointments in the monthly changes in staff list.

RICHARD CLEGG, Chief Clerk.

H. M. Prison at

---

CIRCULAR MEMORANDUM.

General Prisons Board, Dublin Castle,
9th September, 1882.

To GOVERNORS of Local Prisons, &c.

All applications from subordinate officers for leave, annual increments of salary, lodging allowances, &c., &c., are to be accompanied by the conduct sheet of the officer.

Please bear this instruction in mind in all such cases in the future.

By order,

RICHARD CLEGG, Chief Clerk.

---

OFFICERS' UNIFORMS.

CIRCULAR MEMO.
18,310/82.

General Prisons Board, Dublin Castle,
12th September, 1882.

I am directed by the General Prisons Board to inform you that in future the date of issue of articles of Uniform to Warders, shall be computed from the date on which the officer actually receives his first issue after entering the service.

This regulation shall apply to all Warders who have not yet received a second issue of any article of uniform.

GEO. SPROULE, Superintendent of Stores.

The Governor——Prison.

---

Circular No. 240.
18,957.

General Prisons Board, Dublin Castle,
14th September, 1882.

SIR,

I am directed by the General Prisons Board to forward to you the enclosed copy of Instructions approved of by His Excellency the Lord Lieutenant, for the guidance of the Governors of Local Prisons and others, with reference to the course to be followed upon the committal of a prisoner for trial on Change of Venue, under the Prevention of

**Crimes Act; and to request your compliance with the Rules laid down therein relating to prison matters and duties.**

**I am, sir, your obedient servant,**

**RICHARD CLEGG, Chief Clerk.**

**To the Governors, H. M. Prisons.**

---

"COPY OF INSTRUCTIONS referred to in CIRCULAR No. 340.

"In order that proper arrangements may in future be made for the safe custody of prisoners, when a Change of Venue under Section 11 of the Prevention of Crimes Act has been decided on, His Excellency desires that the following instructions may be observed:

"I. When the Governor of the Prison from which prisoners are to be removed receives information of the change of Venue, he shall:—

(*a*.) Enquire from the General Prisons Board the name of the Prison to which the prisoners are to be sent.

(*b*.) Apply to the County Inspector for a sufficient escort. The County Inspector will, if necessary, consult the Inspector-General as to the strength of the escort.

"II. On receipt of communication from the Governor of the Prison, the General Prisons Board will report to the Lord Lieutenant the name of the Local Prison to which they recommend that the prisoners should be transferred, and also state, if necessary, any special reason they may have for thinking that the prisoners should be detained in some Prison other than the Local Prison, under the warrant of the Lord Lieutenant.

"III. The Governor of a Prison on receipt of an intimation that certain prisoners are to be transferred to his custody for trial on change of Venue, shall at once report to the General Prisons Board as to whether, in his opinion, it will be necessary to place a special guard over the Prison during the temporary detention of the class of prisoners in question.

"The General Prisons Board will, if they concur in the recommendations of the Governor, submit the same to the Executive for approval.

"When the prisoners have to be taken to Court and back for Trial, the Governor of the Prison in whose legal custody they are, to make proper arrangements for their safe custody during transit, with the Chief Commissioner of the Dublin Metropolitan Police, or with the Constabulary County Inspector. These Officers to be responsible that a sufficient escort is provided.

"IV. After sentence, the Governor of the Prison to which the Prisoners have to be conveyed, and whose duty it is under paragraph 4 of the Order in Council of July 10, 1882, to take the prisoners into his charge, will make necessary arrangements for their safe custody during transit, in communication with the Inspector-General, who will be responsible that a sufficient escort is provided.

"V. The Crown Solicitor of the County from which the trial is to be removed will give intimation of the date fixed for the trial, and of the removal of the prisoners to the Governor of the Gaol in time to enable the latter to make proper arrangements, and to comply with these instructions."

---

CONVICTS.

General Prisons Board, Dublin Castle,

MEMO. 28th September, 1882.

Referring to Circular of 27 January, 1857, as to treatment of Convicts in punishment cells.

The General Prisons Board direct that in future all convicts placed in punishment cells, shall be supplied during the first three nights with pillow and bedding, such as is now supplied after the third night.

By order, RICHARD CLEGG, Chief Clerk.

I. The Governor, Spike Island Prison.

II. The Governor, Mountjoy Male Prison.

CONVICTS.

Memo.

General Prisons Board, Dublin Castle,
26th September, 1881.

The General Prisons Board direct that a copy of the New Dietary for Convicts recently introduced, be placed in each convict's cell.

Pasteboard cards for the above already sent you, can be had by sending a requisition to this office, stating number required.

By order,

RICHARD OLDEN, Chief Clerk.

I. The Governor, Spike Island Prison.
II. The Governor, Mountjoy Male Prison.
III. The Superintendent, Mountjoy Female Prison.

---

EXEMPTION from STAMP DUTY of BANK CHEQUES used by OFFICERS of PUBLIC DEPARTMENTS in drawing upon PUBLIC ACCOUNTS, Receipts for Imprests, &c., also exempt.

Circular No. 243.
16,688/83.

FINANCE.

General Prisons Board, Dublin Castle,
Sir, 5th October, 1883.

The attached copy of a communication on the above subject, which has been received from the Lords Commissioners of Her Majesty's Treasury, is forwarded for your information, and you are requested to comply with the instructions therein contained.

I am, sir, your obedient servant,

C. F. BOURKE, Chairman.

To the Governor and Sub-Accounting Officer of each Prison.

14,431/83. [Copy.]

Treasury Chambers,
Gentlemen, 31st August, 1883.

I am desired by the Lords Commissioners of Her Majesty's Treasury to append for your information a copy of the 18th Section of the Act 46/47 Vict., cap. 55.

Under this enactment the cheques provided by banks to be used by Officers of Public Departments in drawing upon Public Accounts kept at such banks will, in future, be exempt from stamp duty.

This exemption applies only to cheques drawn upon banking accounts which are opened solely for public purposes, and which consist exclusively of public moneys.

In case any special form of cheque is printed by a bank for the use of your Department, any stock of these cheques upon which the bank may have paid the duty may, to avoid inconvenience to the bank, be supplied to you and paid for. With this exception no charge in respect of stamped cheques will in future arise.

The last part of the enactment, of which a copy is appended, dispenses with stamps upon acknowledgments of receipts given by officers of Public Departments for money paid to them as imprests, or in adjustment of public accounts where they derive no personal benefit therefrom. This exemption has heretofore only partially operated in regard to documents of the above nature. It will now become general.

I have the honour to be, your obedient servant,

(Signed), R. R. W. LINGEN.

The General Prisons Board, Dublin Castle.

COPY of SECTION 10 of the REVENUE, FRIENDLY SOCIETIES, and NATIONAL DEBT ACT, 1882 (45 and 46 Vict., cap. 72).

No stamp duty shall be chargeable upon the following instruments (that is to say),

Draft or order drawn upon any banker in the United Kingdom by an officer of a public department of the State for the payment of money out of a public account.

Receipt given by an officer of a public department of the State, for money paid by way of imprest or advance, or in adjustment of an account where he derives no personal benefit therefrom.

---

Circular No. 241.
20234/82.

General Prisons Board, Dublin Castle,
10th October, 1882.

SIR,

The General Prisons Board direct me to inform you that Prisoners in Punishment Cells are to be permitted to attend Divine Service in the Prison Chapel on Sundays and Holidays, except in any case where the Governor has reason to believe a prisoner would be guilty of misconduct there.

I am, sir, your obedient servant,
RICHARD CLEGG, Chief Clerk.

To Governors of Local Prisons.

---

Circular No. 242.
20,608.

General Prisons Board, Dublin Castle,
13th October, 1882.

SIR,

I am directed to inform you that it is the desire of the General Prisons Board that whenever an officer is transferred from the staff of the Prison under your charge to that of another, you will forthwith furnish to the Governor of that Prison a confidential report as to the character, conduct, &c., of the officer so transferred, for his information and guidance.

I am, sir, your obedient servant,
RICHARD CLEGG, Chief Clerk.

The Governors of H. M. Prisons.

---

CIRCULAR MEMO. TO GOVERNORS AND SUPERINTENDENTS OF CONVICT PRISONS.

General Prisons Board, Dublin Castle,
13th October, 1882.

The attention of the General Prisons Board having been called to the necessity of fixing some definite rule whereby to determine the number of marks which a convict must be given to earn on being removed from the old system of classification and placed under the new system, the Board have agreed to the following proposal with regard thereto :—

The number of months remission which still remains unforfeited by the convict at the time of his being placed under the new system of classification is to be calculated in the usual way (any exceptional cases of males and all cases of females to be referred to the Board for instructions). This period is then to be deducted from the portion of the convict's sentence remaining unexpired at the time of his being placed under the new system. The difference between these two periods being reduced to days, and the number of days being multiplied by 8 (in the case of females by 6), will give the number of marks which the convict must earn before release on licence, which number is to be placed at the head of his card. If, therefore, the convict thenceforth earns the full number of marks, daily, he will lose none of the remission standing to his credit at the time of his being placed under the new system of classification.

This rules applies to the cases of convicts who have already been placed under the new system of classification.

By order,

Richard Clegg, Chief Clerk.

---

Circular 245.
21,161.

General Prisons Board, Dublin Castle,
31st October, 1882.

Sir,

I am directed by the General Prisons Board to inform you, in reference to Rule 36, page 33, Rules for Local Prisons, that the beards of convicted prisoners are to be *clipped* and not shaven.

Any untried prisoner, who before his committal was in the habit of shaving, may be permitted, a prison officer being present, to shave himself, unless the Governor has special reasons for objecting to his so doing.

A supply of scissors, suitable for the purpose, will be supplied on your submitting a requisition on Book Form No. 11.

I am, sir, your obedient servant,

Richard Clegg, Chief Clerk.

The Governors of Local Prisons.

---

Circular No. 246.
21,979.

General Prisons Board, Dublin Castle,
16th November, 1882.

Sir,

I am to inform you in reference to Circular No. 106, 21st April, 1879, that the General Prisons Board direct that, in future, the private clothes of convicted prisoners under order of transfer from one prison to another, shall be made up in one or two parcels, and directed to the Governor of the Prison to which the prisoners are being sent.

The parcels will be carried to the railway by such prisoners as you may detail for the purpose, and then sent on in charge of the railway officials as passenger's luggage.

From the terminus the prisoners will carry the parcels to the prison.

Prisoners are to be warned that if reported for disobedience of this order they will be treated as guilty of a prison offence.

I am, sir, your obedient servant,

Richard Clegg, Chief Clerk.

The Governor, H. M.'s Prisons.

See Circular No. 167.

General Prisons Board, Dublin Castle,
30th November, 1882.

CIRCULAR MEMO.

Referring to Circular Memo. of 28th October, 1879, sending certain forms to be issued to officers for explanation of any charges brought against them, I am directed by the General Prisons Board to request that in all cases such forms may be issued and the officer's written reply received before you proceed to decide the case.

RICHARD CLEGG, Chief Clerk.

The Governors of H. M. Prisons.

---

DEATHS OF PERSONS IN GAOL OTHER THAN PRISONERS.

Circular No. 247.
12,856.

General Prisons Board, Dublin Castle,
6th December, 1882.

SIR,

I am directed by the General Prisons Board to request you to inform the Medical Officer of the Prison that the Board are of opinion that it is desirable, in case of the death of any person in the Prison, he should make an entry in his Journal as to the cause of death, and state, for the information of the Governor, whether he considers an inquest necessary.

If the Medical Officer considers that an inquest should be held the Governor will take the steps pointed out by Rules in case of the death of a prisoner.

I am, sir, your obedient servant,
RICHARD CLEGG, Chief Clerk.

To Governors of Prisons.

---

DIETARIES OF THE LOCAL PRISONS.

General Prisons Board, Dublin Castle,
16th December, 1882.

It having been reported to the General Prisons Board that the term "Month" in the Dietary Schedule is differently construed in the various Prisons, I am to inform you that the word "Month" used in such a case shall mean a "Calendar" Month.

By order,
RICHARD CLEGG, Chief Clerk.

The Governors, H. M. Prisons.

---

Circular No. 248.
14,221

General Prisons Board, Dublin Castle,
30th December, 1882.

SIR,

Referring to Circular No. 235, dated 30th May, 1882, I am directed by the General Prisons Board to inform you that it is the desire of His Excellency the Lord Lieutenant, that Military prisoners under sentence of imprisonment only, shall not be permitted to memorial for the mitigation of their sentences until at least two-thirds of their sentences shall have been completed, unless under some extraordinary circumstances which you consider justify such a proceeding.

I am, sir, your obedient servant,
RICHARD CLEGG, Chief Clerk.

The Governors, H. M. Prisons.

Circular No. 249.

General Prisons Board, Dublin Castle,
6th January, 1883.

Sir,

I am directed by the General Prisons Board to send you the following addendum to Circular 207, dated 12th April, 1881.

Every order directing a Prisoner to wear either of the dresses referred to is to be submitted for reconsideration at termination of each succeeding three months.

I am, sir, your obedient servant,

Richard Clegg, Chief Clerk.

To Governors of Prisons.

---

Circular No. 250.

General Prisons Board, Dublin Castle,
3rd January, 1883.

Sir,

The Inspectors of Lunatic Asylums having brought to the notice of the Executive the difficulties which sometimes arise at Dundrum Criminal Lunatic Asylum in providing funds for the removal of "time expired patients declared of sound mind" to the localities from whence they where committed, His Excellency the Lord Lieutenant has been pleased to direct that for the future in such cases the Medical Superintendent shall apply to the Governor of the Prison from which the patient was received for the required amount; and, I am to inform you that it is the desire of the General Prisons Board that you shall transmit such sum to him, taking credit for such advances in your Cash Book under the proper heading.

A Voucher, Form No. 14, should be sent with each such remittance for the purpose of obtaining a receipt signed by the prisoner and countersigned by the Medical Superintendent.

I am, sir, your obedient servant,

Richard Clegg, Chief Clerk.

The Governors, H. M. Prisons.

---

264/83.

General Prisons Board, Dublin Castle,
15th January, 1883.

Circular Memo.

When filling up the column headed "county where convicted and date of conviction" in Memorial Forms, you will please in every case state the exact *place* of conviction as well as the county.

By order,

Richard Clegg, Chief Clerk.

The Governors, H. M. Prisons.

---

Convicts.

General Prisons Board, Dublin Castle,
19th January, 1883.

Circular Memo.

I am directed by the General Prisons Board to forward for your information and guidance, the accompanying Regulations approved by the Board, for the treatment of Convicts sentenced to undergo a period of second probation, &c., and I am at the same time to request that all convicts so sentenced, shall be reported on at the end of three months of second probation, and afterwards monthly.

By order, RICHARD CLEGG, Chief Clerk.

I. The Governor, Spike Island Prison.
II. The Governor, Mountjoy Male Prison.
III. The Superintendent, Mountjoy Female Prison.
IV. The Governor, Maryborough Prison.

REGULATIONS for the TREATMENT of CONVICTS sentenced to undergo a period of SECOND PROBATION.

1. Any convict whose misconduct, after removal to a Public Works Prison, proves that he has not profited by the discipline he has previously undergone, and shows that his character is such as to exercise a pernicious influence on other prisoners, may, besides any punishment to which he may be sentenced for any special offence, be ordered by the General Prisons Board to undergo a second period of probation, not exceeding nine months, and generally not less than six months, which period may be shortened under the operation of the mark system.

2. Convicts ordered to undergo second probation are to be located in a part of the prison assigned for the purpose, where they will be kept altogether separate from the general body of prisoners, and treated like prisoners undergoing in separate confinement, the first portion of the probation class, except that they will continue to earn marks at the usual rate.

3. Such convicts, after passing through this stage of separate confinement, will not return to work among the general body of prisoners, but will, as a measure of prevention, but not as a punishment, continue to be kept apart from them, and be employed in separate working parties until there is reason to think that they will no longer exercise a bad influence among the others. They will have the same opportunities as other convicts of earning the highest number of marks.

4. In such working parties may, as a measure of prevention, be placed prisoners, who, without themselves incurring punishment, are yet known to exercise a bad influence over other prisoners.

---

Circular No. 252.
869

General Prisons Board, Dublin Castle,
22nd January, 1883.

SIR,

I am directed by the General Prisons Board to request that you will carry out the directions in the subjoined Order, having reference to Classification of Local Prisoners detained by Illness in Hospital.

I am, sir, your obedient servant,

The Governors of Prisons. RICHARD CLEGG, Chief Clerk.

CLASSIFICATION of LOCAL PRISONERS in HOSPITAL.

Prisoners detained by illness in Hospital and thus unable to earn marks to qualify for advance in Classification, are on the termination of the periods usually required for such advance from one class to another, to have their cases specially submitted for the consideration of the Board.

N.B.—It is not intended by this Order that any money is to be given for marks unless when earned by industry.

---

General Prisons Board, Dublin Castle,
30th January, 1883.

CIRCULAR MEMO.

I am directed by the General Prisons Board to send you two copies of the amended Rules for Prison Surgeons, one of which you will please hand to the Surgeon of the Prison under your charge, for his information and guidance.

RICHARD CLEGG, Chief Clerk.

The Governors of the larger Prisons.

DIETARIES OF LOCAL PRISONS.

Circular No. 253.
3217/83.

General Prisons Board, Dublin Castle,
12th March, 1883.

SIR,

I am directed to inform you that the four ounces of beef to be given at dinner on Sundays to Prisoners entitled to Class III. diet, is to be considered as the quantity to be allowed to each prisoner *after* the meat is cooked.

I am, sir, your obedient servant,

RICHARD CLEGG, Chief Clerk.

The Governors of Local Prisons.

---

General Prisons Board, Dublin Castle,
17th March, 1883.

MEMO.

Instructions have been given to the Governor of Mountjoy Prison to supply you with two canvas suits, to be kept in store, for issue to prisoners who may wilfully destroy their own private clothing while in custody. Two of those suits should always be kept in store.

Please also note that a similar suit has been supplied to each Minor Prison and Bridewell under your charge with similar instructions to the above.

GEO. SPROULE, Superintendent of Stores.

The Governor.

---

POLITICAL INFLUENCE.

Circular No. 254.
3612/83.

Dublin Castle,
27th March, 1883.

SIR,

I am directed by the General Prisons Board to send you the accompanying Copies of a Circular Letter received by them from the Under Secretary to the Lord Lieutenant, covering a copy of a Minute of the Lords Commissioners of Her Majesty's Treasury, cautioning Civil servants against the use of Political Influence for obtaining increase of salary, &c., and to request that you will bring its terms to the notice of each of the Officers of the Prison (and Bridewells, if any) under your charge, and return one copy of the Circular Letter to this Department with the signature of each Officer on the margin thereof, as evidence of his or her knowledge of its contents.

I am, sir, your obedient servant,

RICHARD CLEGG, Chief Clerk.

The Governors, &c., of Her Majesty's Prisons.

---

6421.

CIRCULAR LETTER to the HEADS of GOVERNMENT DEPARTMENTS in IRELAND.

Dublin Castle,
12th March, 1883.

SIR,

I am directed by the Lord Lieutenant to acquaint you that from various communications which have lately been received, it appears to His Excellency to be doubtful whether the contents of the Treasury Minute of 2nd May, 1867, prohibiting the practice of seeking Political Influence in support of claims for Increase of Salary, or Additional Retiring Allowance, are fully and generally known.

His Excellency, therefore, desires me to transmit to you the enclosed copy of the Minute in question, and to request that you will be good enough to take the necessary steps for promulgating it amongst all the Officers of the Department under your control.

I am, sir, your obedient servant,

H. G. C. Harrison.

To the Chairman, General Prisons Board, Dublin Castle.

Political Influence.

*Treasury Minute, dated 2nd May, 1867, cautioning Civil Servants against use of, for obtaining increase of Salary, &c.*

My Lords have observed with much regret a growing practice on the part of gentlemen employed in the public service, to endeavour to influence this Board to accede to their applications for increase of salary or additional retiring allowance, by means of the private solicitation of Members of Parliament and other persons of political influence.

It is the duty as well as the wish of their Lordships to give the most careful consideration to every representation made to them in the recognised way on behalf of any public servant (whatever be his social status or his official rank), with regard to his position, salary, and prospects of promotion, and also with regard to the amount of his retiring allowance on his quitting the public service.

It is the practice of their Lordships to consider questions of salary with reference to the duties and responsibilities of the individual or class whose case is brought before them, and to decide upon them after communication with the heads of the departments concerned.

In fixing the amount of the retiring allowance in those cases where the Legislature has left them a discretion, my Lords are in the habit of proceeding upon certain principles which they have prescribed for themselves, and within the limit of those principles they endeavour to deal with each case impartially upon its merits.

It appears to their Lordships that any attempt on the part of an officer to approach them on these matters through the private intervention of persons unconnected with his department, is virtually imputing to this Board either that it is likely to turn a deaf ear to a reasonable application, unless supported by political influence, or that it may be induced to accede to an unreasonable application if such influence be brought to bear upon it.

My Lords disclaim either alternative, and in order to prevent for the future any misapprehension upon this subject, they wish it to be understood by every public officer that any attempt made by him to obtain the sanction of this Board to his application by any such solicitation as is hereinbefore referred to will be treated by them as an admission on the part of such officer that his case is not good upon its merits, and such application will be dealt with by their Lordships accordingly.

Let a copy of this Minute be sent to every public Department.

---

**Circular No. 255.**

**General Prisons Board, Dublin Castle,**
**30th March, 1883.**

The Governor, —— Prison.

Herewith, I send you Forms of Prison Books for use in Local Prisons and Bridewells, approved of by the General Prisons Board.

When making requisitions, from time to time, for any of these books please refer to them by the number as well as by the title given in the book.

A copy has been sent to each Minor Prison and Bridewell.

**By order,**

**Richard Clarke, Chief Clerk.**

# TABLES

TABLE I.—NUMBER of COMMITMENTS to LOCAL PRISONS

| Names of Prisons. | Convicted. At Assizes and Quarter Sessions. Found Guilty. | | Found Insane. | | Summarily. Offences under Prevention of Crimes Act. | | Offences under Larceny Act. | | Misdemeanants. | | Under Revenue Laws. | | Under Poor Law Act. | | [illegible] | [illegible] | Under Vagrancy Act. | | Drunkards. | |
|---|---|---|---|---|---|---|---|---|---|---|---|---|---|---|---|---|---|---|---|---|
| **Larger Prisons.** | M. | F. | M. | F. | M. | F. | M. | F. | M. | F. | M. | F. | M. | F. | M. | M. | M. | F. | M. | F. |
| Armagh, | 24 | 8 | – | – | 2 | – | 42 | 10 | 179 | 22 | 4 | – | 8 | 1 | 5 | 6 | 32 | 23 | 224 | 8 |
| Belfast, | 77 | 22 | 1 | – | 6 | – | 184 | 118 | 1,227 | 621 | 5 | 12 | 8 | 4 | 7 | 17 | 38 | 27 | 1,429 | 1,010 |
| Castlebar, | 15 | 14 | 6 | – | 7 | 1 | 91 | 6 | 104 | 41 | 11 | 3 | 7 | 6 | 6 | 8 | 8 | – | 185 | 52 |
| Clonmel, | 42 | – | – | – | 16 | – | 18 | 6 | 188 | 15 | – | – | – | – | 10 | 8 | 6 | – | 416 | 15 |
| Cork, Male, | 128 | – | – | – | 22 | – | 119 | – | 701 | – | – | – | 18 | – | 22 | – | 34 | – | 632 | – |
| Cork, Female, | – | 83 | – | 8 | – | 4 | – | 71 | – | 941 | – | – | – | 60 | – | – | – | – | – | 1,030 |
| Downpatrick, | 67 | 8 | 1 | – | 1 | – | 8 | 6 | 79 | 16 | – | – | 2 | – | 1 | – | 60 | 4 | 97 | 32 |
| Drogheda, | – | 6 | – | – | – | – | – | 20 | 4 | 34 | – | – | – | – | – | – | – | 22 | 17 | 8 |
| Dundalk, | 27 | – | – | – | 14 | – | 37 | – | 106 | – | 8 | – | 81 | – | 42 | 6 | 1 | – | 148 | – |
| Galway, | 78 | 17 | – | – | 54 | – | 7 | 8 | 207 | 78 | 6 | 8 | 5 | – | 62 | 1 | 11 | – | 246 | 128 |
| Grangegorman, | 14 | 102 | – | 8 | 5 | – | 61 | 67 | 1,108 | 1,169 | – | – | – | 8 | 8 | – | 28 | 44 | 673 | 1,086 |
| Kilkenny, | 122 | 4 | – | – | 7 | – | 21 | 6 | 164 | 26 | – | 4 | – | – | 14 | 8 | 22 | 6 | 176 | 44 |
| Kilmainham, | 68 | – | 1 | – | 6 | – | 63 | – | 406 | – | 8 | – | 34 | – | 44 | – | 98 | – | 398 | – |
| Limerick, Male, | 81 | – | 1 | – | 56 | – | 70 | – | 328 | – | 16 | – | 21 | – | 88 | 14 | 106 | – | 308 | – |
| Limerick, Female, | – | 82 | – | – | – | – | – | 67 | – | 801 | – | – | – | – | – | – | – | 82 | – | 187 |
| Londonderry, | 36 | 14 | 4 | – | 4 | – | 46 | 11 | 218 | 77 | 17 | 4 | 6 | 6 | 6 | 6 | 10 | 24 | 214 | 122 |
| Maryborough, | 18 | 9 | 1 | – | 4 | – | 6 | 1 | 62 | 5 | – | – | 7 | 4 | 44 | 6 | 8 | 1 | 88 | 9 |
| Mullingar, | 67 | 17 | 8 | 8 | 12 | – | 46 | 12 | 207 | 60 | 18 | – | – | – | 27 | 7 | 8 | 4 | 222 | 62 |
| Naas, | 14 | 4 | – | – | 6 | – | 16 | 6 | 48 | 78 | 11 | – | 6 | 1 | 152 | – | 8 | 8 | 167 | 70 |
| Nenagh, | 12 | – | – | – | 4 | – | 3 | – | 144 | – | – | – | 18 | – | 8 | – | 1 | – | 167 | – |
| Omagh, | 87 | 4 | – | – | 12 | – | 84 | 7 | 66 | 12 | 4 | – | 8 | – | 8 | 8 | 16 | 4 | 113 | 14 |
| Richmond, | 148 | – | 6 | – | – | – | 371 | – | 701 | – | 5 | – | 5 | – | – | 84 | 22 | – | 67 | – |
| Sligo, | 43 | 4 | 1 | 1 | 18 | 6 | 61 | 7 | 108 | 36 | 6 | – | 12 | 8 | 4 | 8 | 14 | 8 | 126 | 44 |
| Tralee, | 84 | 6 | – | – | 88 | 6 | 84 | 10 | 258 | 34 | – | – | 8 | – | – | – | 8 | 1 | 234 | 57 |
| Tullamore, | 17 | 6 | – | – | 4 | – | 4 | 9 | 64 | 24 | – | – | – | – | 121 | – | 6 | 1 | 152 | 97 |
| Waterford, | 17 | 8 | – | – | 84 | – | 88 | 16 | 207 | 113 | 8 | – | 9 | 1 | 14 | 8 | – | 4 | 249 | 108 |
| Wexford, | 32 | 3 | 1 | – | 3 | – | 31 | 12 | 126 | 18 | 18 | – | 9 | 18 | 7 | 1 | 6 | 4 | 80 | 14 |
| **Minor Prisons.** | | | | | | | | | | | | | | | | | | | | |
| Carlow, | – | – | – | – | – | – | 3 | 4 | 12 | 6 | – | – | – | – | – | – | 3 | 4 | 50 | 12 |
| Carrick-on-Shannon, | 4 | – | – | – | – | – | 2 | – | 68 | 3 | – | – | 3 | 1 | 6 | 6 | – | – | 66 | 16 |
| Cavan, | – | – | – | – | 2 | – | – | 1 | 4 | 2 | – | – | – | – | – | – | 1 | – | 77 | 31 |
| Ennis, | – | – | – | – | 4 | 2 | 1 | – | 24 | 8 | – | – | 8 | 2 | 4 | – | – | – | 61 | 16 |
| Enniskillen, | – | – | – | – | – | – | 16 | 4 | – | – | – | – | – | – | – | – | – | – | 100 | 18 |
| Lifford, | – | – | – | – | – | – | – | – | – | – | – | – | 1 | – | – | – | 8 | – | 87 | 4 |
| Longford, | – | – | – | – | – | – | 2 | 2 | 22 | 19 | – | – | – | – | – | 1 | 8 | – | 72 | 16 |
| Monaghan, | 7 | – | – | – | – | – | 2 | – | 18 | 2 | – | – | – | – | 2 | 1 | 2 | – | 47 | 22 |
| Roscommon, | 1 | 1 | – | 1 | – | – | 1 | 2 | 21 | 3 | – | – | 1 | – | – | 1 | – | – | 66 | 27 |
| Trim, | 11 | 4 | – | – | 7 | 2 | – | – | 37 | 7 | – | – | – | – | – | 3 | 17 | 1 | 82 | 14 |
| Wicklow, | 37 | 1 | – | – | – | – | – | – | 11 | 2 | 8 | – | 8 | – | – | 6 | – | – | 64 | 16 |
| Total, Males, | 1,620 | – | 82 | – | 450 | – | 1,304 | – | [illegible] | – | 156 | – | 203 | – | [illegible] | [illegible] | [illegible] | – | [illegible] | – |
| Total, Females, | – | [illegible] | – | 16 | – | 14 | – | [illegible] | – | [illegible] | – | 28 | – | 64 | – | – | – | [illegible] | – | [illegible] |
| Total, M. and F., | 1,760 | | 82 | | 480 | | 1,670 | | 11,604 | | 187 | | 267 | | 771 | | 746 | | 18,300 | |

from 1st April, 1882, to 31st March, 1883.

| Totals. | | Not Convicted: Acquitted on Trial. | | Not Convicted: For further Examination, Remanded, and Discharged. | | Not Convicted: Totals. | | Untried Prisoners in Custody on 31st March, 1883. | | Total Commitments. | | | Names of Prisons. |
|---|---|---|---|---|---|---|---|---|---|---|---|---|---|
| M. | F. | M. | F. | M. | F. | M. | F. | M. | F. | M. | F. | M. & F. | *Local Prisons.* |
| [illegible] | [illegible] | [illegible] | [illegible] | [illegible] | [illegible] | [illegible] | [illegible] | [illegible] | [illegible] | [illegible] | [illegible] | [illegible] | Armagh. |
| [illegible] | [illegible] | [illegible] | [illegible] | [illegible] | [illegible] | [illegible] | [illegible] | [illegible] | [illegible] | [illegible] | [illegible] | [illegible] | Belfast. |
| [illegible] | [illegible] | [illegible] | [illegible] | [illegible] | [illegible] | [illegible] | [illegible] | [illegible] | [illegible] | [illegible] | [illegible] | [illegible] | Castlebar. |
| [illegible] | [illegible] | [illegible] | [illegible] | [illegible] | [illegible] | [illegible] | [illegible] | [illegible] | [illegible] | [illegible] | [illegible] | [illegible] | Clonmel. |
| [illegible] | [illegible] | [illegible] | [illegible] | [illegible] | [illegible] | [illegible] | [illegible] | [illegible] | [illegible] | [illegible] | [illegible] | [illegible] | Cork, Male. |
| [illegible] | [illegible] | [illegible] | [illegible] | [illegible] | [illegible] | [illegible] | [illegible] | [illegible] | [illegible] | [illegible] | [illegible] | [illegible] | Cork, Female. |
| [illegible] | [illegible] | [illegible] | [illegible] | [illegible] | [illegible] | [illegible] | [illegible] | [illegible] | [illegible] | [illegible] | [illegible] | [illegible] | Downpatrick. |
| [illegible] | [illegible] | [illegible] | [illegible] | [illegible] | [illegible] | [illegible] | [illegible] | [illegible] | [illegible] | [illegible] | [illegible] | [illegible] | Drogheda. |
| [illegible] | [illegible] | [illegible] | [illegible] | [illegible] | [illegible] | [illegible] | [illegible] | [illegible] | [illegible] | [illegible] | [illegible] | [illegible] | Dundalk. |
| [illegible] | [illegible] | [illegible] | [illegible] | [illegible] | [illegible] | [illegible] | [illegible] | [illegible] | [illegible] | [illegible] | [illegible] | [illegible] | Galway. |
| [illegible] | [illegible] | [illegible] | [illegible] | [illegible] | [illegible] | [illegible] | [illegible] | [illegible] | [illegible] | [illegible] | [illegible] | [illegible] | Grangegorman. |
| [illegible] | [illegible] | [illegible] | [illegible] | [illegible] | [illegible] | [illegible] | [illegible] | [illegible] | [illegible] | [illegible] | [illegible] | [illegible] | Kilkenny. |
| [illegible] | [illegible] | [illegible] | [illegible] | [illegible] | [illegible] | [illegible] | [illegible] | [illegible] | [illegible] | [illegible] | [illegible] | [illegible] | Kilmainham. |
| [illegible] | [illegible] | [illegible] | [illegible] | [illegible] | [illegible] | [illegible] | [illegible] | [illegible] | [illegible] | [illegible] | [illegible] | [illegible] | Limerick, Male. |
| [illegible] | [illegible] | [illegible] | [illegible] | [illegible] | [illegible] | [illegible] | [illegible] | [illegible] | [illegible] | [illegible] | [illegible] | [illegible] | Limerick, Female. |
| [illegible] | [illegible] | [illegible] | [illegible] | [illegible] | [illegible] | [illegible] | [illegible] | [illegible] | [illegible] | [illegible] | [illegible] | [illegible] | Londonderry. |
| [illegible] | [illegible] | [illegible] | [illegible] | [illegible] | [illegible] | [illegible] | [illegible] | [illegible] | [illegible] | [illegible] | [illegible] | [illegible] | Maryborough. |
| [illegible] | [illegible] | [illegible] | [illegible] | [illegible] | [illegible] | [illegible] | [illegible] | [illegible] | [illegible] | [illegible] | [illegible] | [illegible] | Mullingar. |
| [illegible] | [illegible] | [illegible] | [illegible] | [illegible] | [illegible] | [illegible] | [illegible] | [illegible] | [illegible] | [illegible] | [illegible] | [illegible] | Naas. |
| [illegible] | [illegible] | [illegible] | [illegible] | [illegible] | [illegible] | [illegible] | [illegible] | [illegible] | [illegible] | [illegible] | [illegible] | [illegible] | Nenagh. |
| [illegible] | [illegible] | [illegible] | [illegible] | [illegible] | [illegible] | [illegible] | [illegible] | [illegible] | [illegible] | [illegible] | [illegible] | [illegible] | Omagh. |
| [illegible] | [illegible] | [illegible] | [illegible] | [illegible] | [illegible] | [illegible] | [illegible] | [illegible] | [illegible] | [illegible] | [illegible] | [illegible] | Richmond. |
| [illegible] | [illegible] | [illegible] | [illegible] | [illegible] | [illegible] | [illegible] | [illegible] | [illegible] | [illegible] | [illegible] | [illegible] | [illegible] | Sligo. |
| [illegible] | [illegible] | [illegible] | [illegible] | [illegible] | [illegible] | [illegible] | [illegible] | [illegible] | [illegible] | [illegible] | [illegible] | [illegible] | Tralee. |
| [illegible] | [illegible] | [illegible] | [illegible] | [illegible] | [illegible] | [illegible] | [illegible] | [illegible] | [illegible] | [illegible] | [illegible] | [illegible] | Tullamore. |
| [illegible] | [illegible] | [illegible] | [illegible] | [illegible] | [illegible] | [illegible] | [illegible] | [illegible] | [illegible] | [illegible] | [illegible] | [illegible] | Waterford. |
| [illegible] | [illegible] | [illegible] | [illegible] | [illegible] | [illegible] | [illegible] | [illegible] | [illegible] | [illegible] | [illegible] | [illegible] | [illegible] | Wexford. |
| | | | | | | | | | | | | | *Minor Prisons.* |
| [illegible] | [illegible] | [illegible] | [illegible] | [illegible] | [illegible] | [illegible] | [illegible] | [illegible] | [illegible] | [illegible] | [illegible] | [illegible] | Carlow. |
| [illegible] | [illegible] | [illegible] | [illegible] | [illegible] | [illegible] | [illegible] | [illegible] | [illegible] | [illegible] | [illegible] | [illegible] | [illegible] | Carrick-on-Shannon. |
| [illegible] | [illegible] | [illegible] | [illegible] | [illegible] | [illegible] | [illegible] | [illegible] | [illegible] | [illegible] | [illegible] | [illegible] | [illegible] | Cavan. |
| [illegible] | [illegible] | [illegible] | [illegible] | [illegible] | [illegible] | [illegible] | [illegible] | [illegible] | [illegible] | [illegible] | [illegible] | [illegible] | Ennis. |
| [illegible] | [illegible] | [illegible] | [illegible] | [illegible] | [illegible] | [illegible] | [illegible] | [illegible] | [illegible] | [illegible] | [illegible] | [illegible] | Enniskillen. |
| [illegible] | [illegible] | [illegible] | [illegible] | [illegible] | [illegible] | [illegible] | [illegible] | [illegible] | [illegible] | [illegible] | [illegible] | [illegible] | Lifford. |
| [illegible] | [illegible] | [illegible] | [illegible] | [illegible] | [illegible] | [illegible] | [illegible] | [illegible] | [illegible] | [illegible] | [illegible] | [illegible] | Longford. |
| [illegible] | [illegible] | [illegible] | [illegible] | [illegible] | [illegible] | [illegible] | [illegible] | [illegible] | [illegible] | [illegible] | [illegible] | [illegible] | Monaghan. |
| [illegible] | [illegible] | [illegible] | [illegible] | [illegible] | [illegible] | [illegible] | [illegible] | [illegible] | [illegible] | [illegible] | [illegible] | [illegible] | Roscommon. |
| [illegible] | [illegible] | [illegible] | [illegible] | [illegible] | [illegible] | [illegible] | [illegible] | [illegible] | [illegible] | [illegible] | [illegible] | [illegible] | Trim. |
| [illegible] | [illegible] | [illegible] | [illegible] | [illegible] | [illegible] | [illegible] | [illegible] | [illegible] | [illegible] | [illegible] | [illegible] | [illegible] | Wicklow. |
| [illegible] | — | [illegible] | — | [illegible] | — | [illegible] | — | [illegible] | — | [illegible] | — | — | Total, Males. |
| — | [illegible] | — | [illegible] | — | [illegible] | — | [illegible] | — | [illegible] | — | [illegible] | — | Total, Females. |
| [illegible] | | [illegible] | | [illegible] | | [illegible] | | [illegible] | | [illegible] | | [illegible] | Total, M. and F. |

TABLE II.—NUMBER of ORDINARY PRISONERS in each PRISON on the First

| Prisons. | 1st April, 1862. | | | 1st May, 1862. | | | 1st June, 1862. | | | 1st July, 1862. | | | 1st August, 1862. | | | 1st September, 1862. | | |
|---|---|---|---|---|---|---|---|---|---|---|---|---|---|---|---|---|---|---|
| | M. | F. | Tot. | M. | F. | Tot. | M. | F. | Tot. | M. | F. | Tot. | M. | F. | Tot. | M. | F. | Tot. |
| **Larger Prisons.** | | | | | | | | | | | | | | | | | | |
| Armagh, | 77 | – | 77 | [illegible] | – | [illegible] | [illegible] | – | [illegible] | [illegible] | 1 | [illegible] | [illegible] | [illegible] | 71 | [illegible] | 10 | 74 |
| Belfast, | [illegible] | [illegible] | [illegible] | [illegible] | [illegible] | 461 | [illegible] | [illegible] | [illegible] | [illegible] | [illegible] | 467 | [illegible] | 118 | [illegible] | [illegible] | [illegible] | [illegible] |
| Castlebar, | [illegible] | [illegible] | [illegible] | [illegible] | [illegible] | 34 | 24 | [illegible] | [illegible] | [illegible] | 11 | 37 | [illegible] | [illegible] | [illegible] | [illegible] | [illegible] | [illegible] |
| Clonmel, | [illegible] | – | [illegible] | [illegible] | – | [illegible] | [illegible] | – | [illegible] | [illegible] | – | [illegible] | [illegible] | – | [illegible] | [illegible] | – | [illegible] |
| Cork, Male, | [illegible] | – | [illegible] | [illegible] | – | [illegible] | [illegible] | – | [illegible] | [illegible] | – | [illegible] | [illegible] | – | [illegible] | [illegible] | – | [illegible] |
| Cork, Female, | – | [illegible] | [illegible] | – | [illegible] | [illegible] | – | [illegible] | [illegible] | – | [illegible] | [illegible] | – | [illegible] | [illegible] | – | [illegible] | [illegible] |
| Downpatrick, | [illegible] | [illegible] | [illegible] | [illegible] | [illegible] | [illegible] | [illegible] | [illegible] | [illegible] | [illegible] | [illegible] | [illegible] | [illegible] | [illegible] | 102 | [illegible] | [illegible] | [illegible] |
| Drogheda, | – | [illegible] | [illegible] | – | [illegible] | [illegible] | – | [illegible] | [illegible] | – | [illegible] | [illegible] | – | [illegible] | [illegible] | – | [illegible] | [illegible] |
| Dundalk, | [illegible] | – | [illegible] | [illegible] | – | [illegible] | [illegible] | – | [illegible] | [illegible] | – | [illegible] | [illegible] | – | [illegible] | [illegible] | – | [illegible] |
| Galway, | [illegible] | [illegible] | [illegible] | [illegible] | [illegible] | [illegible] | [illegible] | [illegible] | [illegible] | [illegible] | [illegible] | [illegible] | [illegible] | [illegible] | [illegible] | [illegible] | [illegible] | [illegible] |
| Grangegorman, | [illegible] | [illegible] | [illegible] | [illegible] | [illegible] | [illegible] | [illegible] | [illegible] | [illegible] | [illegible] | [illegible] | [illegible] | [illegible] | [illegible] | [illegible] | [illegible] | [illegible] | [illegible] |
| Kilkenny, | [illegible] | – | [illegible] | [illegible] | – | [illegible] | [illegible] | – | [illegible] | [illegible] | – | [illegible] | [illegible] | – | [illegible] | [illegible] | – | [illegible] |
| Kilmainham, | [illegible] | – | [illegible] | [illegible] | – | [illegible] | [illegible] | – | [illegible] | [illegible] | – | [illegible] | [illegible] | – | [illegible] | [illegible] | – | [illegible] |
| Limerick, Male, | [illegible] | – | [illegible] | [illegible] | – | [illegible] | [illegible] | – | [illegible] | [illegible] | – | [illegible] | [illegible] | – | [illegible] | [illegible] | – | [illegible] |
| Limerick, Female, | – | [illegible] | [illegible] | – | [illegible] | [illegible] | – | [illegible] | [illegible] | – | [illegible] | [illegible] | – | [illegible] | [illegible] | – | [illegible] | [illegible] |
| Londonderry, | [illegible] | [illegible] | [illegible] | [illegible] | [illegible] | [illegible] | [illegible] | [illegible] | [illegible] | [illegible] | [illegible] | [illegible] | [illegible] | [illegible] | [illegible] | [illegible] | [illegible] | [illegible] |
| Maryboro', | [illegible] | [illegible] | [illegible] | [illegible] | [illegible] | [illegible] | [illegible] | [illegible] | [illegible] | [illegible] | [illegible] | [illegible] | [illegible] | [illegible] | [illegible] | [illegible] | – | [illegible] |
| Mullingar, | [illegible] | [illegible] | [illegible] | [illegible] | [illegible] | [illegible] | [illegible] | [illegible] | [illegible] | [illegible] | [illegible] | [illegible] | [illegible] | [illegible] | [illegible] | [illegible] | 14 | [illegible] |
| Naas, | [illegible] | – | [illegible] | [illegible] | – | [illegible] | [illegible] | – | [illegible] | [illegible] | – | [illegible] | [illegible] | – | [illegible] | [illegible] | [illegible] | [illegible] |
| Nenagh, | [illegible] | – | [illegible] | [illegible] | – | [illegible] | [illegible] | – | [illegible] | [illegible] | – | [illegible] | [illegible] | – | [illegible] | [illegible] | – | [illegible] |
| Omagh, | [illegible] | – | [illegible] | [illegible] | – | [illegible] | [illegible] | – | [illegible] | [illegible] | – | [illegible] | [illegible] | – | [illegible] | [illegible] | – | [illegible] |
| Richmond, | [illegible] | – | [illegible] | [illegible] | – | [illegible] | [illegible] | – | [illegible] | [illegible] | – | [illegible] | [illegible] | – | [illegible] | [illegible] | – | [illegible] |
| Sligo, | [illegible] | [illegible] | [illegible] | [illegible] | [illegible] | [illegible] | [illegible] | [illegible] | [illegible] | [illegible] | [illegible] | [illegible] | [illegible] | [illegible] | [illegible] | [illegible] | [illegible] | [illegible] |
| Tralee, | [illegible] | [illegible] | [illegible] | [illegible] | [illegible] | [illegible] | [illegible] | [illegible] | [illegible] | [illegible] | [illegible] | [illegible] | [illegible] | [illegible] | [illegible] | [illegible] | [illegible] | [illegible] |
| Tullamore, | [illegible] | [illegible] | [illegible] | [illegible] | [illegible] | [illegible] | [illegible] | [illegible] | [illegible] | [illegible] | [illegible] | [illegible] | [illegible] | [illegible] | [illegible] | [illegible] | [illegible] | [illegible] |
| Waterford, | [illegible] | [illegible] | [illegible] | [illegible] | [illegible] | [illegible] | [illegible] | [illegible] | [illegible] | [illegible] | [illegible] | [illegible] | [illegible] | [illegible] | [illegible] | [illegible] | [illegible] | [illegible] |
| Wexford, | [illegible] | [illegible] | [illegible] | [illegible] | [illegible] | [illegible] | [illegible] | [illegible] | [illegible] | [illegible] | [illegible] | [illegible] | [illegible] | [illegible] | [illegible] | [illegible] | [illegible] | [illegible] |
| **Minor Prisons.** | | | | | | | | | | | | | | | | | | |
| Carlow, | [illegible] | [illegible] | [illegible] | [illegible] | [illegible] | [illegible] | [illegible] | – | [illegible] | [illegible] | [illegible] | [illegible] | – | [illegible] | 1 | [illegible] | 1 | [illegible] |
| Car.-on-Shannon, | [illegible] | – | [illegible] | [illegible] | – | [illegible] | 1 | – | [illegible] | [illegible] | – | [illegible] | [illegible] | – | [illegible] | [illegible] | 1 | [illegible] |
| Cavan, | 3 | – | [illegible] | [illegible] | – | [illegible] | [illegible] | – | [illegible] | [illegible] | [illegible] | [illegible] | [illegible] | [illegible] | [illegible] | [illegible] | 1 | [illegible] |
| Ennis, | [illegible] | – | [illegible] | [illegible] | – | [illegible] | [illegible] | – | [illegible] | [illegible] | – | [illegible] | [illegible] | – | [illegible] | [illegible] | [illegible] | [illegible] |
| Enniskillen, | [illegible] | – | [illegible] | [illegible] | [illegible] | [illegible] | [illegible] | – | [illegible] | [illegible] | [illegible] | [illegible] | [illegible] | – | [illegible] | [illegible] | 1 | [illegible] |
| Lifford, | [illegible] | – | [illegible] | – | [illegible] | [illegible] | – | – | – | – | – | – | – | – | – | [illegible] | – | [illegible] |
| Longford, | [illegible] | – | [illegible] | [illegible] | [illegible] | [illegible] | [illegible] | – | [illegible] | [illegible] | [illegible] | [illegible] | [illegible] | 1 | [illegible] | [illegible] | 1 | [illegible] |
| Monaghan, | [illegible] | – | [illegible] | [illegible] | – | [illegible] | [illegible] | [illegible] | [illegible] | [illegible] | [illegible] | [illegible] | [illegible] | – | [illegible] | [illegible] | – | [illegible] |
| [illegible] | [illegible] | – | [illegible] | [illegible] | – | [illegible] | [illegible] | [illegible] | [illegible] | [illegible] | – | [illegible] | [illegible] | [illegible] | [illegible] | [illegible] | – | [illegible] |
| Trim, | 1 | [illegible] | [illegible] | [illegible] | – | [illegible] | [illegible] | – | [illegible] | [illegible] | – | [illegible] | [illegible] | – | [illegible] | [illegible] | – | [illegible] |
| Wicklow, | [illegible] | 1 | [illegible] | – | – | – | [illegible] | – | [illegible] | [illegible] | – | [illegible] | [illegible] | [illegible] | [illegible] | – | 1 | [illegible] |
| **Convict Prisons—** | | | | | | | | | | | | | | | | | | |
| Mountjoy, Male, | [illegible] | – | [illegible] | [illegible] | – | [illegible] | [illegible] | – | [illegible] | [illegible] | – | [illegible] | [illegible] | – | [illegible] | [illegible] | – | [illegible] |
| Mountjoy, Fem., | – | [illegible] | [illegible] | – | [illegible] | [illegible] | – | [illegible] | [illegible] | – | [illegible] | [illegible] | – | [illegible] | [illegible] | – | [illegible] | [illegible] |
| Total, 1862-63, | [illegible] | [illegible] | [illegible] | [illegible] | [illegible] | [illegible] | [illegible] | [illegible] | [illegible] | [illegible] | [illegible] | [illegible] | [illegible] | [illegible] | [illegible] | [illegible] | [illegible] | [illegible] |

Day of each Month during the Year ended 31st March, 1883 (at Lock-up).

| 1st October, 1882. | | | 1st November, 1882. | | | 1st December, 1882. | | | 1st January, 1883. | | | 1st February, 1883. | | | 1st March, 1883. | | | Prisons. |
|---|---|---|---|---|---|---|---|---|---|---|---|---|---|---|---|---|---|---|
| M. | F. | Tot. | M. | F. | Tot. | M. | F. | Tot. | M. | F. | Tot. | M. | F. | Tot. | M. | F. | Tot. | |
| | | | | | | | | | | | | | | | | | | **Larger Prisons.** |
| 67 | [illegible] | [illegible] | [illegible] | [illegible] | [illegible] | 61 | [illegible] | [illegible] | 47 | [illegible] | [illegible] | [illegible] | [illegible] | [illegible] | [illegible] | [illegible] | [illegible] | Armagh. |
| [illegible] | [illegible] | [illegible] | [illegible] | [illegible] | [illegible] | [illegible] | [illegible] | [illegible] | [illegible] | [illegible] | [illegible] | [illegible] | [illegible] | [illegible] | [illegible] | [illegible] | [illegible] | Belfast. |
| [illegible] | [illegible] | [illegible] | [illegible] | [illegible] | [illegible] | [illegible] | [illegible] | [illegible] | [illegible] | [illegible] | [illegible] | [illegible] | [illegible] | [illegible] | [illegible] | [illegible] | [illegible] | Castlebar. |
| [illegible] | – | [illegible] | [illegible] | – | [illegible] | 64 | – | [illegible] | [illegible] | – | [illegible] | [illegible] | – | [illegible] | 47 | [illegible] | [illegible] | Clonmel. |
| [illegible] | – | [illegible] | [illegible] | – | [illegible] | 161 | – | [illegible] | [illegible] | – | [illegible] | [illegible] | – | [illegible] | [illegible] | – | [illegible] | Cork, Male. |
| – | [illegible] | [illegible] | – | [illegible] | [illegible] | – | [illegible] | [illegible] | – | [illegible] | [illegible] | – | [illegible] | [illegible] | – | [illegible] | [illegible] | Cork, Female. |
| [illegible] | [illegible] | [illegible] | [illegible] | [illegible] | [illegible] | [illegible] | [illegible] | [illegible] | [illegible] | [illegible] | [illegible] | [illegible] | [illegible] | [illegible] | [illegible] | [illegible] | [illegible] | Downpatrick. |
| – | [illegible] | [illegible] | – | [illegible] | [illegible] | – | [illegible] | [illegible] | [illegible] | [illegible] | [illegible] | – | – | – | [illegible] | [illegible] | [illegible] | Drogheda. |
| [illegible] | – | [illegible] | [illegible] | – | [illegible] | [illegible] | – | [illegible] | [illegible] | – | [illegible] | [illegible] | – | [illegible] | [illegible] | – | [illegible] | Dundalk. |
| [illegible] | [illegible] | [illegible] | [illegible] | [illegible] | [illegible] | [illegible] | [illegible] | [illegible] | [illegible] | [illegible] | [illegible] | [illegible] | [illegible] | [illegible] | [illegible] | [illegible] | [illegible] | Galway. |
| [illegible] | [illegible] | [illegible] | [illegible] | [illegible] | [illegible] | [illegible] | [illegible] | [illegible] | [illegible] | [illegible] | [illegible] | [illegible] | [illegible] | [illegible] | [illegible] | [illegible] | [illegible] | Grangegorman. |
| [illegible] | – | [illegible] | [illegible] | [illegible] | [illegible] | [illegible] | [illegible] | [illegible] | [illegible] | [illegible] | [illegible] | [illegible] | [illegible] | [illegible] | [illegible] | [illegible] | [illegible] | Kilkenny. |
| [illegible] | – | [illegible] | [illegible] | – | [illegible] | [illegible] | – | [illegible] | [illegible] | – | [illegible] | [illegible] | – | [illegible] | [illegible] | – | [illegible] | Kilmainham. |
| [illegible] | – | [illegible] | [illegible] | – | [illegible] | [illegible] | – | [illegible] | [illegible] | – | [illegible] | [illegible] | – | [illegible] | [illegible] | – | [illegible] | Limerick, Male. |
| – | [illegible] | [illegible] | – | [illegible] | [illegible] | – | [illegible] | [illegible] | – | [illegible] | [illegible] | – | [illegible] | [illegible] | – | [illegible] | [illegible] | Limerick, Female. |
| [illegible] | [illegible] | [illegible] | [illegible] | [illegible] | [illegible] | [illegible] | [illegible] | [illegible] | [illegible] | [illegible] | [illegible] | [illegible] | [illegible] | [illegible] | [illegible] | [illegible] | [illegible] | Londonderry. |
| [illegible] | – | [illegible] | [illegible] | – | [illegible] | [illegible] | – | [illegible] | [illegible] | – | [illegible] | [illegible] | – | [illegible] | [illegible] | – | [illegible] | Maryboro'. |
| [illegible] | [illegible] | [illegible] | [illegible] | [illegible] | [illegible] | [illegible] | [illegible] | [illegible] | [illegible] | [illegible] | [illegible] | [illegible] | [illegible] | [illegible] | [illegible] | [illegible] | [illegible] | Mullingar. |
| [illegible] | [illegible] | [illegible] | [illegible] | [illegible] | [illegible] | [illegible] | [illegible] | [illegible] | [illegible] | [illegible] | [illegible] | [illegible] | [illegible] | [illegible] | [illegible] | [illegible] | [illegible] | Naas. |
| [illegible] | – | [illegible] | [illegible] | – | [illegible] | [illegible] | – | [illegible] | [illegible] | – | [illegible] | [illegible] | – | [illegible] | [illegible] | | [illegible] | Nenagh. |
| 47 | [illegible] | [illegible] | [illegible] | [illegible] | [illegible] | [illegible] | [illegible] | [illegible] | [illegible] | [illegible] | [illegible] | [illegible] | [illegible] | [illegible] | [illegible] | [illegible] | [illegible] | Omagh. |
| [illegible] | – | [illegible] | [illegible] | – | [illegible] | [illegible] | – | [illegible] | [illegible] | – | [illegible] | [illegible] | – | [illegible] | [illegible] | – | [illegible] | Richmond. |
| [illegible] | [illegible] | [illegible] | [illegible] | [illegible] | [illegible] | [illegible] | [illegible] | [illegible] | [illegible] | [illegible] | [illegible] | [illegible] | [illegible] | [illegible] | [illegible] | [illegible] | [illegible] | Sligo. |
| [illegible] | [illegible] | [illegible] | [illegible] | [illegible] | [illegible] | [illegible] | [illegible] | [illegible] | [illegible] | [illegible] | [illegible] | [illegible] | [illegible] | [illegible] | [illegible] | [illegible] | [illegible] | Tralee. |
| [illegible] | [illegible] | [illegible] | [illegible] | [illegible] | [illegible] | [illegible] | [illegible] | [illegible] | [illegible] | [illegible] | [illegible] | [illegible] | [illegible] | [illegible] | [illegible] | [illegible] | [illegible] | Tullamore. |
| [illegible] | [illegible] | [illegible] | [illegible] | [illegible] | [illegible] | [illegible] | [illegible] | [illegible] | [illegible] | [illegible] | [illegible] | [illegible] | [illegible] | [illegible] | [illegible] | [illegible] | [illegible] | Waterford. |
| [illegible] | [illegible] | [illegible] | [illegible] | [illegible] | [illegible] | [illegible] | [illegible] | [illegible] | [illegible] | [illegible] | [illegible] | [illegible] | [illegible] | [illegible] | [illegible] | [illegible] | [illegible] | Wexford. |
| | | | | | | | | | | | | | | | | | | **Minor Prisons.** |
| [illegible] | [illegible] | [illegible] | – | – | – | [illegible] | [illegible] | [illegible] | – | [illegible] | [illegible] | – | – | – | [illegible] | – | [illegible] | Carlow. |
| [illegible] | – | [illegible] | [illegible] | – | [illegible] | – | [illegible] | [illegible] | [illegible] | [illegible] | [illegible] | – | – | – | [illegible] | – | [illegible] | Carrick-on-Shannon. |
| [illegible] | [illegible] | [illegible] | [illegible] | [illegible] | [illegible] | [illegible] | [illegible] | [illegible] | – | – | – | – | – | – | [illegible] | [illegible] | [illegible] | Cavan. |
| [illegible] | [illegible] | [illegible] | [illegible] | [illegible] | [illegible] | [illegible] | [illegible] | [illegible] | [illegible] | [illegible] | [illegible] | [illegible] | [illegible] | [illegible] | [illegible] | – | [illegible] | Ennis. |
| – | – | – | [illegible] | [illegible] | [illegible] | [illegible] | – | [illegible] | [illegible] | [illegible] | [illegible] | [illegible] | [illegible] | [illegible] | [illegible] | – | [illegible] | Enniskillen. |
| [illegible] | [illegible] | [illegible] | [illegible] | – | [illegible] | [illegible] | – | – | [illegible] | – | [illegible] | [illegible] | [illegible] | [illegible] | [illegible] | [illegible] | [illegible] | Lifford. |
| [illegible] | [illegible] | [illegible] | – | [illegible] | [illegible] | [illegible] | – | [illegible] | [illegible] | – | [illegible] | [illegible] | [illegible] | [illegible] | [illegible] | – | [illegible] | Longford. |
| [illegible] | [illegible] | [illegible] | [illegible] | – | [illegible] | [illegible] | [illegible] | [illegible] | [illegible] | [illegible] | [illegible] | [illegible] | [illegible] | [illegible] | – | [illegible] | [illegible] | Monaghan. |
| [illegible] | [illegible] | [illegible] | [illegible] | – | [illegible] | – | – | – | – | – | [illegible] | [illegible] | – | [illegible] | [illegible] | [illegible] | [illegible] | Roscommon. |
| [illegible] | – | [illegible] | [illegible] | – | [illegible] | – | – | – | – | – | [illegible] | – | – | [illegible] | [illegible] | – | [illegible] | Trim. |
| [illegible] | – | [illegible] | [illegible] | – | [illegible] | [illegible] | [illegible] | [illegible] | [illegible] | – | [illegible] | – | – | [illegible] | [illegible] | [illegible] | [illegible] | Wicklow. |
| | | | | | | | | | | | | | | | | | | Convict Prisons— |
| [illegible] | – | [illegible] | [illegible] | – | [illegible] | [illegible] | – | [illegible] | [illegible] | – | [illegible] | [illegible] | – | [illegible] | [illegible] | – | [illegible] | Mountjoy, Male. |
| – | [illegible] | [illegible] | – | [illegible] | [illegible] | – | [illegible] | [illegible] | – | [illegible] | [illegible] | – | [illegible] | [illegible] | – | [illegible] | [illegible] | Mountjoy, Fem. |
| [illegible] | [illegible] | [illegible] | [illegible] | [illegible] | [illegible] | [illegible] | [illegible] | [illegible] | [illegible] | [illegible] | [illegible] | [illegible] | [illegible] | [illegible] | [illegible] | [illegible] | [illegible] | Total, 1882-83. |

TABLE III.—DAILY AVERAGE NUMBER of PRISONERS in CUSTODY, &c., &c., from 1st April, 1882, to 31st March, 1883.

| NAMES OF PRISONS. | Daily Average Number of Prisoners. | | | Highest Number confined at any one time (with Date). | | Lowest Number confined at any one time (with Date). | | Highest Number of Male Prisoners confined at any one time. | | Highest Number of Female Prisoners confined at any one time. | | Lowest Number of Male Prisoners confined at any one time. | | Lowest Number of Female Prisoners confined at any one time. | |
|---|---|---|---|---|---|---|---|---|---|---|---|---|---|---|---|
| | M. | F. | Total. | No. | Date. | No. | Date. | No. | Date. | No. | Date. | No. | Date. | No. | Date. |
| Larger Prisons. | | | | | | | | | | | | | | | |
| Armagh, | [illegible] | [illegible] | [illegible] | [illegible] | [illegible] | [illegible] | [illegible] | [illegible] | [illegible] | [illegible] | [illegible] | [illegible] | [illegible] | [illegible] | [illegible] |
| Belfast, | [illegible] | [illegible] | [illegible] | [illegible] | [illegible] | [illegible] | [illegible] | [illegible] | [illegible] | [illegible] | [illegible] | [illegible] | [illegible] | [illegible] | [illegible] |
| Castlebar, | [illegible] | [illegible] | [illegible] | [illegible] | [illegible] | [illegible] | [illegible] | [illegible] | [illegible] | [illegible] | [illegible] | [illegible] | [illegible] | [illegible] | [illegible] |
| Clonmel, | [illegible] | [illegible] | [illegible] | [illegible] | [illegible] | [illegible] | [illegible] | [illegible] | [illegible] | [illegible] | [illegible] | [illegible] | [illegible] | [illegible] | [illegible] |
| Cork, Male, | [illegible] | [illegible] | [illegible] | [illegible] | [illegible] | [illegible] | [illegible] | [illegible] | [illegible] | [illegible] | [illegible] | [illegible] | [illegible] | [illegible] | [illegible] |
| Cork, Female, | [illegible] | [illegible] | [illegible] | [illegible] | [illegible] | [illegible] | [illegible] | [illegible] | [illegible] | [illegible] | [illegible] | [illegible] | [illegible] | [illegible] | [illegible] |
| Downpatrick, | [illegible] | [illegible] | [illegible] | [illegible] | [illegible] | [illegible] | [illegible] | [illegible] | [illegible] | [illegible] | [illegible] | [illegible] | [illegible] | [illegible] | [illegible] |
| Drogheda, | [illegible] | [illegible] | [illegible] | [illegible] | [illegible] | [illegible] | [illegible] | [illegible] | [illegible] | [illegible] | [illegible] | [illegible] | [illegible] | [illegible] | [illegible] |
| Dundalk, | [illegible] | [illegible] | [illegible] | [illegible] | [illegible] | [illegible] | [illegible] | [illegible] | [illegible] | [illegible] | [illegible] | [illegible] | [illegible] | [illegible] | [illegible] |
| Galway, | [illegible] | [illegible] | [illegible] | [illegible] | [illegible] | [illegible] | [illegible] | [illegible] | [illegible] | [illegible] | [illegible] | [illegible] | [illegible] | [illegible] | [illegible] |
| Grangegorman, | [illegible] | [illegible] | [illegible] | [illegible] | [illegible] | [illegible] | [illegible] | [illegible] | [illegible] | [illegible] | [illegible] | [illegible] | [illegible] | [illegible] | [illegible] |
| Kilkenny, | [illegible] | [illegible] | [illegible] | [illegible] | [illegible] | [illegible] | [illegible] | [illegible] | [illegible] | [illegible] | [illegible] | [illegible] | [illegible] | [illegible] | [illegible] |
| Kilmainham, | [illegible] | [illegible] | [illegible] | [illegible] | [illegible] | [illegible] | [illegible] | [illegible] | [illegible] | [illegible] | [illegible] | [illegible] | [illegible] | [illegible] | [illegible] |
| Limerick, Male, | [illegible] | [illegible] | [illegible] | [illegible] | [illegible] | [illegible] | [illegible] | [illegible] | [illegible] | [illegible] | [illegible] | [illegible] | [illegible] | [illegible] | [illegible] |
| Limerick, Female, | [illegible] | [illegible] | [illegible] | [illegible] | [illegible] | [illegible] | [illegible] | [illegible] | [illegible] | [illegible] | [illegible] | [illegible] | [illegible] | [illegible] | [illegible] |
| Londonderry, | [illegible] | [illegible] | [illegible] | [illegible] | [illegible] | [illegible] | [illegible] | [illegible] | [illegible] | [illegible] | [illegible] | [illegible] | [illegible] | [illegible] | [illegible] |
| Maryborough, | [illegible] | [illegible] | [illegible] | [illegible] | [illegible] | [illegible] | [illegible] | [illegible] | [illegible] | [illegible] | [illegible] | [illegible] | [illegible] | [illegible] | [illegible] |
| Mullingar, | [illegible] | [illegible] | [illegible] | [illegible] | [illegible] | [illegible] | [illegible] | [illegible] | [illegible] | [illegible] | [illegible] | [illegible] | [illegible] | [illegible] | [illegible] |
| Naas, | [illegible] | [illegible] | [illegible] | [illegible] | [illegible] | [illegible] | [illegible] | [illegible] | [illegible] | [illegible] | [illegible] | [illegible] | [illegible] | [illegible] | [illegible] |
| Nenagh, | [illegible] | [illegible] | [illegible] | [illegible] | [illegible] | [illegible] | [illegible] | [illegible] | [illegible] | [illegible] | [illegible] | [illegible] | [illegible] | [illegible] | [illegible] |
| Omagh, | [illegible] | [illegible] | [illegible] | [illegible] | [illegible] | [illegible] | [illegible] | [illegible] | [illegible] | [illegible] | [illegible] | [illegible] | [illegible] | [illegible] | [illegible] |
| Richmond, | [illegible] | [illegible] | [illegible] | [illegible] | [illegible] | [illegible] | [illegible] | [illegible] | [illegible] | [illegible] | [illegible] | [illegible] | [illegible] | [illegible] | [illegible] |
| Sligo, | [illegible] | [illegible] | [illegible] | [illegible] | [illegible] | [illegible] | [illegible] | [illegible] | [illegible] | [illegible] | [illegible] | [illegible] | [illegible] | [illegible] | [illegible] |
| Tralee, | [illegible] | [illegible] | [illegible] | [illegible] | [illegible] | [illegible] | [illegible] | [illegible] | [illegible] | [illegible] | [illegible] | [illegible] | [illegible] | [illegible] | [illegible] |
| Tullamore, | [illegible] | [illegible] | [illegible] | [illegible] | [illegible] | [illegible] | [illegible] | [illegible] | [illegible] | [illegible] | [illegible] | [illegible] | [illegible] | [illegible] | [illegible] |
| Waterford, | [illegible] | [illegible] | [illegible] | [illegible] | [illegible] | [illegible] | [illegible] | [illegible] | [illegible] | [illegible] | [illegible] | [illegible] | [illegible] | [illegible] | [illegible] |
| Wexford, | [illegible] | [illegible] | [illegible] | [illegible] | [illegible] | [illegible] | [illegible] | [illegible] | [illegible] | [illegible] | [illegible] | [illegible] | [illegible] | [illegible] | [illegible] |
| Minor Prisons. | | | | | | | | | | | | | | | |
| Carlow, | [illegible] | [illegible] | [illegible] | [illegible] | [illegible] | [illegible] | [illegible] | [illegible] | [illegible] | [illegible] | [illegible] | [illegible] | [illegible] | [illegible] | [illegible] |
| Carrick-on-Shannon, | [illegible] | [illegible] | [illegible] | [illegible] | [illegible] | [illegible] | [illegible] | [illegible] | [illegible] | [illegible] | [illegible] | [illegible] | [illegible] | [illegible] | [illegible] |
| Cavan, | [illegible] | [illegible] | [illegible] | [illegible] | [illegible] | [illegible] | [illegible] | [illegible] | [illegible] | [illegible] | [illegible] | [illegible] | [illegible] | [illegible] | [illegible] |
| Ennis, | [illegible] | [illegible] | [illegible] | [illegible] | [illegible] | [illegible] | [illegible] | [illegible] | [illegible] | [illegible] | [illegible] | [illegible] | [illegible] | [illegible] | [illegible] |
| Enniskillen, | [illegible] | [illegible] | [illegible] | [illegible] | [illegible] | [illegible] | [illegible] | [illegible] | [illegible] | [illegible] | [illegible] | [illegible] | [illegible] | [illegible] | [illegible] |
| Lifford, | [illegible] | [illegible] | [illegible] | [illegible] | [illegible] | [illegible] | [illegible] | [illegible] | [illegible] | [illegible] | [illegible] | [illegible] | [illegible] | [illegible] | [illegible] |
| Longford, | [illegible] | [illegible] | [illegible] | [illegible] | [illegible] | [illegible] | [illegible] | [illegible] | [illegible] | [illegible] | [illegible] | [illegible] | [illegible] | [illegible] | [illegible] |
| Monaghan, | [illegible] | [illegible] | [illegible] | [illegible] | [illegible] | [illegible] | [illegible] | [illegible] | [illegible] | [illegible] | [illegible] | [illegible] | [illegible] | [illegible] | [illegible] |
| Roscommon, | [illegible] | [illegible] | [illegible] | [illegible] | [illegible] | [illegible] | [illegible] | [illegible] | [illegible] | [illegible] | [illegible] | [illegible] | [illegible] | [illegible] | [illegible] |
| Trim, | [illegible] | [illegible] | [illegible] | [illegible] | [illegible] | [illegible] | [illegible] | [illegible] | [illegible] | [illegible] | [illegible] | [illegible] | [illegible] | [illegible] | [illegible] |
| Wicklow, | [illegible] | [illegible] | [illegible] | [illegible] | [illegible] | [illegible] | [illegible] | [illegible] | [illegible] | [illegible] | [illegible] | [illegible] | [illegible] | [illegible] | [illegible] |
| County Prisons in Mountjoy, Male, | [illegible] | [illegible] | [illegible] | [illegible] | [illegible] | [illegible] | [illegible] | [illegible] | [illegible] | [illegible] | [illegible] | [illegible] | [illegible] | [illegible] | [illegible] |
| „ Fem., | [illegible] | [illegible] | [illegible] | [illegible] | [illegible] | [illegible] | [illegible] | [illegible] | [illegible] | [illegible] | [illegible] | [illegible] | [illegible] | [illegible] | [illegible] |
| Total, 1882-83, | [illegible] | [illegible] | [illegible] | – | – | – | – | – | – | – | – | – | – | – | – |
| Total, 1881-82, | [illegible] | [illegible] | [illegible] | – | – | – | – | – | – | – | – | – | – | – | – |

**Table IV.—Deaths in Local Prisons and their Causes from 1st April, 1882, to 31st March, 1883.**

| Prisons in which Deaths occurred. | No. | Initials of Name. | Sex. | Age. | Crime, &c., for which Convicted or charged. | Date of Committal. | Date of Death. | Disease, &c., which caused Death. |
|---|---|---|---|---|---|---|---|---|
| Belfast, | 1 | M. L. | F. | 30 | [illegible] | 25:4:82 | 9:6:82 | Inflammation of lungs. |
| Carrick (Military prison), | 1 | J. W. | M. | [illegible] | Drunkenness, | [illegible] | [illegible] | Erysipelas [illegible] |
| Cork, Male, | 1 | T. M. | M. | [illegible] | Murder, | [illegible] | [illegible] | Executed. |
| Cork Female, | | M. C. | F. | [illegible] | Drunkenness, | 24:7:82 | [illegible] | Consumption (acute). |
| Dundalk, | 1 | T. S. | M. | [illegible] | Murder, | [illegible] | [illegible] | Acute dyspepsia and bronchitis. |
| Galway, | 7 | [illegible] | M. | [illegible] | Murder, | [illegible] | [illegible] | Executed. |
| Kilkenny, | 1 | J. D. | M. | [illegible] | Rape, | [illegible] | [illegible] | [illegible] |
| Kilmainham, | 1 | M. B. | M. | [illegible] | Conspiracy to [illegible] | [illegible] | [illegible] | Congestion of the brain. |
| Limerick, Male, | 1 | F. H. | M. | [illegible] | Murder, | [illegible] | [illegible] | Executed. |
| Tralee, | 2 | [illegible] | M. | [illegible] | Murder, | [illegible] | [illegible] | Executed. |
| County [illegible] Monaghan, Female, | 1 | L. R. | F. | 45 | Drunkenness, | [illegible] | [illegible] | Organic disease of the [illegible] |

**Table V.—Escapes from Local Prisons and Bridewells from 1st April, 1882, to 31st March, 1883.**

| Prisons from which Escapes were effected. | Initials of Name. | Sex. | Age. | Date. | Offence of which convicted or charged. | Tried or Untried. | Whether effected separately or with others. | Whether retaken or not. |
|---|---|---|---|---|---|---|---|---|
| Ennis (Military prison), | A. H. | M. | 19 | [illegible]:1:83 | Desertion, | Untried, | Separately, | Yes. |
| Tralee, | M. W. | M. | 17 | 18:8:82 | Larceny of goods, | Tried, | Separately, | Yes. |

TABLE VI.—NUMBER of INDIVIDUALS, exclusive of DEBTORS, committed to the them who were not known to have been in Prison before that year, and the from their *first* Commitment in *any year*,—to 31st March, 1883.

| Larger Prisons. | Number of Commitments. | | Number of Individuals Committed. | | Number of them which had not been in Prison before 1st April, 18[illegible]. | | Number. | | | | | |
|---|---|---|---|---|---|---|---|---|---|---|---|---|
| | | | | | | | Once only. | | Twice. | | Thrice. | |
| | M. | F. | M. | F. | M. | F. | M. | F. | M. | F. | M. | F. |
| Armagh, | [illegible] | [illegible] | [illegible] | [illegible] | [illegible] | [illegible] | [illegible] | [illegible] | [illegible] | [illegible] | [illegible] | [illegible] |
| Belfast, | [illegible] | [illegible] | [illegible] | [illegible] | [illegible] | [illegible] | [illegible] | [illegible] | [illegible] | [illegible] | [illegible] | [illegible] |
| Castlebar, | [illegible] | [illegible] | [illegible] | [illegible] | [illegible] | [illegible] | [illegible] | [illegible] | [illegible] | [illegible] | [illegible] | [illegible] |
| Clonmel, | [illegible] | [illegible] | [illegible] | [illegible] | [illegible] | [illegible] | [illegible] | 17 | [illegible] | [illegible] | [illegible] | [illegible] |
| Cork, Male, | [illegible] | — | [illegible] | — | [illegible] | — | [illegible] | — | [illegible] | — | [illegible] | — |
| Cork, Female, | — | [illegible] | — | [illegible] | — | [illegible] | — | [illegible] | — | [illegible] | — | [illegible] |
| Downpatrick, | [illegible] | [illegible] | [illegible] | [illegible] | [illegible] | [illegible] | [illegible] | [illegible] | [illegible] | 5 | [illegible] | [illegible] |
| Drogheda, | [illegible] | [illegible] | [illegible] | [illegible] | [illegible] | [illegible] | [illegible] | [illegible] | [illegible] | [illegible] | [illegible] | [illegible] |
| Dundalk, | [illegible] | — | [illegible] | — | [illegible] | — | [illegible] | — | [illegible] | — | [illegible] | — |
| Galway, | [illegible] | [illegible] | [illegible] | [illegible] | [illegible] | [illegible] | [illegible] | [illegible] | [illegible] | [illegible] | [illegible] | [illegible] |
| Grangegorman, | [illegible] | [illegible] | [illegible] | [illegible] | [illegible] | [illegible] | [illegible] | [illegible] | [illegible] | [illegible] | [illegible] | [illegible] |
| Kilkenny, | [illegible] | [illegible] | [illegible] | [illegible] | [illegible] | [illegible] | [illegible] | [illegible] | [illegible] | [illegible] | [illegible] | [illegible] |
| Kilmainham, | [illegible] | — | [illegible] | — | [illegible] | — | [illegible] | — | [illegible] | — | [illegible] | — |
| Limerick, Male, | [illegible] | — | [illegible] | — | [illegible] | — | [illegible] | — | [illegible] | — | [illegible] | — |
| Limerick, Female, | — | [illegible] | — | [illegible] | — | — | — | [illegible] | — | [illegible] | — | [illegible] |
| Londonderry, | [illegible] | [illegible] | [illegible] | [illegible] | [illegible] | [illegible] | [illegible] | [illegible] | [illegible] | [illegible] | [illegible] | [illegible] |
| Maryborough, | [illegible] | [illegible] | [illegible] | [illegible] | [illegible] | [illegible] | [illegible] | [illegible] | [illegible] | [illegible] | [illegible] | [illegible] |
| Mullingar, | [illegible] | [illegible] | [illegible] | [illegible] | [illegible] | [illegible] | [illegible] | [illegible] | [illegible] | [illegible] | [illegible] | [illegible] |
| Naas, | [illegible] | [illegible] | [illegible] | [illegible] | [illegible] | [illegible] | [illegible] | [illegible] | [illegible] | [illegible] | [illegible] | [illegible] |
| Nenagh, | [illegible] | — | [illegible] | — | [illegible] | — | [illegible] | — | [illegible] | — | [illegible] | — |
| Omagh, | [illegible] | [illegible] | [illegible] | [illegible] | [illegible] | [illegible] | [illegible] | [illegible] | [illegible] | [illegible] | [illegible] | [illegible] |
| Richmond, | [illegible] | — | [illegible] | — | [illegible] | — | [illegible] | — | [illegible] | — | [illegible] | — |
| Sligo, | [illegible] | [illegible] | [illegible] | [illegible] | [illegible] | 44 | [illegible] | [illegible] | [illegible] | [illegible] | [illegible] | [illegible] |
| Tralee, | [illegible] | [illegible] | [illegible] | [illegible] | [illegible] | [illegible] | [illegible] | [illegible] | [illegible] | [illegible] | [illegible] | [illegible] |
| Tullamore, | [illegible] | [illegible] | [illegible] | [illegible] | [illegible] | [illegible] | [illegible] | [illegible] | [illegible] | [illegible] | [illegible] | [illegible] |
| Waterford, | [illegible] | [illegible] | [illegible] | [illegible] | [illegible] | [illegible] | [illegible] | [illegible] | [illegible] | [illegible] | [illegible] | [illegible] |
| Wexford, | [illegible] | [illegible] | [illegible] | [illegible] | [illegible] | [illegible] | [illegible] | [illegible] | [illegible] | [illegible] | [illegible] | [illegible] |
| Total, Males, | [illegible] | — | [illegible] | — | [illegible] | — | [illegible] | — | [illegible] | — | [illegible] | — |
| Total, Females, | — | [illegible] | — | [illegible] | — | [illegible] | — | [illegible] | — | [illegible] | — | [illegible] |
| Total, M. and F., | [illegible] | | [illegible] | | [illegible] | | [illegible] | | [illegible] | | [illegible] | |

**undermentioned Prisons from 1st April, 1882, to 31st March, 1883; Number of Number of them who had undergone One, Two, Three, &c., Commitments**

| [illegible] 31st March, 1883, committed— | | | | | | | | | | | | | | Number of Individuals known to have been committed [illegible] up to 31st March, 1883. (Column No. 1.) | | Name of Prison. |
|---|---|---|---|---|---|---|---|---|---|---|---|---|---|---|---|---|
| Three times. | | Five times. | | Six times. | | Seven to Eleven times. | | Twelve to Sixteen times. | | Seventeen to Twenty times. | | Twenty-one times and upwards. | | | | |
| M. | F. | M. | F. | M. | F. | M. | F. | M. | F. | M. | F. | M. | F. | M. | F. | |
| [illegible] | [illegible] | [illegible] | [illegible] | [illegible] | [illegible] | [illegible] | [illegible] | [illegible] | [illegible] | [illegible] | [illegible] | [illegible] | [illegible] | [illegible] | [illegible] | Armagh. |
| [illegible] | [illegible] | [illegible] | [illegible] | [illegible] | [illegible] | [illegible] | [illegible] | [illegible] | [illegible] | [illegible] | [illegible] | [illegible] | [illegible] | [illegible] | [illegible] | Belfast. |
| [illegible] | [illegible] | [illegible] | [illegible] | [illegible] | – | [illegible] | [illegible] | [illegible] | – | – | – | [illegible] | [illegible] | [illegible] | [illegible] | Castlebar. |
| [illegible] | – | [illegible] | 1 | [illegible] | 1 | [illegible] | [illegible] | [illegible] | 1 | – | – | [illegible] | [illegible] | 1,640 | 108 | Clonmel. |
| [illegible] | – | [illegible] | – | [illegible] | – | 101 | – | [illegible] | – | [illegible] | – | [illegible] | – | [illegible] | – | Cork, Male. |
| – | [illegible] | – | [illegible] | – | [illegible] | – | [illegible] | – | [illegible] | – | [illegible] | – | [illegible] | – | [illegible] | Cork, Female. |
| [illegible] | [illegible] | [illegible] | [illegible] | [illegible] | 1 | [illegible] | [illegible] | [illegible] | [illegible] | 1 | [illegible] | [illegible] | [illegible] | [illegible] | [illegible] | Downpatrick. |
| – | [illegible] | [illegible] | [illegible] | – | [illegible] | [illegible] | [illegible] | [illegible] | [illegible] | – | [illegible] | [illegible] | [illegible] | [illegible] | [illegible] | Drogheda. |
| [illegible] | – | [illegible] | – | [illegible] | – | [illegible] | – | [illegible] | – | [illegible] | – | [illegible] | – | [illegible] | – | Dundalk. |
| 17 | 18 | [illegible] | [illegible] | [illegible] | [illegible] | [illegible] | [illegible] | [illegible] | [illegible] | [illegible] | [illegible] | [illegible] | [illegible] | [illegible] | [illegible] | Galway. |
| [illegible] | [illegible] | [illegible] | [illegible] | [illegible] | [illegible] | [illegible] | [illegible] | [illegible] | [illegible] | [illegible] | [illegible] | 1 | [illegible] | [illegible] | [illegible] | Grangegorman. |
| [illegible] | [illegible] | [illegible] | – | [illegible] | [illegible] | [illegible] | [illegible] | [illegible] | [illegible] | [illegible] | [illegible] | [illegible] | [illegible] | [illegible] | [illegible] | Kilkenny. |
| [illegible] | – | [illegible] | – | [illegible] | – | [illegible] | – | [illegible] | – | [illegible] | – | [illegible] | – | [illegible] | – | Kilmainham. |
| [illegible] | – | [illegible] | – | [illegible] | – | [illegible] | – | [illegible] | – | [illegible] | – | [illegible] | – | [illegible] | – | Limerick, Male. |
| – | [illegible] | – | [illegible] | – | [illegible] | – | [illegible] | – | [illegible] | – | [illegible] | – | [illegible] | – | [illegible] | Limerick, Female. |
| [illegible] | [illegible] | [illegible] | [illegible] | [illegible] | [illegible] | [illegible] | [illegible] | [illegible] | [illegible] | [illegible] | [illegible] | [illegible] | [illegible] | [illegible] | [illegible] | Londonderry. |
| [illegible] | – | [illegible] | – | [illegible] | [illegible] | [illegible] | – | [illegible] | – | [illegible] | – | [illegible] | – | [illegible] | [illegible] | Maryborough. |
| [illegible] | [illegible] | [illegible] | [illegible] | [illegible] | [illegible] | [illegible] | [illegible] | [illegible] | [illegible] | [illegible] | [illegible] | [illegible] | [illegible] | [illegible] | [illegible] | Mullingar. |
| [illegible] | [illegible] | [illegible] | [illegible] | [illegible] | [illegible] | [illegible] | [illegible] | [illegible] | [illegible] | [illegible] | [illegible] | [illegible] | [illegible] | [illegible] | [illegible] | Naas. |
| [illegible] | – | [illegible] | – | [illegible] | – | [illegible] | – | [illegible] | – | [illegible] | – | [illegible] | – | [illegible] | – | Nenagh. |
| [illegible] | – | [illegible] | – | [illegible] | [illegible] | [illegible] | [illegible] | [illegible] | [illegible] | – | [illegible] | [illegible] | – | [illegible] | [illegible] | Omagh. |
| [illegible] | – | [illegible] | – | [illegible] | – | [illegible] | – | [illegible] | – | [illegible] | – | [illegible] | – | [illegible] | – | Richmond. |
| [illegible] | [illegible] | [illegible] | [illegible] | [illegible] | [illegible] | [illegible] | [illegible] | [illegible] | [illegible] | [illegible] | [illegible] | [illegible] | [illegible] | [illegible] | [illegible] | Sligo. |
| [illegible] | [illegible] | [illegible] | [illegible] | [illegible] | [illegible] | [illegible] | [illegible] | [illegible] | [illegible] | [illegible] | – | [illegible] | [illegible] | [illegible] | [illegible] | Tralee. |
| [illegible] | [illegible] | [illegible] | [illegible] | [illegible] | – | [illegible] | [illegible] | – | [illegible] | [illegible] | – | [illegible] | 1 | [illegible] | [illegible] | Tullamore. |
| [illegible] | [illegible] | [illegible] | [illegible] | [illegible] | [illegible] | [illegible] | [illegible] | [illegible] | [illegible] | [illegible] | [illegible] | [illegible] | [illegible] | [illegible] | [illegible] | Waterford. |
| [illegible] | – | 2 | – | [illegible] | [illegible] | [illegible] | [illegible] | [illegible] | – | – | – | 1 | – | [illegible] | [illegible] | Wexford. |
| [illegible] | – | [illegible] | – | [illegible] | – | [illegible] | – | [illegible] | – | [illegible] | – | [illegible] | – | [illegible] | – | Total, Males. |
| – | [illegible] | – | [illegible] | – | [illegible] | – | [illegible] | – | [illegible] | – | [illegible] | – | [illegible] | – | [illegible] | Total, Females. |
| [illegible] | | [illegible] | | [illegible] | | [illegible] | | [illegible] | | [illegible] | | [illegible] | | [illegible] | | Total, M. and F. |

TABLE VII.—SENTENCES OF DEATH, PENAL SERVITUDE, IMPRI-

| Prisons. | Death. | | Penal Servitude for: Life. | | Above 15 Years. | | 15 Years and above 10. | | 10 Years and above 7. | | 7 Years. | | 5 Years. | | Imprisonment for: [illegible] Years and above 2. | | [illegible] Years and above 18 Months. | |
|---|---|---|---|---|---|---|---|---|---|---|---|---|---|---|---|---|---|---|
| | M. | F. | M. | F. | M. | F. | M. | F. | M. | F. | M. | F. | M. | F. | M. | F. | M. | F. |
| Armagh, | – | – | – | – | – | – | – | – | – | – | – | – | 9 | – | – | – | 1 | – |
| Belfast, | – | – | – | – | – | – | 1 | – | – | – | 8 | – | 34 | 1 | – | – | – | – |
| Carlow, | – | – | – | – | – | – | – | – | – | – | – | – | – | – | – | – | – | – |
| Carrick-on-Shannon, | – | – | – | – | – | – | – | – | – | – | – | – | – | – | – | – | – | – |
| Castlebar, | – | – | – | – | – | – | – | – | – | – | – | 1 | – | 6 | – | – | – | – |
| Cavan, | – | – | – | – | – | – | – | – | – | – | – | – | – | – | – | – | – | – |
| Clonmel, | – | – | – | – | – | – | – | – | – | – | 1 | – | 1 | – | – | – | 2 | – |
| Cork, Male, | 8 | – | 6 | – | 1 | – | 1 | – | 1 | – | 9 | – | 6 | – | – | – | 3 | – |
| Cork, Female, | – | – | – | – | – | – | – | – | – | – | – | – | – | 6 | – | – | – | 1 |
| Downpatrick, | – | – | – | – | – | – | – | – | – | – | 1 | 1 | 2 | – | – | – | – | – |
| Drogheda, | – | – | – | – | – | – | – | – | – | – | – | – | – | – | – | – | – | – |
| Dundalk, | – | – | – | – | – | – | – | – | – | – | – | – | – | – | – | – | 8 | – |
| Ennis, | – | – | – | – | – | – | – | – | – | – | – | – | – | – | – | – | – | – |
| Enniskillen, | – | – | – | – | – | – | – | – | – | – | – | – | – | – | – | – | – | – |
| Galway, | 7 | – | 6 | – | – | – | – | – | – | – | – | – | 2 | – | – | – | – | – |
| Grangegorman, | – | – | – | – | – | – | – | – | – | – | – | 6 | – | 4 | – | – | – | – |
| Kilkenny, | 1 | – | – | – | 1 | – | – | – | 1 | – | – | – | 2 | – | – | – | – | – |
| Kilmainham, | – | – | 1 | – | – | – | 1 | – | 1 | – | 8 | – | 10 | – | – | – | 2 | – |
| Lifford, | – | – | – | – | – | – | – | – | – | – | – | – | – | – | – | – | – | – |
| Limerick, Male, | 1 | – | – | – | – | – | – | – | – | – | – | – | 1 | – | – | – | – | – |
| Limerick, Female, | – | – | – | – | – | – | – | – | – | – | – | – | – | 1 | – | – | – | – |
| Londonderry, | – | – | – | – | – | – | – | – | – | – | 1 | 1 | 9 | – | – | – | – | – |
| Longford, | – | – | – | – | – | – | – | – | – | – | – | – | – | – | – | – | – | – |
| Maryborough, | – | – | – | – | – | – | – | – | – | – | – | – | 3 | – | – | – | – | – |
| Monaghan, | – | – | – | – | – | – | – | – | – | – | – | – | – | – | – | – | – | – |
| Mullingar, | – | – | – | – | – | – | – | – | – | – | 1 | – | 4 | 6 | – | – | 8 | – |
| Naas, | – | 1 | – | – | – | – | – | – | – | – | 1 | – | – | – | – | – | 4 | – |
| Nenagh, | – | – | – | – | 1 | – | – | – | 1 | – | – | – | 1 | – | – | – | – | – |
| Omagh, | – | – | – | – | – | – | – | – | – | – | 9 | – | – | – | – | – | 1 | – |
| Richmond, | – | – | – | – | 1 | – | – | – | 3 | – | 6 | – | 64 | – | – | – | 3 | – |
| Roscommon, | – | – | – | – | – | – | – | – | – | – | – | – | – | – | – | – | – | – |
| Sligo, | – | – | – | – | – | – | – | – | – | – | 1 | 3 | 1 | 1 | – | – | – | – |
| Tralee, | 2 | – | – | – | 1 | – | 1 | – | 4 | – | 6 | – | 3 | – | – | – | 1 | – |
| Trim, | – | – | – | – | – | – | 1 | – | – | – | – | 1 | – | – | – | – | – | – |
| Tullamore, | – | – | – | – | – | – | – | – | – | – | – | – | – | – | – | – | – | – |
| Waterford, | – | – | – | – | – | – | – | – | – | – | – | – | – | – | – | – | 3 | – |
| Wexford, | – | – | – | – | – | – | – | – | – | – | – | – | – | 1 | 1 | – | 1 | – |
| Wicklow, | – | – | – | – | 2 | – | – | – | 1 | – | 1 | – | 2 | – | – | – | 1 | – |
| Total, Males, | 14 | – | 3 | – | 7 | – | 5 | – | 12 | – | 57 | – | 161 | – | 1 | – | 24 | – |
| Total, Females, | – | 1 | – | – | – | – | – | – | – | – | – | 9 | – | 19 | – | – | – | 1 |
| Total, M. and F., | 15 | | 3 | | 7 | | 5 | | 12 | | 66 | | 180 | | 1 | | 25 | |

SOBRIETY, &c., passed from 1st April, 1882, to 31st March, 1883.

| IMPRISONMENT (cont.) | | | | | | | | | | | | |
|---|---|---|---|---|---|---|---|---|---|---|---|---|
| 18 Months and above 12. | | 12 Months only. | | Under 12 Months and above 9. | | 9 Months and above 6. | | 6 Months only. | | Under 6 Months and above 3. | | PRISONS. |
| M. | F. | M. | F. | M. | F. | M. | F. | M. | F. | M. | F. | |
| 6 | – | 5 | 3 | – | – | 2 | – | 21 | 3 | 9 | 2 | Armagh. |
| 9 | – | 61 | 6 | 1 | 1 | 23 | 11 | 183 | 61 | 41 | 11 | Belfast. |
| – | – | – | – | – | – | – | – | – | – | – | – | Carlow. |
| – | – | – | – | – | – | – | – | – | – | – | – | Carrick-on-Shannon. |
| 2 | – | 1 | 1 | – | – | 2 | – | 4 | 2 | 4 | – | Castlebar. |
| – | – | – | – | – | – | – | – | – | – | – | – | Cavan. |
| – | – | 5 | – | – | – | 7 | – | 8 | 3 | 12 | – | Clonmel. |
| 15 | – | 17 | – | 3 | – | 6 | – | 25 | – | 14 | – | Cork, Male. |
| – | 2 | – | 4 | – | – | – | 2 | – | 7 | – | 9 | Cork, Female. |
| 2 | 1 | 5 | – | 1 | – | 2 | 3 | 10 | 8 | 13 | 8 | Downpatrick. |
| – | – | – | – | – | – | – | 1 | – | – | – | 6 | Drogheda. |
| – | – | 13 | – | – | – | 6 | – | 20 | – | 20 | – | Dundalk. |
| – | – | – | – | – | – | – | – | – | – | – | – | Ennis. |
| – | – | – | – | – | – | – | – | – | – | – | – | Enniskillen. |
| 6 | – | 10 | 2 | 1 | – | 3 | 2 | 16 | 2 | 6 | – | Galway. |
| – | 2 | – | 16 | – | – | – | 7 | – | [illegible] | – | 17 | Grangegorman. |
| – | 1 | 8 | – | – | – | 1 | – | 10 | – | 9 | – | Kilkenny. |
| 6 | – | 10 | – | – | – | 9 | – | 21 | – | 14 | – | Kilmainham. |
| – | – | – | – | – | – | – | – | – | – | – | – | Lifford. |
| 3 | – | 14 | – | – | – | 8 | – | 48 | – | 9 | – | Limerick, Male. |
| – | 8 | – | 2 | – | 1 | – | – | – | [illegible] | – | – | Limerick, Female. |
| – | – | 7 | 8 | 3 | – | 8 | – | 34 | 14 | 24 | 6 | Londonderry. |
| – | – | – | – | – | – | – | – | – | – | – | – | Longford. |
| – | – | 4 | – | 13 | – | – | – | 11 | – | 9 | – | Maryborough. |
| – | – | – | – | – | – | – | – | – | – | – | – | Monaghan. |
| 2 | – | 8 | – | 6 | – | 10 | – | 37 | 6 | 11 | – | Mullingar. |
| 1 | – | 14 | 1 | 2 | – | 6 | – | 21 | 1 | 21 | 2 | Naas. |
| 2 | – | 9 | – | – | – | 9 | – | 4 | – | 9 | – | Nenagh. |
| – | – | 8 | – | – | – | 1 | – | 15 | 4 | 6 | 2 | Omagh. |
| 65 | – | 103 | – | – | – | 46 | – | 291 | – | [illegible] | – | Richmond. |
| – | – | – | – | – | – | – | – | – | – | – | – | Roscommon. |
| 1 | – | – | – | 3 | – | 1 | – | 5 | – | 5 | 1 | Sligo. |
| 3 | – | 11 | – | – | – | – | – | 10 | 4 | 7 | – | Tralee. |
| 1 | – | – | 2 | – | – | – | – | 2 | – | 2 | 1 | Trim. |
| – | – | 20 | 1 | 1 | – | 11 | – | 20 | 1 | 11 | 1 | Tullamore. |
| – | – | 2 | 1 | 6 | – | – | – | 4 | 5 | 5 | – | Waterford. |
| – | – | 8 | – | – | – | 7 | – | 13 | – | 2 | 2 | Wexford. |
| – | – | 5 | – | – | – | 0 | – | 6 | – | – | – | Wicklow. |
| 17 | – | 326 | – | 60 | – | 162 | – | 711 | – | 311 | – | Total, Males. |
| – | 8 | – | 43 | – | 9 | – | 26 | – | 169 | – | 41 | Total, Females. |
| 25 | | 317 | | 69 | | 188 | | 880 | | 352 | | Total, M. and F. |

(continued.

TABLE VII, *concluded.*—SENTENCES of DEATH, PENAL SERVITUDE,

| Prisons. | Imprisonment for: 6 Months only. | | Under 6 Months and above 3. | | 3 Months and above 1. | | 1 Month and above 14 Days. | | 14 Days and above 7. | | 7 Days and above 48 Hours. | |
|---|---|---|---|---|---|---|---|---|---|---|---|---|
| | M. | F. | M. | F. | M. | F. | M. | F. | M. | F. | M. | F. |
| Armagh, | 26 | 11 | 24 | 7 | 109 | 66 | 189 | 48 | 89 | 61 | 78 | 68 |
| Belfast, | 161 | 81 | 3 | 4 | 810 | 61 | 837 | 712 | 434 | 465 | 816 | 439 |
| Carlow, | – | – | – | – | – | – | – | – | – | – | 67 | 50 |
| Carrick-on-Shannon, | – | – | – | – | – | – | – | – | – | – | 60 | 30 |
| Castlebar, | 14 | 1 | – | 1 | 65 | 7 | 68 | 30 | 61 | 21 | 147 | 48 |
| Cavan, | – | – | – | – | – | – | – | – | – | – | 63 | 58 |
| Clonmel, | 20 | – | 1 | 1 | 28 | 9 | 96 | 10 | 76 | 5 | 297 | 16 |
| Cork, Male, | 60 | – | 24 | – | 190 | – | 408 | – | 842 | – | 740 | – |
| Cork, Female, | – | 26 | – | 5 | – | 63 | – | 566 | – | 526 | – | 530 |
| Downpatrick, | 10 | 6 | 14 | 6 | 10 | 7 | 81 | 7 | 38 | 10 | 70 | 18 |
| Drogheda, | – | 7 | – | 30 | – | 30 | – | 64 | – | 39 | 19 | 9 |
| Dundalk, | 29 | – | 4 | – | 48 | – | 160 | – | 97 | – | 197 | – |
| Ennis, | – | – | – | – | – | – | 1 | – | 4 | – | 65 | 30 |
| Enniskillen, | – | – | – | – | – | – | – | – | – | – | 71 | 16 |
| Galway, | 5 | 8 | – | – | 18 | 8 | 209 | 47 | 167 | 36 | 262 | 77 |
| Grangegorman, | – | 46 | – | 3 | – | 116 | [illegible] | [illegible] | 414 | 447 | 949 | 1,840 |
| Kilkenny, | 18 | 2 | – | – | 18 | 7 | 97 | 84 | 68 | 10 | 148 | 30 |
| Kilmainham, | 41 | – | 6 | – | 110 | – | 254 | – | 220 | – | 240 | – |
| Lifford, | – | – | – | – | – | – | – | – | – | – | 91 | 3 |
| Limerick, Male, | 67 | – | – | – | 118 | – | 878 | – | 845 | – | 877 | – |
| Limerick, Female, | – | 46 | – | 6 | – | 87 | – | 270 | – | 179 | – | 164 |
| Londonderry, | 66 | 81 | 11 | 7 | 90 | 14 | 185 | 60 | 162 | 61 | 187 | 118 |
| Longford, | – | – | – | – | – | – | – | – | – | – | 60 | 18 |
| Maryborough, | 11 | – | 1 | – | 18 | 2 | 48 | 5 | 34 | 3 | 70 | 8 |
| Monaghan, | – | – | – | – | – | – | – | – | – | – | 60 | 65 |
| Mullingar, | 40 | 7 | 11 | 8 | 85 | 4 | 120 | 73 | 104 | 64 | 118 | 80 |
| Naas, | 18 | 8 | 18 | 1 | 33 | 7 | 87 | 63 | 97 | 17 | 79 | 36 |
| Nenagh, | 11 | – | – | – | 30 | – | 49 | – | 38 | – | 111 | – |
| Omagh, | 13 | 6 | 4 | – | 41 | 7 | 63 | 19 | 73 | 6 | 34 | 8 |
| Richmond, | 294 | – | 34 | – | 494 | – | 150 | – | 90 | – | 28 | – |
| Roscommon, | – | – | – | – | – | – | – | – | – | – | 48 | 19 |
| Sligo, | 37 | 6 | – | – | 68 | 4 | 128 | 41 | 90 | 20 | 77 | 16 |
| Tralee, | 16 | 5 | – | – | 41 | 7 | 190 | 43 | 120 | 39 | 291 | 65 |
| Trim, | 7 | 1 | – | – | 4 | 1 | 2 | 1 | 3 | – | 66 | 11 |
| Tullamore, | 47 | 2 | – | – | 60 | 5 | 47 | 6 | 36 | 12 | 67 | 31 |
| Waterford, | 17 | 7 | 6 | – | 65 | 5 | 60 | 87 | 198 | 29 | 144 | 85 |
| Wexford, | 16 | – | – | – | 65 | 5 | 40 | 18 | 90 | 5 | 69 | 19 |
| Wicklow, | 8 | – | – | – | 3 | 1 | – | – | – | – | 50 | 14 |
| Total, Males, | 1,641 | – | 157 | – | 1,750 | – | 4,326 | – | 3,256 | – | 6,146 | – |
| Total, Females, | – | 574 | – | 79 | – | 437 | – | 2,529 | – | 1,745 | – | 3,[illegible] |
| Total, M. and F., | 2,2[illegible] | | 2[illegible] | | 2,180 | | 6,8[illegible] | | 4,[illegible] | | 9,[illegible]16 | |

IMPRISONMENT, &c., passed from 1st April, 1892, to 31st March, 1893.

| Imprisonment for 48 Hours. M. | F. | [illegible] Hours and under. M. | F. | Fine without any alternative Imprisonment. M. | F. | Unstated. M. | F. | Sentences respited and not passed. M. | F. | Total Number of Sentences. M. | F. | Prisons. |
|---|---|---|---|---|---|---|---|---|---|---|---|---|
| 14 | 9 | 84 | 5 | – | – | 5 | – | – | – | [illegible] | [illegible] | Armagh. |
| 18 | 3 | 147 | 47 | – | – | 10 | – | – | – | 6,072 | 1,[illegible] | Belfast. |
| 4 | 8 | 4 | – | – | – | – | – | – | – | 73 | [illegible] | Carlow. |
| 5 | – | – | 1 | – | – | 5 | – | 4 | – | 91 | 21 | Carrick-on-Shannon. |
| [illegible] | 10 | 15 | 4 | – | – | 3 | – | – | – | 877 | [illegible] | Castlebar. |
| [illegible] | 7 | 5 | 1 | – | – | – | – | – | – | 84 | 97 | Cavan. |
| 1 | – | 1 | – | – | – | 3 | – | – | – | 878 | [illegible] | Clonmel. |
| [illegible] | – | 12 | – | – | – | – | – | – | – | 1,801 | – | Cork, Male. |
| – | [illegible] | – | [illegible] | – | – | – | – | – | – | – | 1,548 | Cork, Female. |
| 37 | 6 | 24 | 8 | – | – | 1 | – | – | – | 819 | 73 | Downpatrick. |
| 8 | 4 | – | – | – | – | – | – | – | – | [illegible] | 187 | Drogheda. |
| [illegible] | – | 19 | – | – | – | 5 | – | – | – | 937 | – | Dundalk. |
| [illegible] | 8 | 5 | – | – | – | 4 | – | – | – | [illegible] | [illegible] | Ennis. |
| 19 | 8 | 24 | 5 | – | – | – | – | – | – | 134 | 20 | Enniskillen. |
| 108 | 48 | [illegible] | 15 | – | – | – | – | – | – | [illegible] | [illegible] | Galway. |
| 417 | 774 | 121 | 176 | – | – | – | 6 | – | – | 8,158 | 8,211 | Grangegorman. |
| 41 | 8 | 9 | 2 | – | – | 3 | – | – | – | 417 | [illegible] | Kilkenny. |
| [illegible] | – | [illegible] | – | – | – | 1 | – | – | – | 1,080 | – | Kilmainham. |
| 8 | 1 | 2 | 1 | – | – | – | – | – | – | 81 | 4 | Lifford. |
| [illegible] | – | 167 | – | – | – | 14 | – | – | – | 1,[illegible] | – | Limerick, Male. |
| – | [illegible] | – | [illegible] | – | – | – | – | – | – | – | 734 | Limerick, Female. |
| [illegible] | [illegible] | 18 | 16 | 2 | – | 7 | – | 7 | 1 | [illegible] | [illegible] | Londonderry. |
| [illegible] | 8 | 14 | 10 | – | – | 1 | – | – | – | 168 | 87 | Longford. |
| [illegible] | 8 | 8 | – | – | – | 4 | – | – | – | [illegible] | [illegible] | Maryborough. |
| 8 | 4 | 8 | 2 | – | – | 1 | – | – | – | 78 | 84 | Monaghan. |
| 16 | 1 | 10 | 8 | – | – | 19 | 8 | – | – | [illegible] | [illegible] | Mullingar. |
| [illegible] | 61 | 74 | 11 | – | – | – | – | – | – | [illegible] | 173 | Naas. |
| 6 | – | [illegible] | – | – | – | – | – | – | – | [illegible] | – | Nenagh. |
| 18 | 1 | 6 | – | – | – | 5 | – | – | – | [illegible] | 48 | Omagh. |
| [illegible] | – | 6 | – | – | – | 20 | – | [illegible] | – | 1,710 | – | Richmond. |
| [illegible] | 8 | – | 1 | – | – | 1 | 1 | 8 | 1 | 84 | [illegible] | Roscommon. |
| [illegible] | [illegible] | 19 | 4 | – | – | 8 | 1 | – | – | 426 | 159 | Sligo. |
| 4 | 1 | 5 | 8 | – | – | – | – | [illegible] | – | [illegible] | 154 | Tralee. |
| 8 | – | 2 | 8 | – | – | 2 | – | – | – | 84 | [illegible] | Trim. |
| 18 | 8 | 58 | 3 | – | – | – | – | – | – | 877 | [illegible] | Tullamore. |
| 377 | 46 | 157 | [illegible] | – | – | 6 | – | – | – | 719 | [illegible] | Waterford. |
| 18 | 7 | 11 | 8 | – | – | – | – | 1 | – | 601 | 48 | Wexford. |
| 16 | 8 | – | – | – | – | – | – | – | – | 109 | 18 | Wicklow. |
| 1,423 | – | [illegible] | – | 8 | – | 182 | – | 68 | – | 61,107 | – | Total, Males. |
| – | 1,114 | – | 431 | – | – | – | 8 | – | 2 | – | 10,109 | Total, Females. |
| 4,537 | | 1,[illegible] | | 8 | | 190 | | 71 | | 61,216 | | Total, M. and F. |

TABLE VIII.—AGES, EDUCATIONAL CONDITION ON COMMITMENT, and RELIGIOUS [illegible]
1st April, 1882, to 31st March,

| Local Prisons. | Total Number of Commitments. | | | Ages. Under 12 Years. | | 12 and not exceeding 16 Years. | | Above 16 to 21 Years. | | 21 to 31 Years. | | 31 to 41 Years. | |
|---|---|---|---|---|---|---|---|---|---|---|---|---|---|
| | M. | F. | M. & F. | M. | F. | M. | F. | M. | F. | M. | F. | M. | F. |
| Armagh, . . | [illegible] | 184 | [illegible] | 4 | 1 | 20 | 2 | 158 | 21 | 222 | 64 | 165 | [illegible] |
| Belfast, . . | 3,351 | 1,022 | 4,373 | 18 | 2 | 112 | 11 | 787 | 282 | 1,244 | 782 | 686 | 482 |
| Castlebar, . . | 496 | 122 | 678 | 1 | – | 27 | 10 | 183 | 37 | 183 | 42 | 68 | [illegible] |
| Clonmel, . . | 720 | 62 | 782 | – | – | 16 | 1 | 168 | 31 | 222 | 16 | 144 | 4 |
| Cork, Male, . . | 2,732 | – | 2,732 | 11 | – | [illegible] | – | 568 | – | 748 | – | 497 | – |
| Cork, Female, . | – | 1,017 | 1,017 | – | 8 | – | 8 | – | 128 | – | 661 | – | 530 |
| Downpatrick, . . | 246 | 68 | 317 | – | – | 8 | – | 29 | 18 | 64 | 24 | 68 | 15 |
| Drogheda, . . | 27 | 203 | 232 | – | – | – | 6 | 8 | 31 | 16 | 44 | 6 | 50 |
| Dundalk, . . | 609 | – | 609 | 2 | – | 7 | – | 167 | – | 691 | – | 168 | – |
| Galway, . . | 676 | 646 | 1,322 | 2 | – | 46 | 6 | 277 | 42 | 365 | 72 | 106 | 77 |
| Grangegorman, . | 2,168 | 3,436 | 3,076 | – | 6 | 6 | 86 | 618 | 718 | 742 | 1,463 | 484 | 646 |
| Kilkenny, . . | 456 | 91 | 548 | 8 | – | 11 | 1 | 64 | 16 | 200 | 24 | 64 | 27 |
| Kilmainham, . . | 1,316 | – | 1,316 | 11 | – | 65 | – | 296 | – | 468 | – | 168 | – |
| Limerick, Male, . | 1,000 | – | 1,000 | 6 | – | 44 | – | 442 | – | 726 | – | 300 | – |
| Limerick, Female, . | – | 616 | 616 | – | – | – | 6 | – | 103 | – | 272 | – | 227 |
| Londonderry, . . | 726 | 376 | 1,102 | 6 | 6 | 36 | 2 | 168 | 72 | 285 | 171 | 116 | 82 |
| Maryborough, . . | 273 | 28 | 300 | 1 | – | 1 | – | 47 | 5 | 130 | 6 | 62 | 8 |
| Mullingar, . . | 682 | 226 | 1,023 | 7 | – | 82 | 4 | 166 | 88 | 265 | 64 | 160 | 72 |
| Naas, . . | 412 | 174 | 586 | 1 | 1 | 6 | 2 | 67 | 6 | 174 | 64 | 74 | 6 |
| Nenagh, . . | 324 | – | 324 | – | – | 5 | – | 67 | – | 182 | – | 60 | – |
| Omagh, . . | 242 | 32 | 304 | 6 | – | 16 | – | 36 | 4 | 114 | 15 | 77 | 16 |
| Richmond, . . | 2,401 | – | 2,401 | 30 | – | 127 | – | 692 | – | 888 | – | 287 | – |
| Sligo, . . | 545 | 142 | 687 | 2 | – | 15 | 6 | 146 | 17 | 199 | 64 | 79 | 64 |
| Tralee, . . | 867 | 122 | 1,022 | 6 | – | 44 | 6 | 283 | 14 | 333 | 62 | 128 | 62 |
| Tullamore, . . | 412 | 64 | 476 | 1 | – | 6 | 1 | 76 | 6 | 180 | 16 | 74 | 24 |
| Waterford, . . | 782 | 326 | 1,110 | 6 | 1 | 17 | 2 | 147 | 68 | 314 | 116 | 176 | 102 |
| Wexford, . . | 218 | 62 | 278 | 2 | – | 16 | 6 | 76 | 10 | 197 | 16 | 87 | 17 |
| Total, Males, . | 23,031 | – | – | 122 | – | 678 | – | 5,462 | – | 8,738 | – | 4,186 | – |
| Total, Females, . | – | 10,380 | – | – | 10 | – | 178 | – | 1,626 | – | 4,077 | – | 2,727 |
| Total, M. and F., . | – | – | 33,446 | 130 | | 853 | | 7,088 | | 13,016 | | 6,886 | |

Professions of all Persons Committed to the undermentioned Prisons from 1883, exclusive of Debtors.

| Ages. | | | | Education of Committees. | | | | | | | | | | | | | |
|---|---|---|---|---|---|---|---|---|---|---|---|---|---|---|---|---|---|
| [illegible] Years and upwards. | | Age could not be ascertained. | | Read and Write. | | Read Imperfectly. | | Know Spelling. | | Know Alphabet. | | Wholly Illiterate. | | Education not ascertained. | | Local Prisons. |
| M. | F. | M. | F. | M. | F. | M. | F. | M. | F. | M. | F. | M. | F. | M. | F. | |
| 84 | 8[illegible] | – | – | [illegible] | 84 | 104 | 87 | 84 | 21 | [illegible] | [illegible] | 10[illegible] | 76 | – | – | Armagh. |
| 370 | 87[illegible] | – | – | 4,074 | 941 | 451 | 455 | – | – | – | – | 816 | [illegible] | – | – | Belfast. |
| 87 | [illegible] | – | – | 120 | [illegible] | 48 | 15 | – | – | – | – | [illegible] | [illegible] | – | – | Castlebar. |
| 200 | [illegible] | – | – | 864 | 19 | [illegible] | 0 | – | – | – | – | [illegible] | 17 | – | – | Clonmel. |
| 377 | – | – | – | 1,1[illegible] | – | 151 | – | [illegible] | – | [illegible] | – | [illegible] | – | – | – | Cork, Male. |
| – | 377 | – | – | – | 819 | – | [illegible] | – | 46 | – | [illegible] | – | [illegible] | – | – | Cork, Female. |
| 43 | [illegible] | 1 | – | 174 | 14 | [illegible] | [illegible] | – | – | – | – | 4[illegible] | [illegible] | – | – | Downpatrick. |
| 0 | [illegible] | – | – | [illegible] | [illegible] | [illegible] | [illegible] | – | – | [illegible] | [illegible] | [illegible] | 10[illegible] | – | – | Dun[illegible]. |
| 10[illegible] | – | – | – | 271 | – | [illegible] | – | [illegible] | – | [illegible] | – | 2[illegible] | – | – | – | Dundalk. |
| [illegible] | 47 | – | – | [illegible] | [illegible] | [illegible] | [illegible] | – | – | [illegible] | – | [illegible] | 177 | [illegible] | – | Galway. |
| 281 | 4[illegible] | – | – | [illegible] | 1,0[illegible] | [illegible] | 73[illegible] | – | – | – | – | [illegible] | 1,[illegible] | – | – | Grangegorman. |
| 87 | 10 | – | – | 2[illegible] | [illegible] | [illegible] | [illegible] | – | – | – | – | [illegible] | 4[illegible] | – | – | Kilkenny. |
| 15[illegible] | – | [illegible] | – | [illegible] | – | 7[illegible] | – | – | – | 4 | – | 4[illegible] | – | [illegible] | – | Kilmainham. |
| [illegible] | – | – | – | 1,081 | – | 17[illegible] | – | 1[illegible] | – | [illegible] | – | 4[illegible] | – | – | – | Limerick, Male. |
| – | 10[illegible] | – | – | – | 1[illegible] | – | 81 | – | – | – | – | – | [illegible] | – | – | Limerick, Female. |
| 10[illegible] | 87 | – | – | [illegible] | 64 | 14[illegible] | 7[illegible] | 4[illegible] | 1[illegible] | [illegible] | [illegible] | [illegible] | 2[illegible] | – | – | Londonderry. |
| 49 | [illegible] | – | – | 141 | [illegible] | [illegible] | [illegible] | [illegible] | [illegible] | [illegible] | [illegible] | 61 | [illegible] | – | – | Maryborough. |
| 163 | [illegible] | – | – | [illegible] | 17[illegible] | – | – | – | – | – | – | 20[illegible] | 4[illegible] | – | – | Mullingar. |
| 74 | 2[illegible] | – | – | [illegible] | [illegible] | [illegible] | [illegible] | – | – | [illegible] | – | 1[illegible] | [illegible] | – | – | Naas. |
| 74 | – | – | – | 19[illegible] | – | [illegible] | – | – | – | – | – | 1[illegible] | – | – | – | Nenagh. |
| [illegible] | 1[illegible] | – | – | 1[illegible] | [illegible] | [illegible] | 14 | 1 | – | [illegible] | – | 11[illegible] | [illegible] | – | – | Omagh. |
| 1[illegible] | – | [illegible] | – | 1,[illegible] | – | [illegible] | – | – | – | 11[illegible] | – | [illegible] | – | [illegible] | – | Richmond. |
| 1[illegible] | 64 | – | – | [illegible] | [illegible] | 4[illegible] | [illegible] | [illegible] | – | 1[illegible] | [illegible] | 1[illegible] | [illegible] | – | – | Sligo. |
| 110 | 87 | – | 1 | 41[illegible] | 74 | 6[illegible] | 1[illegible] | [illegible] | [illegible] | – | – | 81[illegible] | 71 | [illegible] | [illegible] | Tralee. |
| [illegible] | 1[illegible] | – | – | [illegible] | 1[illegible] | 4[illegible] | 91 | 7 | [illegible] | [illegible] | – | 10[illegible] | [illegible] | – | – | Tullamore. |
| [illegible] | [illegible] | – | – | 309 | [illegible] | 7[illegible] | [illegible] | – | – | – | – | [illegible] | [illegible] | – | – | Waterford. |
| 6[illegible] | 17 | – | – | 100 | [illegible] | 1[illegible] | [illegible] | – | – | – | – | 14[illegible] | [illegible] | – | – | Wexford. |
| [illegible] | – | 4[illegible] | – | [illegible] | – | [illegible] | – | 1[illegible] | – | [illegible] | – | 7,[illegible] | – | [illegible] | – | Total, Males. |
| – | 1,87[illegible] | – | [illegible] | – | 2,0[illegible] | – | 2,161 | – | [illegible] | – | [illegible] | – | [illegible] | – | [illegible] | Total, Females. |
| 4,864 | | 60 | | 15,283 | | 4,8[illegible] | | 2[illegible] | | 816 | | 10,[illegible] | | 64 | | Total, M. and F. |

[continued.

TABLE VIII., *concluded*.—AGES, EDUCATIONAL CONDITION ON COMMITMENT, and RELIGIOUS PROFESSIONS of all Persons Committed to the undermentioned Prisons from 1st April, 1882, to 31st March, 1883, exclusive of Debtors.

| Larger Prisons. | Religious Professions. | | | | | | | | | | Total Number of Commitments. | | |
|---|---|---|---|---|---|---|---|---|---|---|---|---|---|
| | Protestant Episcopalians of Ireland. | | Presbyterians. | | Roman Catholics. | | Other Religious Professions. | | Could not be ascertained. | | | | |
| | M. | F. | M. | F. | M. | F. | M. | F. | M. | F. | M. | F. | M. & F. |
| Armagh, | [illegible] | [illegible] | [illegible] | 6 | [illegible] | [illegible] | 1 | – | – | – | [illegible] | [illegible] | [illegible] |
| Belfast, | [illegible] | 473 | 814 | [illegible] | [illegible] | 1,210 | 1 | – | – | – | [illegible] | [illegible] | [illegible] |
| Castlebar, | [illegible] | 1 | – | – | [illegible] | [illegible] | – | – | – | – | [illegible] | [illegible] | 670 |
| Clonmel, | [illegible] | 1 | 3 | – | [illegible] | [illegible] | – | – | – | – | [illegible] | [illegible] | [illegible] |
| Cork, Male, | [illegible] | – | 8 | – | [illegible] | – | [illegible] | – | – | – | [illegible] | – | [illegible] |
| Cork, Female, | – | [illegible] | – | 2 | – | [illegible] | – | [illegible] | – | – | – | 1,817 | 1,817 |
| Downpatrick, | [illegible] | 10 | [illegible] | 18 | [illegible] | [illegible] | – | – | – | – | [illegible] | [illegible] | 317 |
| Drogheda, | [illegible] | [illegible] | – | – | [illegible] | [illegible] | – | – | – | – | [illegible] | [illegible] | [illegible] |
| Dundalk, | [illegible] | – | 47 | – | [illegible] | – | [illegible] | – | [illegible] | – | [illegible] | – | [illegible] |
| Galway, | [illegible] | [illegible] | – | – | [illegible] | [illegible] | [illegible] | – | 1 | – | [illegible] | [illegible] | [illegible] |
| Grangegorman, | [illegible] | [illegible] | [illegible] | [illegible] | [illegible] | [illegible] | [illegible] | – | – | [illegible] | [illegible] | [illegible] | [illegible] |
| Kilkenny, | [illegible] | [illegible] | – | – | [illegible] | [illegible] | – | – | – | – | [illegible] | [illegible] | 550 |
| Kilmainham, | [illegible] | – | [illegible] | – | [illegible] | – | [illegible] | – | – | – | [illegible] | – | [illegible] |
| Limerick, Male, | [illegible] | – | [illegible] | – | [illegible] | – | [illegible] | – | 1 | – | [illegible] | – | [illegible] |
| Limerick, Female, | – | [illegible] | – | – | – | [illegible] | – | – | – | – | – | [illegible] | [illegible] |
| Londonderry, | [illegible] | [illegible] | 97 | 22 | [illegible] | [illegible] | – | – | – | – | [illegible] | 370 | [illegible] |
| Maryborough, | [illegible] | – | [illegible] | – | [illegible] | [illegible] | [illegible] | – | – | – | [illegible] | [illegible] | [illegible] |
| Mullingar, | [illegible] | [illegible] | [illegible] | – | [illegible] | [illegible] | – | – | – | – | [illegible] | [illegible] | [illegible] |
| Naas, | [illegible] | [illegible] | [illegible] | – | [illegible] | [illegible] | [illegible] | – | – | – | [illegible] | [illegible] | [illegible] |
| Nenagh, | [illegible] | – | [illegible] | – | [illegible] | – | – | – | – | – | [illegible] | – | [illegible] |
| Omagh, | [illegible] | [illegible] | [illegible] | [illegible] | [illegible] | [illegible] | – | – | – | – | [illegible] | [illegible] | [illegible] |
| Richmond, | [illegible] | – | [illegible] | – | [illegible] | – | [illegible] | – | [illegible] | – | [illegible] | – | [illegible] |
| Sligo, | [illegible] | [illegible] | – | – | [illegible] | [illegible] | – | – | – | – | [illegible] | [illegible] | [illegible] |
| Tralee, | [illegible] | [illegible] | – | – | [illegible] | [illegible] | – | – | – | [illegible] | [illegible] | [illegible] | [illegible] |
| Tullamore, | [illegible] | 4 | [illegible] | – | [illegible] | [illegible] | – | – | – | – | [illegible] | [illegible] | [illegible] |
| Waterford, | [illegible] | [illegible] | – | – | [illegible] | [illegible] | – | – | – | – | [illegible] | [illegible] | 1,110 |
| Wexford, | [illegible] | [illegible] | – | – | [illegible] | [illegible] | – | – | – | – | [illegible] | [illegible] | [illegible] |
| Total, Males, | [illegible] | – | [illegible] | – | [illegible] | – | [illegible] | – | [illegible] | – | [illegible] | – | – |
| Total Females, | – | [illegible] | – | [illegible] | – | [illegible] | – | [illegible] | – | [illegible] | – | [illegible] | – |
| Total M. and F., | [illegible] | | [illegible] | | [illegible] | | [illegible] | | [illegible] | | [illegible] | | |

TABLE IX.—SCHOOLS.—NUMBER of PRISONERS in Attendance; Number of Days Schools were held; Number of Teachers, &c., from 1st April, 1882, to 31st March, 1883, in under-mentioned Prisons.

| LOCAL PRISONS. | Number of Individual Prisoners who attended School. | | Number of Days School was held. | | Average Daily Number of Pupils. | | Number of Teachers. | | Number of Hours allotted daily for Instruction of each Prisoner. | |
|---|---|---|---|---|---|---|---|---|---|---|
| | M. | F. | M. | F. | M. | F. | M. | F. | M. | F. |
| Armagh, . . | 43 | 24 | 180 | 152 | 10 | 7 | 1 | 1 | 1 | 1 |
| Belfast, . . . | 120 | 140 | 868 | 289 | 16 | 16 | 1 | 1 | 1 | 1 |
| Castlebar, . . | 26 | – | 250 | – | 4 | – | 1 | | 10 m. | – |
| Clonmel, . . | – | – | – | – | – | – | – | – | – | – |
| Cork, Male, . . | 54 | – | 288 | – | 13 | – | 1 | – | 1 | – |
| Cork, Female, . | – | 18 | – | 307 | – | 7 | – | 1 | – | 1 |
| Downpatrick, . | 61 | 25 | 88 | 184 | 3 | 3 | 1 | 1 | 3 | 2 |
| Drogheda, . . | – | – | – | – | – | – | – | – | – | – |
| Dundalk, . . | 107 | – | 302 | – | 14 | – | 1 | – | 2 | – |
| Galway, . . . | 58 | – | 313 | – | 8 | – | 1 | – | 2 | – |
| Grangegorman, . | 352 | – | 297 | – | 14 | – | 1 | – | 2 | – |
| Kilkenny, . . | – | – | – | – | – | – | – | – | – | – |
| Kilmainham, . . | 99 | – | 314 | – | 14 | – | 1 | – | 1 | – |
| Limerick, Male, . | 31 | – | 3 | – | 2 | – | 1 | – | 1 | – |
| Limerick, Female, . | – | – | – | – | – | – | – | – | – | – |
| Londonderry, . . | 58 | – | 308 | – | 5 | – | 1 | – | 1 | – |
| Maryborough, . | – | – | – | – | – | – | – | – | – | – |
| Mullingar, . . | – | – | – | – | – | – | – | – | – | – |
| Naas, . . . | 72 | – | 181 | – | 24·75 | – | 1 | – | 1 | – |
| Nenagh, . . | 41 | – | 240 | – | 4 | – | 1 | – | 10 m. | – |
| Omagh, . . . | 38 | 8 | 304 | 97 | 13 | 2 | 1 | 1 | 1 | 1 |
| Richmond, . . | – | – | – | – | – | – | – | – | – | – |
| Sligo, . . . | 73 | 14 | 225 | 285 | 4 | 1 | 1 | 1 | 1 | 1 |
| Tralee, . . . | – | – | – | – | – | – | – | – | – | – |
| Tullamore, . . | 109 | – | 261 | – | 3 | – | 1 | – | 1 | – |
| Waterford, . . | – | – | – | – | – | – | – | – | – | – |
| Wexford, . . | – | – | – | – | – | – | – | – | – | – |
| County prisoners in Mountjoy, Male, . | 137 | – | 270 | – | 40·1 | – | 3 | – | 1 | – |
| Mountjoy, Female, | – | 46 | – | 303 | – | 34 | – | 3 | – | 1 |
| Total, 1882-83, . | 1,437 | 260 | 3,815 | 1,413 | 208·23 | 75 | 17 | 8 | – | – |
| Total, 1881-82, . | 1,261 | 418 | 3,187 | 1,316 | 204·76 | 73 | – | – | – | – |

TABLE X.—RETURN of PRISON OFFENCES and PUNISHMENTS in

| Prisons. | Total number of Prisoners during the Year. | | Irons or Handcuffs. | | Prison Punishments. Punishment Cells. | | Prison Punishments. Dietary Punishment. | | Total number of Prisoners punished. | | [illegible] | |
|---|---|---|---|---|---|---|---|---|---|---|---|---|
| | M. | F. | M. | F. | M. | F. | M. | F. | M. | F. | M. | F. |
| Armagh, | 701 | 195 | 1 | – | 12 | 6 | 46 | 7 | 52 | 9 | 1 | – |
| Belfast, | 2,836 | 2,113 | – | – | 150 | 47 | 1,077 | 617 | 1,185 | 674 | 36 | 56 |
| Carlow, | 103 | 27 | – | – | – | – | 23 | 1 | 19 | 1 | – | – |
| Carrick-on-Shannon, | 106 | 15 | – | – | – | – | – | – | – | – | – | – |
| Castlebar, | 871 | 115 | – | – | 31 | – | 73 | – | 59 | – | – | – |
| Cavan, | 125 | 24 | – | – | 1 | – | 1 | – | 2 | – | – | – |
| Clonmel, | 748 | 39 | – | – | 18 | 1 | 165 | – | 177 | 1 | 1 | – |
| Cork, Male, | 2,431 | – | – | – | 115 | – | [illegible] | – | 645 | – | – | – |
| Cork, Female, | – | 744 | – | – | – | 65 | – | 187 | – | 96 | – | – |
| Downpatrick, | 803 | 16 | – | – | 42 | – | 163 | 15 | 208 | 10 | 6 | – |
| Dungannon, | 25 | 150 | – | – | – | 7 | – | 80 | – | 97 | – | 8 |
| Dundalk, | 607 | – | – | – | [illegible] | – | 250 | – | 205 | – | 6 | – |
| Ennis, | 316 | 62 | – | – | – | – | 37 | – | 28 | – | – | – |
| Enniskillen, | 183 | 43 | – | – | – | – | 15 | – | 18 | – | 1 | – |
| Galway, | 721 | 187 | – | – | 1 | 4 | 287 | 45 | 288 | 49 | – | – |
| Grangegorman, | 1,080 | 1,727 | – | – | 58 | 66 | 171 | 83 | 228 | [illegible] | 4 | 10 |
| Kilkenny, | 479 | 48 | – | – | 30 | – | 470 | 86 | 274 | 16 | 4 | – |
| Kilmainham, | 1,991 | – | – | – | 1 | – | 164 | – | 148 | 1 | – | – |
| Lifford, | 60 | 7 | – | – | – | – | – | – | – | – | – | – |
| Limerick, Male, | 1,286 | – | – | – | 62 | – | 280 | – | 259 | – | – | – |
| Limerick, Female, | – | 877 | – | 6 | – | 23 | – | – | – | 20 | – | 8 |
| Londonderry, | 914 | 446 | – | – | 24 | – | 503 | 65 | 413 | 44 | 1 | – |
| Longford, | 195 | 34 | – | – | – | – | 4 | 1 | 4 | 1 | – | – |
| Maryborough, | 147 | – | – | – | – | – | 95 | – | 84 | – | 8 | – |
| Monaghan, | [illegible] | 34 | – | – | 6 | – | 15 | – | 28 | – | – | – |
| Mullingar, | 946 | 224 | – | – | 1 | 4 | 251 | 16 | 265 | 30 | 1 | 6 |
| Naas, | 579 | 75 | – | – | 2 | 4 | 83 | – | 44 | 4 | 1 | – |
| Nenagh, | 637 | – | – | – | 5 | – | 121 | – | 73 | – | 6 | – |
| Omagh, | 392 | 67 | – | – | 35 | – | 91 | 10 | 110 | 16 | 1 | – |
| Richmond, | 2,593 | – | – | – | 149 | – | 461 | – | 458 | – | 6 | – |
| Roscommon, | 147 | 44 | – | – | – | – | – | – | – | – | – | – |
| Sligo, | 461 | 87 | – | – | 31 | 6 | 75 | 52 | 65 | 52 | 4 | – |
| Tralee, | 914 | 102 | – | – | 4 | – | 165 | 1 | 169 | 1 | – | – |
| Trim, | 182 | 24 | – | – | – | – | – | – | – | – | – | – |
| Tullamore, | 434 | 94 | – | – | 14 | – | 128 | 2 | 65 | 2 | 4 | 1 |
| Waterford, | 600 | 379 | – | – | 9 | 6 | 152 | 16 | 191 | 21 | – | – |
| Wexford, | 598 | 101 | – | – | – | – | 186 | 1 | 188 | 1 | – | – |
| Wicklow, | 161 | 31 | – | – | – | – | – | – | – | – | – | – |
| * Mountjoy, Male, | 504 | – | 5 | – | 67 | – | 41 | – | 131 | – | 8 | – |
| * " Female, | – | 124 | – | 19 | – | 18 | – | 19 | – | 45 | – | 16 |
| Total, Males, | 23,070 | – | 4 | – | 890 | – | 6,472 | – | 6,090 | – | 109 | – |
| Total, Females, | – | 9,216 | – | 15 | – | 245 | – | 1,029 | – | 1,033 | – | 63 |
| Total, M. and F., | 32,187 | | 19 | | 1,178 | | 7,501 | | 7,073 | | 191 | |

* Convict Prisoners.

**Local Prisons from 1st April, 1882, to 31st March, 1883.**

| Prison Offences. | | | | | | | | | | |
|---|---|---|---|---|---|---|---|---|---|---|
| Forgery and Attempts to Escape. | | Offences. | | Other Breaches of Regulations. | | Total Offences. | | Deprivation of Marks or Stage. | | Prisons. |
| M. | F. | M. | F. | M. | F. | M. | F. | M. | F. | |
| — | — | 58 | 8 | 57 | 5 | 99 | 13 | 1 | — | Armagh. |
| — | 1 | 401 | 102 | 706 | 289 | 1,108 | 374 | 380 | 24 | Belfast. |
| — | — | 18 | 1 | 8 | — | 26 | 1 | — | — | Carlow. |
| — | — | — | — | — | — | — | — | — | — | Carrick-on-Shannon. |
| — | — | 150 | — | 108 | — | 258 | — | 3 | — | Castlebar. |
| — | — | — | — | 8 | — | 8 | — | — | — | Cavan. |
| — | — | 46 | — | 126 | 1 | 161 | 1 | 1 | — | Clonmel. |
| — | — | 231 | — | 696 | — | 927 | — | 107 | — | Cork, Male. |
| — | — | — | 7 | — | 110 | — | 117 | — | 8 | Cork, Female. |
| — | — | 71 | 7 | 150 | 31 | 221 | 38 | — | — | Downpatrick. |
| — | — | — | 8 | — | 88 | — | 97 | — | — | Drogheda. |
| — | — | 126 | — | 200 | — | 326 | — | 130 | — | Dundalk. |
| 1 | — | 9 | — | 20 | — | 30 | — | — | — | Ennis. |
| — | — | 1 | — | 11 | — | 12 | — | 12 | — | Enniskillen. |
| — | — | 103 | 5 | 151 | 44 | 256 | 49 | 8 | 3 | Galway. |
| — | — | 116 | 42 | 102 | 60 | [illegible] | 102 | 9 | 24 | Grangegorman. |
| — | — | 354 | 13 | 320 | 8 | 674 | 21 | 66 | 1 | Kilkenny. |
| — | — | 68 | — | 39 | — | 107 | — | — | — | Kilmainham. |
| — | — | — | — | — | — | — | — | — | — | Lifford. |
| — | — | 65 | — | 244 | — | 309 | — | — | — | Limerick, Male. |
| — | — | — | 6 | — | 18 | — | 23 | — | 9 | Limerick, Female. |
| — | — | 328 | 32 | 545 | 33 | 873 | [illegible] | 11 | — | Londonderry. |
| — | — | 1 | — | 8 | 3 | 9 | 3 | — | — | Longford. |
| — | — | 86 | — | 56 | — | 142 | — | — | — | Maryborough. |
| — | — | — | — | 24 | — | 24 | — | 4 | — | Monaghan. |
| — | — | 36 | 8 | 231 | 8 | 267 | 16 | 4 | 2 | Mullingar. |
| — | — | 12 | — | 31 | [illegible] | 43 | 4 | — | — | Naas. |
| — | — | 24 | — | 101 | — | 125 | — | 5 | — | Nenagh. |
| — | — | 93 | 2 | 26 | 8 | 119 | 10 | 4 | — | Omagh. |
| — | — | 282 | — | 418 | — | 700 | — | 66 | — | Richmond. |
| — | — | — | — | — | — | — | — | — | — | Roscommon. |
| — | — | 28 | 8 | 65 | 12 | 93 | 20 | 11 | 3 | Sligo. |
| 1 | — | 66 | — | 217 | 1 | 284 | 1 | 18 | — | Tralee. |
| — | — | — | — | — | — | — | — | — | — | Trim. |
| — | — | 67 | — | 71 | 1 | 138 | [illegible] | 18 | — | Tullamore. |
| — | — | 71 | 1 | 120 | 30 | 191 | 31 | — | — | Waterford. |
| — | — | 33 | 1 | 100 | — | 133 | 1 | — | — | Wexford. |
| — | — | — | — | — | — | — | — | — | — | Wicklow. |
| — | — | 39 | — | 156 | — | 195 | — | 120 | — | Mountjoy, Male. |
| — | — | — | — | — | 66 | — | 66 | — | 18 | Mountjoy, Female. |
| 2 | — | [illegible] | — | 5,147 | — | [illegible] | — | 969 | — | Total, Males. |
| — | 1 | — | 218 | — | 768 | — | 1,180 | — | 140 | Total, Females. |
| 3 | | [illegible] | | 5,915 | | 9,368 | | 1,109 | | Total, M. and F. |

TABLE XI.—OFFENCES and COMMITMENTS of JUVENILES, *i.e.*, PRISONERS
Included in

| PRISONS. | COMMITMENTS. | | | | | | | | |
|---|---|---|---|---|---|---|---|---|---|
| | CONVICTED | | | | | | | | |
| | AT ASSIZES AND QUARTER SESSIONS. | | | | SUMMARILY. | | | | BY SPECIAL MAGISTRATES AND DIRECTORS. |
| | Under 12 Years. | | 12 and not exceeding 16 Years. | | Under 12 Years. | | 12 and not exceeding 16 Years. | | 12 and not exceeding 16 Years. |
| | M. | F. | M. | F. | M. | F. | M. | F. | M. |
| Armagh, | – | – | – | – | 6 | 1 | 18 | 2 | – |
| Belfast, | – | – | – | – | 13 | 3 | 79 | 10 | – |
| Carlow, | – | – | – | – | – | – | – | – | – |
| Carrick-on-Shannon, | – | – | – | – | – | – | – | – | – |
| Castlebar, | – | – | – | – | 1 | – | 17 | 4 | – |
| Cavan, | – | – | – | – | – | – | – | – | – |
| Clonmel, | – | – | – | – | – | – | 18 | – | – |
| Cork, Male, | – | – | 3 | – | 11 | – | 80 | – | – |
| Cork, Female, | – | – | – | 1 | – | – | – | 6 | – |
| Downpatrick, | – | – | 2 | – | – | – | – | – | – |
| Drogheda, | – | – | – | 1 | – | – | – | 4 | – |
| Dundalk, | 1 | – | 3 | – | 1 | – | 1 | – | 1 |
| Ennis, | – | – | – | – | – | – | 2 | – | – |
| Enniskillen, | – | – | – | – | – | – | – | – | – |
| Galway, | – | – | 1 | – | 2 | – | 31 | 8 | – |
| Grangegorman, | – | – | – | 1 | – | 3 | 6 | 84 | – |
| Kilkenny, | – | – | 1 | – | 1 | – | 6 | – | – |
| Kilmainham, | – | – | 4 | – | 6 | – | 44 | – | – |
| Lifford, | – | – | – | – | – | – | – | – | – |
| Limerick, Male, | – | – | 1 | – | 4 | – | 34 | – | – |
| Limerick, Female, | – | – | – | – | – | 1 | – | 5 | – |
| Londonderry, | 2 | – | 3 | 1 | 2 | – | 34 | 1 | – |
| Longford, | – | – | – | – | 1 | – | 2 | – | – |
| Maryborough, | – | – | – | – | 1 | – | 1 | – | – |
| Monaghan, | – | – | – | – | – | – | 1 | – | – |
| Mullingar, | 1 | – | 3 | 2 | 8 | – | 22 | 2 | – |
| Naas, | – | – | – | 1 | 1 | – | 2 | 1 | – |
| Nenagh, | – | – | – | – | – | – | 8 | – | – |
| Omagh, | – | – | 1 | – | 3 | – | 18 | – | – |
| Richmond, | – | – | 21 | – | 18 | – | 181 | – | – |
| Roscommon, | – | – | 1 | – | – | – | 1 | – | – |
| Sligo, | – | – | 1 | – | 6 | – | 13 | 2 | – |
| Tralee, | – | – | 4 | – | 5 | – | 28 | 4 | – |
| Trim, | – | – | 1 | – | – | – | 1 | – | – |
| Tullamore, | – | – | 3 | – | 1 | – | 2 | 1 | – |
| Waterford, | – | – | – | – | 11 | – | 13 | 1 | – |
| Wexford, | – | – | 1 | – | 1 | – | 10 | 3 | – |
| Wicklow, | – | – | – | – | – | – | – | – | – |
| Total, 1882-83, | 4 | – | 55 | 7 | 81 | 6 | 674 | 90 | 1 |
| Total, 1881-82, | 3 | – | 46 | 2 | 89 | 10 | 576 | 123 | – |

not exceeding 16 years of age, from 1st April, 1882, to 31st March, 1883, foregoing Tables.

| Commitments. Total Convicted. Under 12 Years. M. | F. | 12 and not exceeding 16 Years. M. | F. | Not Convicted and Untried. Under 12 Years. M. | F. | 12 and not exceeding 16 Years. M. | F. | Total Number of Commitments. Under 12 Years. M. | F. | 12 and not exceeding 16 Years. M. | F. | Prisons. |
|---|---|---|---|---|---|---|---|---|---|---|---|---|
| 6 | 1 | 19 | 8 | – | – | 1 | – | 6 | 1 | 20 | 8 | Armagh. |
| 18 | 8 | 79 | 16 | 8 | – | 62 | 1 | 19 | 8 | 116 | 11 | Belfast. |
| – | – | – | – | – | – | – | – | – | – | – | – | Carlow. |
| – | – | – | – | – | – | – | – | – | – | – | – | Carrick-on-Shannon. |
| 1 | – | 17 | 4 | – | – | 4 | 5 | 1 | – | 21 | 9 | Castlebar. |
| – | – | – | – | – | – | 1 | – | – | – | 1 | – | Cavan. |
| – | – | 18 | – | – | – | 1 | 1 | – | – | 19 | 1 | Clonmel. |
| 11 | – | 50 | – | – | – | 19 | – | 11 | – | 69 | – | Cork, Male. |
| – | – | – | 9 | – | 1 | – | – | – | 1 | – | 9 | Cork, Female. |
| – | – | 2 | – | – | – | – | – | – | – | 2 | – | Downpatrick. |
| – | – | – | 6 | – | – | – | – | – | – | – | 6 | Drogheda. |
| 2 | – | 4 | – | – | – | 3 | – | 2 | – | 7 | – | Dundalk. |
| – | – | 2 | – | 1 | – | 4 | 1 | 1 | – | 6 | 1 | Ennis. |
| – | – | – | – | – | – | – | – | – | – | – | – | Enniskillen. |
| 3 | – | 32 | 4 | – | – | 8 | – | 3 | – | 40 | 4 | Galway. |
| – | 2 | 4 | 35 | – | – | – | – | – | 2 | 4 | 35 | Grangegorman. |
| 8 | – | 6 | – | 1 | – | 5 | 1 | 9 | – | 11 | 1 | Kilkenny. |
| 6 | – | 40 | – | 6 | – | 23 | – | 12 | – | 63 | – | Kilmainham. |
| – | – | – | – | – | – | – | – | – | – | – | – | Lifford. |
| 5 | – | 26 | – | 1 | – | 9 | – | 6 | – | 35 | – | Limerick, Male. |
| – | 1 | – | 5 | – | – | – | – | – | 1 | – | 5 | Limerick, Female. |
| 5 | – | 37 | 3 | 3 | 3 | 3 | – | 8 | 3 | 40 | 3 | Londonderry. |
| 1 | – | 3 | – | 1 | – | – | – | 2 | – | 3 | – | Longford. |
| 1 | – | 1 | – | – | – | – | – | 1 | – | 1 | – | Maryborough. |
| – | – | 1 | – | – | – | – | – | – | – | 1 | – | Monaghan. |
| 7 | – | 25 | 1 | – | – | 2 | – | 7 | – | 27 | 1 | Mullingar. |
| 1 | – | 3 | 2 | – | 1 | – | – | 1 | 1 | 3 | 2 | Naas. |
| – | – | 3 | – | – | – | – | – | – | – | 3 | – | Nenagh. |
| 6 | – | 17 | – | – | – | 1 | – | 6 | – | 18 | – | Omagh. |
| 18 | – | 153 | – | 10 | – | 74 | – | 28 | – | 227 | – | Richmond. |
| – | – | 2 | – | – | – | 5 | – | – | – | 7 | – | Roscommon. |
| 3 | – | 14 | 3 | – | – | 1 | 1 | 3 | – | 15 | 4 | Sligo. |
| 3 | – | 30 | 6 | – | – | 12 | 1 | 3 | – | 42 | 7 | Tralee. |
| – | – | 3 | – | 1 | – | – | – | 1 | – | 3 | – | Trim. |
| 1 | – | 4 | 1 | – | – | 1 | – | 1 | – | 5 | 1 | Tullamore. |
| 8 | – | 10 | 1 | – | 1 | 4 | 1 | 8 | 1 | 14 | 2 | Waterford. |
| 1 | – | 19 | 3 | – | – | 1 | – | 1 | – | 20 | 3 | Wexford. |
| – | – | – | – | 1 | – | – | – | 1 | – | – | – | Wicklow. |
| 85 | 6 | 640 | 97 | 33 | 6 | 198 | 14 | 118 | 12 | 838 | 111 | Total, 1882–83. |
| 98 | 10 | 566 | 125 | 20 | 8 | 159 | 16 | 118 | 18 | 725 | 141 | Total, 1881–82. |

TABLE XII.—SENTENCES of PENAL SERVITUDE and IMPRISONMENT passed

| LOCAL PRISONS. | Penal Servitude for 5 Years and upwards. | | IMPRISONMENT FOR: 12 Months and upwards. | | 9 Months and above 6. | | 6 Months only. | | Under 6 Months and above 3. | | 3 Months only. | | 3 Months and above 2. | | 2 Months and above 1. | |
|---|---|---|---|---|---|---|---|---|---|---|---|---|---|---|---|---|
| | M. | F. | M. | F. | M. | F. | M. | F. | M. | F. | M. | F. | M. | F. | M. | F. |
| Armagh, | – | – | – | – | – | – | – | – | – | – | – | – | 1 | – | 2 | – |
| Belfast, | – | – | – | – | – | – | 3 | – | 1 | – | 5 | – | – | – | 7 | 1 |
| Castlebar, | – | – | – | – | – | – | – | – | – | – | – | – | – | – | 1 | – |
| Clonmel, | – | – | – | – | – | – | – | – | – | – | – | – | – | – | – | – |
| Cork, Male, | 1 | – | – | – | – | – | – | – | – | – | – | – | – | – | 4 | – |
| Cork, Female, | – | – | – | – | – | – | – | – | – | 1 | – | – | – | – | – | – |
| Downpatrick, | – | – | – | – | – | – | – | – | – | – | – | – | – | – | 1 | – |
| Drogheda, | – | – | – | – | – | – | – | – | – | 1 | – | – | – | – | – | – |
| Dundalk, | – | – | 1 | – | – | – | – | – | 1 | – | 1 | – | – | – | – | – |
| Galway, | 1 | – | – | – | – | – | – | – | – | – | – | – | – | – | 1 | – |
| Grangegorman, | – | – | – | – | – | – | – | – | – | 1 | – | – | – | – | – | – |
| Kilkenny, | – | – | – | – | – | – | 1 | – | – | – | – | – | – | – | – | – |
| Kilmainham, | – | – | – | – | – | – | 1 | – | 2 | – | 2 | – | – | – | 4 | – |
| Limerick, Male, | – | – | – | – | – | – | – | – | – | – | 5 | – | – | – | 1 | – |
| Limerick, Female, | – | – | – | – | – | – | – | – | – | – | – | 1 | – | – | – | – |
| Londonderry, | – | – | – | – | – | – | 1 | – | – | – | 1 | – | – | – | 1 | – |
| Maryborough, | – | – | – | – | – | – | – | – | – | – | – | – | – | – | – | – |
| Mullingar, | – | – | – | – | – | – | 1 | – | 1 | – | – | – | – | – | 2 | – |
| Naas, | – | – | – | – | – | – | – | – | – | – | – | – | – | – | – | – |
| Nenagh, | – | – | – | – | – | – | – | – | – | – | – | – | – | – | – | – |
| Omagh, | 4 | – | 1 | – | – | – | 1 | – | – | – | – | – | 1 | – | 4 | – |
| Richmond, | – | – | – | – | – | – | 3 | – | – | – | 4 | – | 2 | – | 17 | – |
| Sligo, | – | – | – | – | – | – | – | – | – | – | – | – | – | – | – | – |
| Tralee, | 1 | – | – | – | – | – | 2 | – | – | – | – | – | – | – | – | – |
| Tullamore, | – | – | – | – | – | – | – | – | – | – | – | – | – | – | 1 | – |
| Waterford, | – | – | – | – | – | – | 1 | – | – | – | – | – | – | – | – | – |
| Wexford, | – | – | – | – | 2 | – | – | – | – | – | 1 | – | – | – | – | – |
| Total, Males, | 7 | – | 2 | – | 2 | – | 14 | – | 5 | – | 19 | – | 4 | – | 46 | – |
| Total, Females, | – | – | – | – | – | – | – | – | – | 3 | – | 1 | – | – | – | 1 |
| Total, M. and F. | 7 | | 3 | | 2 | | 14 | | 8 | | 20 | | 4 | | 47 | |

on JUVENILE PRISONERS from the 1st April, 1882, to 31st March, 1883.

| IMPRISONMENT FOR | | | | | | | | | | Sentences [illegible] and not passed. | | Total. | | LOCAL PRISONS. |
|---|---|---|---|---|---|---|---|---|---|---|---|---|---|---|
| 1 Month and above 14 Days. | | 14 Days and above 7. | | 7 Days and above 48 Hours. | | 48 Hours. | | 24 Hours. | | | | | | |
| M. | F. | M. | F. | M. | F. | M. | F. | M. | F. | M. | F. | M. | F. | |
| 11 | 6 | 5 | – | – | – | 1 | – | 1 | – | – | – | 18 | 6 | Armagh. |
| 50 | 4 | 81 | 5 | 12 | 3 | 1 | – | 11 | – | – | – | [illegible] | 12 | Belfast. |
| 6 | 3 | 6 | 1 | 6 | [illegible] | 6 | – | – | – | – | – | 16 | 4 | Castlebar. |
| 8 | – | 6 | – | 7 | – | – | – | – | – | – | – | 16 | – | Clonmel. |
| 8 | – | 37 | – | 18 | – | 3 | – | 1 | – | – | – | 61 | – | Cork, Male. |
| – | – | – | 5 | – | 5 | – | – | – | – | – | – | – | 8 | Cork, Female. |
| – | – | 1 | – | – | – | – | – | – | – | – | – | 1 | – | Downpatrick. |
| – | – | – | 4 | – | 1 | – | – | – | – | – | – | – | 5 | Drogheda. |
| 5 | – | 1 | – | – | – | 1 | – | – | – | – | – | 7 | – | Dundalk. |
| 6 | 1 | 18 | 6 | 13 | 3 | 6 | – | – | – | – | – | 84 | 8 | Galway. |
| 1 | – | 4 | 16 | – | 7 | – | – | – | 11 | – | – | 5 | 37 | Grangegorman. |
| 3 | – | 6 | – | 8 | – | – | – | – | – | – | – | 7 | – | Kilkenny. |
| 8 | – | 31 | – | 9 | – | 8 | – | – | – | – | – | 64 | – | Kilmainham. |
| 6 | – | 18 | – | 16 | – | – | – | – | – | – | – | 40 | – | Limerick, Male. |
| – | – | – | 4 | – | – | – | – | – | 1 | – | – | – | 5 | Limerick, Female. |
| 14 | 1 | 9 | 1 | 9 | – | 5 | – | 4 | – | – | – | 42 | 2 | Londonderry. |
| – | – | 1 | – | 1 | – | – | – | – | – | – | – | 2 | – | Maryborough. |
| 4 | 1 | 15 | 1 | 9 | 3 | – | – | – | – | – | – | 31 | 4 | Mullingar. |
| – | – | 8 | 2 | 1 | – | – | – | – | – | – | – | 8 | 2 | Naas. |
| – | – | 2 | – | – | – | – | – | – | – | – | – | 2 | – | Nenagh. |
| 4 | – | 3 | – | 1 | – | 1 | – | – | – | – | – | 20 | – | Omagh. |
| 53 | – | 76 | – | 31 | – | 9 | – | 6 | – | – | – | 180 | – | Richmond. |
| 6 | 1 | 7 | 1 | 4 | – | – | – | – | – | – | – | 17 | 2 | Sligo. |
| – | 2 | 15 | – | 17 | 2 | – | – | 1 | – | – | – | 33 | 4 | Tralee. |
| 5 | – | 2 | – | – | – | – | 1 | – | – | – | – | 5 | 1 | Tullamore. |
| 3 | – | 6 | – | 6 | – | 1 | – | 4 | 1 | – | – | 21 | 1 | Waterford. |
| 2 | 2 | 6 | – | 3 | 1 | – | – | – | – | – | – | 18 | 6 | Wexford. |
| 138 | – | 301 | – | 142 | – | 62 | 1 | 27 | 13 | – | – | 731 | – | Total, Males. |
| – | 17 | – | 44 | – | 23 | – | – | – | – | – | – | – | 106 | Total, Females. |
| 155 | | 345 | | 165 | | 63 | | 40 | | – | | 837 | | Total, M. and F. |

TABLE XIII.—CONDITION of JUVENILES as to

| LARGER PRISONS. | EDUCATION OF | | | | | | | | | | | |
|---|---|---|---|---|---|---|---|---|---|---|---|---|
| | Read and Write. | | | | Read Imperfectly. | | | | Know Spelling. | | | |
| | Under 12 years. | | 12 and not exceeding 16 years. | | Under 12 years. | | 12 and not exceeding 16 years. | | Under 12 years. | | 12 and not exceeding 16 years. | |
| | M. | F. | M. | F. | M. | F. | M. | F. | M. | F. | M. | F. |
| Armagh, . . . | 9 | – | 3 | – | – | – | 3 | 1 | – | – | 4 | – |
| Belfast, . . . | 11 | 1 | 58 | 7 | 6 | – | 6 | 1 | – | – | – | – |
| Castlebar, . . . | – | – | 7 | 4 | – | – | – | – | – | – | – | – |
| Clonmel, . . . | – | – | 6 | 1 | – | – | 1 | – | – | – | – | – |
| Cork, Male, . . | 4 | – | 83 | – | 1 | – | 8 | – | – | – | – | – |
| Cork, Female, . . | – | – | – | 4 | – | – | – | 2 | – | – | – | 1 |
| Downpatrick, . . | – | – | – | – | – | – | 1 | – | – | – | – | – |
| Drogheda, . . . | – | – | – | 1 | – | – | – | – | – | – | – | – |
| Dundalk, . . . | 1 | – | 4 | – | 1 | – | – | – | – | – | – | – |
| Galway, . . . | 1 | – | 18 | 2 | – | – | – | – | – | – | – | – |
| Grangegorman, . . | – | 1 | 8 | 18 | – | – | 2 | 3 | – | – | – | – |
| Kilkenny, . . . | – | – | 7 | 1 | 1 | – | 5 | – | – | – | – | – |
| Kilmainham, . . | 2 | – | 37 | – | 1 | – | 4 | – | – | – | – | – |
| Limerick, Male, . . | 8 | – | 83 | – | – | – | 8 | – | – | – | 2 | – |
| Limerick, Female, . | – | – | – | – | – | – | – | 1 | – | 1 | – | – |
| Londonderry, . . | 1 | – | 10 | – | 1 | – | 2 | – | – | – | 8 | – |
| Maryborough, . . | 1 | – | – | – | – | – | – | – | – | – | – | – |
| Mullingar, . . . | 4 | – | 10 | 3 | – | – | – | – | – | – | – | – |
| Naas, . . . | 1 | 1 | 1 | 1 | – | – | – | – | – | – | – | – |
| Nenagh, . . . | – | – | 8 | – | – | – | – | – | – | – | – | – |
| Omagh, . . . | 1 | – | 9 | – | – | – | 2 | – | – | – | 1 | – |
| Richmond, . . . | 3 | – | 128 | – | 4 | – | 49 | – | 12 | – | 5 | – |
| Sligo, . . . | 2 | – | 5 | 1 | – | – | 6 | 8 | 1 | – | – | – |
| Tralee, . . . | 2 | – | 27 | 4 | – | – | 6 | – | – | – | 4 | – |
| Tullamore, . . | 1 | – | 9 | – | – | – | – | 1 | – | – | – | – |
| Waterford, . . . | – | – | 6 | 1 | – | – | – | – | – | – | – | – |
| Wexford . . . | – | – | 10 | 1 | – | – | 1 | – | – | – | – | – |
| Total, Males, . | 43 | – | 413 | – | 14 | – | 88 | – | 13 | – | 21 | – |
| Total, Females, . | – | 5 | – | 47 | – | – | – | 10 | – | 1 | – | 1 |
| Total, M. and F., . | 48 | | 460 | | 14 | | 98 | | 14 | | 22 | |

EDUCATION and RELIGION in 1882–83.

| Continued. | | | | | | | | | | | | | | | | |
|---|---|---|---|---|---|---|---|---|---|---|---|---|---|---|---|---|
| Knew Alphabet. | | | | Wholly Illiterate. | | | | Could not be ascertained. | | | | Total. | | | | Local Prisons. |
| Under 12 years. | | 12 and not exceeding 16 years. | | Under 12 years. | | 12 and not exceeding 16 years. | | Under 12 years. | | 12 and not exceeding 16 years. | | Under 12 years. | | 12 and not exceeding 16 years. | | |
| M. | F. | M. | F. | M. | F. | M. | F. | M. | F. | M. | F. | M. | F. | M. | F. | |
| – | 1 | 2 | 1 | 6 | – | 6 | – | – | – | – | – | 9 | 1 | 20 | 5 | Armagh. |
| – | – | – | – | 6 | 1 | 26 | 8 | – | – | – | – | 19 | 2 | 119 | 11 | Belfast. |
| – | – | – | – | 1 | – | 14 | 5 | – | – | – | – | 1 | – | 21 | 10 | Castlebar. |
| – | – | – | – | – | – | 12 | – | – | – | – | – | – | – | 19 | 1 | Clonmel. |
| 4 | – | 7 | – | 8 | – | 18 | – | – | – | – | – | 11 | – | 65 | – | Cork, Male. |
| – | – | – | 1 | – | 1 | – | 1 | – | – | – | – | – | 1 | – | 9 | Cork, Female. |
| – | – | – | – | – | – | 1 | – | – | – | – | – | – | – | 6 | – | Downpatrick. |
| – | – | – | 1 | – | – | – | 4 | – | – | – | – | – | – | – | 6 | Drogheda. |
| – | – | 1 | – | – | – | 1 | – | – | – | – | – | 9 | – | 7 | – | Dundalk. |
| – | – | – | – | 1 | – | 25 | 4 | – | – | – | – | 9 | – | 40 | 8 | Galway. |
| – | – | – | – | – | 1 | 1 | 16 | – | – | – | – | – | 8 | 5 | 85 | Grangegorman. |
| – | – | – | – | 1 | – | 1 | – | – | – | – | – | 8 | – | 11 | 1 | Kilkenny. |
| 3 | – | 1 | – | 8 | – | 19 | – | – | – | – | – | 11 | – | 69 | – | Kilmainham. |
| – | – | 6 | – | 4 | – | 11 | – | – | – | – | – | 6 | – | 44 | – | Limerick, Male. |
| – | – | – | – | – | – | – | 4 | – | – | – | – | – | 1 | – | 5 | Limerick, Female. |
| – | – | 13 | 1 | 4 | 8 | 8 | 1 | – | – | – | – | 8 | 2 | 80 | 8 | Londonderry. |
| – | – | 1 | – | – | – | – | – | – | – | – | – | 1 | – | 1 | – | Maryborough. |
| – | – | – | – | 8 | – | 8 | 1 | – | – | – | – | 7 | – | 27 | 4 | Mullingar. |
| – | – | – | 1 | – | – | 1 | – | – | – | | – | 1 | 1 | 9 | 3 | Naas. |
| – | – | – | – | – | – | – | – | – | – | – | – | – | – | 6 | – | Nenagh. |
| 1 | – | 6 | – | 1 | – | 4 | – | – | – | – | – | 6 | – | 18 | – | Omagh. |
| – | – | – | – | 10 | – | 43 | – | – | – | – | – | 89 | – | 667 | – | Richmond. |
| – | – | – | – | 1 | – | 4 | – | – | – | – | – | 3 | – | 15 | 6 | Sligo. |
| – | – | 1 | – | 1 | – | 4 | 1 | – | – | – | – | 5 | – | 43 | 8 | Tralee. |
| – | – | 3 | – | – | – | – | – | – | – | – | – | 1 | – | 6 | 1 | Tullamore. |
| – | – | – | – | 6 | 1 | 9 | 1 | – | – | – | – | 8 | 1 | 17 | 2 | Waterford. |
| – | – | – | – | 1 | – | 8 | 9 | – | – | – | – | 1 | – | 18 | 3 | Wexford. |
| 7 | – | 37 | – | 47 | – | 219 | – | – | – | – | – | 129 | – | 819 | – | Total, Males. |
| – | 1 | – | 5 | – | 5 | – | 43 | – | – | – | – | – | 11 | – | 167 | Total, Females. |
| 8 | | 42 | | 52 | | 254 | | – | | – | | 132 | | 9[illegible] | | Total, M. & F. |

TABLE XIII. *concluded.*—CONDITION of JUVENILES

| LABOUR PRISONS. | RELIGION. | | | | | | | | | | | |
|---|---|---|---|---|---|---|---|---|---|---|---|---|
| | Protestant Episcopalians of Ireland. | | | | Presbyterian. | | | | Roman Catholic. | | | |
| | Under 15 years. | | 15 and not exceeding 16 years. | | Under 15 years. | | 15 and not exceeding 16 years. | | Under 15 years. | | 15 and not exceeding 16 years. | |
| | M. | F. | M. | F. | M. | F. | M. | F. | M. | F. | M. | F. |
| Armagh, | 1 | – | 2 | – | – | – | 1 | – | 4 | 1 | 17 | 2 |
| Belfast, | 4 | 1 | 23 | 3 | 6 | – | 23 | 1 | 9 | 1 | 61 | 7 |
| Castlebar, | – | – | – | – | – | – | – | – | 1 | – | 21 | 10 |
| Clonmel, | – | – | – | – | – | – | – | – | – | – | 19 | 1 |
| Cork, Male, | – | – | – | – | – | – | – | – | 11 | – | 85 | – |
| Cork, Female, | – | – | – | – | – | – | – | – | – | 1 | – | 9 |
| Downpatrick, | – | – | – | – | – | – | – | – | – | – | 2 | – |
| Drogheda, | – | – | – | – | – | – | – | – | – | – | – | 6 |
| Dundalk, | – | – | – | – | – | – | – | – | 6 | – | 7 | – |
| Galway, | – | – | – | – | – | – | – | – | 3 | – | 40 | 6 |
| Grangegorman, | – | – | – | 4 | – | – | – | 1 | – | 2 | 8 | 80 |
| Kilkenny, | – | – | 8 | – | – | – | – | – | 2 | – | 9 | 1 |
| Kilmainham, | 1 | – | 3 | – | – | – | – | – | 10 | – | 60 | – |
| Limerick, Male, | – | – | 2 | – | – | – | – | – | 6 | – | 43 | – |
| Limerick, Female, | – | – | – | – | – | – | – | – | – | 1 | – | 5 |
| Londonderry, | 6 | – | 2 | – | – | – | 6 | – | 4 | 1 | 51 | 2 |
| Maryborough, | – | – | – | – | – | – | – | – | 1 | – | 1 | – |
| Mullingar, | – | – | – | – | – | – | – | – | 7 | – | 27 | 4 |
| Naas, | – | – | – | – | – | – | – | – | 1 | 1 | 8 | 2 |
| Nenagh, | – | – | – | – | – | – | – | – | – | – | 8 | – |
| Omagh, | – | – | 1 | – | – | – | – | – | 3 | – | 17 | – |
| Richmond, | 4 | – | 25 | – | – | – | – | – | 20 | – | 304 | – |
| Sligo, | – | – | – | – | – | – | – | – | 8 | – | 15 | 3 |
| Tralee, | – | – | – | – | – | – | – | – | 3 | – | 43 | 5 |
| Tullamore, | – | – | – | – | – | – | – | – | 1 | – | 6 | 1 |
| Waterford, | – | – | – | – | – | – | – | – | 6 | 1 | 17 | 3 |
| Wexford, | – | – | – | – | – | – | – | – | 1 | – | 16 | 3 |
| Total, Males, | 12 | – | 63 | – | 6 | – | 25 | – | 104 | – | 797 | – |
| Total, Females, | – | 1 | – | 7 | – | – | – | 3 | – | 10 | – | 99 |
| Total, M. and F. | 13 | | 70 | | 6 | | 28 | | 114 | | 896 | |

as to Education and Religion in 1882–83.

| Religion. | | | | | | | | | | | | Lunatic Prisons. |
|---|---|---|---|---|---|---|---|---|---|---|---|---|
| Other Religions. | | | | Could not be ascertained. | | | | Total. | | | | |
| Under 12 years. | | 12 and not exceeding 16 years. | | Under 12 years. | | 12 and not exceeding 16 years. | | Under 12 years. | | 12 and not exceeding 16 years. | | |
| M. | F. | M. | F. | M. | F. | M. | F. | M. | F. | M. | F. | |
| – | – | – | – | – | – | – | – | 3 | 1 | 20 | 2 | Armagh. |
| – | – | – | – | – | – | – | – | 18 | 6 | 112 | 13 | Belfast. |
| – | – | – | – | – | – | – | – | 1 | – | 61 | 10 | Castlebar. |
| – | – | – | – | – | – | – | – | – | – | 18 | 1 | Clonmel. |
| – | – | – | – | – | – | – | – | 21 | – | 63 | – | Cork, Male. |
| – | – | – | – | – | – | – | – | – | 1 | – | 9 | Cork, Female. |
| – | – | – | – | – | – | – | – | – | – | 8 | – | Downpatrick. |
| – | – | – | – | – | – | – | – | – | – | – | 6 | Drogheda. |
| – | – | – | – | – | – | – | – | 2 | – | 7 | – | Dundalk. |
| – | – | – | – | – | – | – | – | 8 | – | 44 | 6 | Galway. |
| – | – | – | – | – | – | – | – | – | 2 | 5 | 85 | Grangegorman. |
| – | – | – | – | – | – | – | – | 3 | – | 11 | 1 | Kilkenny. |
| – | – | – | – | – | – | – | – | 11 | – | 64 | – | Kilmainham. |
| – | – | – | – | – | – | – | – | 6 | – | 44 | – | Limerick, Male. |
| – | – | – | – | – | – | – | – | – | 1 | – | 5 | Limerick, Female. |
| – | – | – | – | – | – | – | – | 6 | 2 | 20 | 2 | Londonderry. |
| – | – | – | – | – | – | – | – | 1 | – | 1 | – | Maryborough. |
| – | – | – | – | – | – | – | – | 7 | – | 27 | 4 | Mullingar. |
| – | – | – | – | – | – | – | – | 1 | 1 | 8 | 6 | Naas. |
| – | – | – | – | – | – | – | – | – | – | 8 | – | Nenagh. |
| – | – | – | – | – | – | – | – | 8 | – | 13 | – | Omagh. |
| – | – | – | – | – | – | – | – | 20 | – | 227 | – | Richmond. |
| – | – | – | – | – | – | – | – | 3 | – | 15 | 3 | Sligo. |
| – | – | – | – | – | – | – | – | 3 | – | 43 | 6 | Tralee. |
| – | – | – | – | – | – | – | – | 1 | – | 6 | 1 | Tullamore. |
| – | – | – | – | – | – | – | – | 6 | 1 | 17 | 2 | Waterford. |
| – | – | – | – | – | – | – | – | 1 | – | 16 | 3 | Wexford. |
| – | – | – | – | – | – | – | – | 129 | – | 810 | – | Total, Males. |
| – | – | – | – | – | – | – | – | – | 11 | – | 105 | Total, Females. |
| – | | – | | – | | – | | [illegible] | | [illegible] | | Total, M. and F. |

TABLE XIV.—No. of CONVICTED PRISONERS in Custody in the following Prisons on

| LARGER PRISONS. | 4 Years Penal Servitude and upwards. | | 3 Years and above 2. | | 2 Years and above 18 Months. | | 18 Months and above 12. | | 12 Months only. | | Under 12 Months and above 6. | | 6 Months and above 3. | |
|---|---|---|---|---|---|---|---|---|---|---|---|---|---|---|
| | M. | F. | M. | F. | M. | F. | M. | F. | M. | F. | M. | F. | M. | F. |
| Armagh, . . | - | - | - | - | 1 | - | 3 | - | 8 | 1 | - | - | 2 | - |
| Belfast, . . | - | - | - | - | 1 | - | 1 | - | 37 | - | 1 | - | 18 | - |
| Castlebar, . . | - | - | - | - | - | - | 2 | - | 1 | - | - | - | - | - |
| Clonmel, . . | - | - | - | - | 1 | - | 1 | - | 8 | - | - | - | 6 | - |
| Cork, Male, . . | - | - | - | - | - | - | 7 | - | 13 | - | - | - | 8 | - |
| Cork, Female, . | - | - | - | - | - | - | - | 3 | - | 1 | - | - | - | 1 |
| Downpatrick, . . | - | - | 2 | - | - | - | 1 | - | 5 | - | - | - | 8 | - |
| Drogheda, . . | - | - | - | - | - | - | - | - | - | - | - | - | - | - |
| Dundalk, . . | - | - | 1 | - | 1 | - | 1 | - | 23 | - | 2 | - | 2 | - |
| Galway, . . | - | - | - | - | 1 | - | - | - | 1 | - | 1 | - | 1 | - |
| Grangegorman, . | - | - | - | - | 8 | - | 1 | 1 | 3 | 6 | - | - | 8 | 2 |
| Kilkenny, . . | - | - | - | - | 1 | - | - | - | 5 | - | - | - | - | - |
| Kilmainham, . . | - | - | - | - | - | - | - | - | 8 | - | - | - | - | - |
| Limerick, Male, . | - | - | - | - | 3 | - | 6 | - | 9 | - | - | - | 8 | - |
| Limerick, Female, . | - | - | - | - | - | - | - | - | - | - | - | - | - | - |
| Londonderry, . . | 2 | - | - | - | 1 | - | - | - | 3 | - | 1 | - | 4 | 1 |
| Maryborough, . | - | - | - | - | - | - | - | - | 5 | - | - | - | - | - |
| Mullingar, . . | - | - | - | - | - | - | 1 | - | 8 | - | 1 | - | 5 | - |
| Naas, . . . | - | - | - | - | - | - | - | - | - | - | - | - | - | - |
| Nenagh, . . | - | - | - | - | - | - | - | - | 8 | - | - | - | 3 | - |
| Omagh, . . | - | - | - | - | - | - | - | - | 3 | - | - | - | 1 | - |
| Richmond, . . | - | - | 4 | - | 9 | - | 19 | - | 97 | - | - | - | 27 | - |
| Sligo, . . . | - | - | - | - | - | - | - | - | 8 | - | - | - | - | - |
| Tralee, . . | - | - | - | - | - | - | - | - | 7 | - | - | - | - | - |
| Tullamore, . . | - | - | - | - | 2 | - | - | 3 | 16 | - | - | - | 6 | - |
| Waterford, . . | - | - | - | - | - | 2 | - | 8 | 3 | 4 | - | - | - | - |
| Wexford, . . | - | - | - | - | - | - | - | - | 6 | - | - | - | 8 | - |
| Total, Males, . | 2 | - | 7 | - | 15 | - | 34 | - | 198 | - | 6 | - | 105 | - |
| Total, Females, . | - | - | - | - | - | 2 | - | 9 | - | 12 | - | - | - | 4 |
| Total, M. and F. | 2 | | 7 | | 17 | | 43 | | 210 | | 6 | | 109 | |

the 31st March, 1883, sentenced to the under-mentioned terms of Imprisonment.

| 6 Months only. | | Under 6 Months and above 3. | | 3 Months only. | | Under 3 Months and above 2. | | 2 Months and above 1. | | 1 Month or Under. | | Local Prisons. |
|---|---|---|---|---|---|---|---|---|---|---|---|---|
| M. | F. | M. | F. | M. | F. | M. | F. | M. | F. | M. | F. | |
| 5 | 2 | 3 | 3 | 2 | 1 | 2 | 1 | 10 | 3 | 9 | 3 | Armagh. |
| 88 | 20 | 6 | 6 | 24 | 13 | 3 | – | 67 | 23 | 107 | 24 | Belfast. |
| 5 | 1 | – | – | 3 | 1 | – | – | 1 | 1 | 8 | 1 | Castlebar. |
| 4 | 2 | 1 | 1 | 6 | 1 | 3 | – | 8 | 1 | 15 | 9 | Clonmel. |
| 9 | – | 1 | – | 14 | – | 1 | – | 55 | – | 41 | – | Cork, Male. |
| – | 7 | – | – | – | 10 | – | 9 | – | 7 | – | 60 | Cork, Female. |
| 7 | 1 | 1 | 1 | 3 | 1 | 5 | 3 | 1 | – | 8 | 7 | Downpatrick. |
| – | – | – | – | – | – | – | – | – | – | 5 | 3 | Drogheda. |
| 7 | – | 2 | – | 14 | – | 4 | – | 4 | – | 12 | – | Dundalk. |
| 1 | 1 | – | – | 1 | 3 | – | 1 | 8 | 4 | 23 | 3 | Galway. |
| 11 | 16 | 1 | 5 | 8 | 5 | – | – | 2 | 15 | 20 | 56 | Grangegorman. |
| 8 | – | 1 | 1 | 1 | – | – | – | 8 | 6 | 4 | 10 | Kilkenny. |
| 1 | – | 3 | – | 6 | – | 1 | – | 11 | – | 30 | – | Kilmainham. |
| 19 | – | 8 | – | 6 | – | 8 | – | 19 | – | 29 | – | Limerick, Male. |
| – | 6 | – | – | – | – | – | 5 | – | 4 | – | 17 | Limerick, Female. |
| 12 | – | 8 | – | 7 | 1 | – | 1 | 6 | 4 | 14 | 10 | Londonderry. |
| – | – | – | – | – | – | – | – | – | – | – | – | Maryborough. |
| 6 | 1 | 5 | 1 | 8 | – | – | – | 13 | – | 10 | 9 | Mullingar. |
| – | – | – | – | – | – | – | – | – | – | – | – | Naas. |
| 8 | – | 1 | – | 1 | – | – | – | 1 | – | 6 | – | Nenagh. |
| 9 | 4 | – | – | 4 | 8 | 1 | – | – | 1 | 7 | 2 | Omagh. |
| 75 | – | 11 | – | 43 | – | 4 | – | 9 | – | 6 | – | Richmond. |
| 9 | – | 2 | 1 | 5 | 1 | – | – | 4 | 1 | 8 | 1 | Sligo. |
| 4 | – | 3 | 2 | 4 | – | – | 1 | 5 | 1 | 7 | 3 | Tralee. |
| 15 | – | – | – | 10 | 2 | – | – | 7 | 8 | 4 | 6 | Tullamore. |
| 8 | – | – | – | 3 | 5 | – | – | 4 | 3 | 16 | 8 | Waterford. |
| – | 10 | – | – | 2 | – | 4 | – | 6 | – | 8 | 6 | Wexford. |

TABLE XV.—RETURN of COMMITTALS, &c., to BRIDEWELLS.

| BRIDEWELLS. | COUNTY. | Number of Direct Committals. | | Number received from other Bridewells on way to County Gaol. | | Number otherwise received. | | Total in Bridewell. | | Number of Drunkards committed from 1st April, 18[illegible], to 31st March, 18[illegible]. | |
|---|---|---|---|---|---|---|---|---|---|---|---|
| | | M. | F. | M. | F. | M. | F. | M. | F. | M. | F. |
| Bailieborough, | Cavan, | 45 | 17 | – | – | – | – | 44 | 17 | 16 | 6 |
| Ballina, | Mayo, | 30 | 3 | – | – | 44 | 21 | 84 | 24 | 22 | 12 |
| Ballinasloe, | Galway, | 209 | 48 | 27 | 10 | – | – | 238 | 58 | 41 | 15 |
| Ballinrobe, | Mayo, | 90 | 7 | – | – | – | – | 90 | 7 | 22 | – |
| Ballymena, | Antrim, | 102 | 8 | – | – | 8 | – | 117 | 8 | 11 | 1 |
| Baltinglass, | Wicklow, | 1 | 2 | – | – | – | – | 1 | 2 | – | – |
| Bantry, | Cork, | 106 | 21 | – | – | – | – | 106 | 21 | 4 | 3 |
| Cahirciveen, | Kerry, | 43 | 6 | – | – | – | – | 46 | 6 | 15 | 2 |
| Clifden, | Galway, | 24 | 1 | – | – | 19 | 3 | 43 | 4 | 18 | 1 |
| Clonakilty, | Cork, | 22 | 11 | – | – | 30 | 6 | 52 | 17 | 31 | 6 |
| Coleraine, | Londonderry, | 72 | 18 | – | – | 19 | 3 | 91 | 21 | 8 | 3 |
| Dingle, | Kerry, | 22 | 3 | – | – | – | – | 22 | 3 | 1 | – |
| Donegal, | Donegal, | 9 | 2 | – | – | 7 | 1 | 16 | 3 | 3 | – |
| Dungannon, | Tyrone, | 96 | 35 | – | – | 23 | 6 | 119 | 41 | 88 | 19 |
| Dungarvan, | Waterford, | 103 | 16 | – | – | 55 | 14 | 157 | 30 | 60 | 7 |
| Fermoy, | Cork, | 106 | 41 | – | – | – | – | 106 | 41 | 40 | 17 |
| Killarney, | Kerry, | 60 | 4 | – | – | 7 | 3 | 67 | 6 | 6 | 3 |
| Kilrush, | Clare, | 51 | 8 | – | – | 24 | 1 | 75 | 9 | 3 | – |
| Letterkenny, | Donegal, | 63 | 60 | 14 | 1 | 2 | 3 | 79 | 64 | 63 | 62 |
| Listowel, | Kerry, | 34 | 19 | – | – | – | – | 84 | 19 | 4 | 3 |
| Loughrea, | Galway, | 131 | 9 | – | – | – | – | 131 | 9 | 33 | 3 |
| Lurgan, | Armagh, | 190 | 28 | – | – | – | – | 190 | 26 | 46 | 7 |
| Mallow, | Cork, | 181 | 44 | – | – | 3 | 2 | 186 | 46 | 20 | 7 |
| Mitchelstown, | Cork, | 54 | 8 | – | – | 17 | 4 | 78 | 12 | 18 | 3 |
| Navan, | Meath, | 50 | 1 | – | – | 34 | 4 | 88 | 5 | 7 | 1 |
| New Ross, | Wexford, | 44 | 31 | 1 | – | – | – | 45 | 31 | 18 | 6 |
| Newry, | Down, | 220 | 38 | – | – | 11 | 6 | 231 | 43 | 142 | 38 |
| Parsonstown, | King's, | 148 | 36 | – | – | – | – | 188 | 40 | 47 | 12 |
| Queenstown, | Cork, | 109 | 14 | – | – | – | – | 109 | 14 | – | – |
| Rathkeale, | Limerick, | 44 | 6 | – | – | – | – | 44 | 6 | – | – |
| Thurles, | Tipperary, | 96 | 18 | – | – | 7 | 4 | 103 | 22 | 9 | 4 |
| Tipperary, | Tipperary, | 151 | 23 | – | – | 12 | 6 | 164 | 29 | 28 | – |
| Tuam, | Galway, | 70 | 7 | – | – | 107 | 16 | 177 | 24 | 25 | 1 |
| Youghal, | Cork, | 41 | 10 | – | – | – | – | 41 | 14 | 14 | 10 |

from 1st April, 1882, to 31st March, 1883.

| Prisoners received and ? during the above Period. | | | | | | | | Greatest number of Males and Females in custody at any one time during above period. | | BRIDEWELLS. |
|---|---|---|---|---|---|---|---|---|---|---|
| 24 Hours and under. | | 48 Hours and above 24 Hours. | | 7 Days and above 48 Hours. | | Above 7 Days. | | | | |
| M. | F. | M. | F. | M. | F. | M. | F. | M. | F. | |
| 4 | – | 7 | 4 | – | – | – | – | 6 | 3 | Bailieborough. |
| – | – | 2 | – | – | – | – | – | 3 | 4 | Ballina. |
| 27 | 8 | 32 | 14 | – | – | – | – | 10 | 2 | Ballinasloe. |
| 6 | – | 9 | – | – | – | – | – | 4 | 2 | Ballinrobe. |
| 24 | 8 | 26 | 1 | – | – | – | – | 6 | 2 | Ballymena. |
| – | – | – | – | – | – | – | – | 2 | 1 | Ballyvaughan. |
| – | – | – | – | – | – | – | – | 6 | 2 | Bantry. |
| 6 | 1 | 14 | 2 | – | – | – | – | 4 | 1 | Castletown. |
| 3 | – | 6 | | 3 | 2 | – | – | 4 | 2 | Clifden. |
| – | – | 1 | – | – | – | – | – | 4 | 2 | Clonakilty. |
| 1 | 3 | 1 | 1 | – | – | – | – | 8 | 2 | Coleraine. |
| – | – | – | – | – | – | – | – | 5 | 1 | Dingle. |
| – | – | 3 | – | – | – | – | – | 5 | 1 | Donegal. |
| 12 | – | 24 | 6 | 41 | 13 | | – | 9 | 4 | Dungannon. |
| 12 | 1 | | 4 | 29 | 12 | 2 | – | 10 | 3 | Dungarvan. |
| 8 | – | 22 | 16 | – | – | – | – | 8 | 4 | Fermoy. |
| 1 | 1 | 4 | – | – | – | – | – | 7 | 2 | Kilkenny. |
| 8 | – | 2 | – | – | – | – | – | 5 | 1 | Kilrush. |
| 36 | 10 | 18 | 17 | – | – | – | – | 4 | 2 | Letterkenny. |
| 8 | 4 | 4 | 1 | – | – | – | – | 6 | 2 | Listowel. |
| 32 | – | 32 | 8 | – | – | – | – | 16 | 1 | Loughrea. |
| 4 | 8 | 30 | 6 | – | – | – | – | 12 | 4 | Lurgan. |
| 8 | 1 | 24 | 3 | 1 | 2 | – | – | 18 | 2 | Mallow. |
| 4 | 3 | 35 | 1 | – | – | – | – | 7 | 3 | Mitchelstown. |
| 1 | 3 | 8 | – | 4 | – | – | – | 8 | 1 | Naas. |
| 1 | – | 8 | – | – | – | – | – | 6 | 2 | New Ross. |
| 107 | 18 | 34 | 23 | – | – | – | – | 8 | 2 | Newry. |
| 4 | – | 13 | 3 | 44 | 13 | – | 1 | 9 | 3 | Parsonstown. |
| – | – | – | – | – | – | – | – | 13 | 2 | Queenstown. |
| – | – | – | – | – | – | – | – | 3 | 2 | Rathkeale. |
| 2 | 2 | 4 | 2 | – | – | – | – | 18 | 3 | Thurles. |
| 23 | 2 | – | – | 17 | 3 | – | – | 16 | 4 | Tipperary. |
| 3 | – | 28 | 1 | – | – | – | – | 13 | 4 | Tuam. |
| 30 | 3 | 7 | 6 | 14 | 2 | – | – | 4 | 2 | Youghal. |
| 357 | – | 367 | – | 135 | – | 2 | – | 231 | – | Total, Males. |
| – | 60 | – | 123 | – | 66 | – | 1 | – | 87 | Total, Females. |
| 417 | | 490 | | 201 | | 3 | | 318 | | Total, M. and F. |

TABLE XVI.—Cases of SICKNESS and LUNACY, from 1st April, 1882, to 31st March, 1883, in the under-mentioned Prisons.

| Local Prisons. | Number in Prison Hospital. | | Daily average Number in Hospital. | | Number of Cases of Illness or Disease prescribed for out of Hospital. | | Number of Lunatics in Custody during the above period. | | Number of Days passed by Lunatics in Gaol. | | Greatest Number Sick at any one time in and out of Hospital, including Lunatics. | |
|---|---|---|---|---|---|---|---|---|---|---|---|---|
| | M. | F. | M. | F. | M. | F. | M. | F. | M. | F. | M. | F. |
| Armagh, | 12 | 3 | ·86 | ·07 | 990 | 83 | – | – | – | – | 9 | 8 |
| Belfast, | 49 | 30 | 3 | 2 | 8,058 | 3,363 | 15 | 8 | 44 | 21 | 16 | 11 |
| Castlebar, | 9 | – | ·1 | – | 234 | 49 | 4 | – | 49 | – | 13 | 3 |
| Clonmel, | 63 | 3 | 2 | – | 858 | 8 | 1 | – | 9 | – | 8 | – |
| Cork, Male, | 64 | – | 1 | – | 1,573 | – | 8 | – | 10 | – | 9 | – |
| Cork, Female, | – | 66 | – | 3 | – | 1,531 | – | 3 | – | 8 | – | 14 |
| Downpatrick, | – | – | – | – | 60 | 18 | 1 | – | 60 | – | 6 | 1 |
| Drogheda, | – | 2 | – | – | – | 55 | – | 3 | – | 13 | – | 8 |
| Dundalk, | 18 | – | ·0416 | – | 30 | – | – | – | – | – | 5 | – |
| Galway, | 7 | 6 | – | – | 272 | 38 | – | – | – | – | 6 | 4 |
| Grangegorman, | 78 | 263 | 5 | 8 | 1,641 | 2,389 | 5 | 3 | 28 | 46 | 14 | 26 |
| Kilkenny, | 8 | 3 | – | – | 782 | 112 | 2 | – | 8 | – | 11 | 6 |
| Kilmainham, | 68 | – | 3 | – | 604 | – | 1 | – | 11 | – | 11 | – |
| Limerick, Male, | 15 | – | ·31 | – | 1,420 | – | 6 | – | 30 | – | 4 | – |
| Limerick, Female, | – | 9 | – | ·00684 | – | 155 | – | 4 | – | 83 | – | 6 |
| Londonderry, | 25 | 4 | 1 | ·1 | 417 | 66 | 4 | – | 33 | – | 3 | 1 |
| Maryborough, | – | – | – | – | 430 | 4 | 1 | – | 13 | – | 7 | 1 |
| Mullingar, | 91 | 13 | 1 | 1 | 170 | 64 | 4 | 3 | 60 | 78 | 5 | 2 |
| Naas, | – | – | – | – | 113 | 36 | 2 | – | 24 | – | 2 | 2 |
| Nenagh, | – | – | – | – | 1,510 | – | 1 | – | 6 | – | 3 | |
| Omagh, | 7 | 8 | ·082 | ·038 | 146 | 40 | 1 | – | 6 | – | 4 | 3 |
| Richmond, | 600 | – | 21·5 | – | 4,066 | – | 17 | – | 478 | – | 57 | – |
| Sligo, | 13 | 7 | ·24 | ·1 | 154 | 40 | 4 | 1 | 38 | 6 | 5 | 2 |
| Tralee, | – | – | – | – | 311 | 109 | 4 | 1 | 116 | 4 | 2 | 8 |
| Tullamore, | 13 | 2 | ·5 | – | 557 | 80 | 1 | – | 14 | – | – | – |
| Waterford, | 7 | 8 | ·1 | ·04 | 418 | 144 | 2 | – | 8 | – | 3 | 4 |
| Wexford, | 7 | 3 | – | – | 108 | 80 | 1 | – | 4 | – | 4 | – |
| County Prisoners in Mountjoy, Male, | 20 | – | 2·33 | – | 1,498 | – | – | – | – | – | 20 | – |
| Mountjoy, Female, | – | 98 | – | 3 | – | 66 | – | – | – | – | – | 13 |
| Total, Males, | 1,377 | – | 40·0806 | – | 25,376 | – | 75 | – | 1,080 | – | 217 | – |
| Total, Females, | – | 608 | – | 17·7208 | – | 8,470 | – | 23 | – | 182 | – | 105 |
| Total, M. and F., | 1,985 | | 58·8014 | | 33,846 | | 97 | | 1,261 | | 322 | |

TABLE XVII.—RETURN of the ACTUAL STAFF of the under-mentioned PRISONS on 31st March, 1883.

| PRISONS. | Governors or Deputy Governors and Female Superintendents. | | Head or Chief Warders. | Chaplains. | Surgeons and Apothecaries. | Clerks, Schoolmasters and Schoolmistresses. | | Matrons and Assistant Matrons. | Warders. | Other Subordinate Officers, including Bridewell Keepers, Nurses, &c. | | Total. | |
|---|---|---|---|---|---|---|---|---|---|---|---|---|---|
| LOCAL PRISONS. | M. | F. | | | | M. | F. | | | M. | F. | M. | F. |
| Armagh, | [illegible] | — | [illegible] | [illegible] | [illegible] | [illegible] | — | [illegible] | [illegible] | 1 | — | [illegible] | 5 |
| Belfast, | [illegible] | — | [illegible] | [illegible] | [illegible] | [illegible] | — | [illegible] | [illegible] | 1 | [illegible] | [illegible] | 11 |
| Castlebar, | [illegible] | — | [illegible] | [illegible] | [illegible] | — | — | [illegible] | [illegible] | [illegible] | — | [illegible] | 8 |
| Clonmel, | [illegible] | — | [illegible] | [illegible] | [illegible] | [illegible] | — | [illegible] | [illegible] | [illegible] | [illegible] | [illegible] | 4 |
| Cork, Male, | [illegible] | — | [illegible] | [illegible] | [illegible] | [illegible] | — | — | [illegible] | [illegible] | [illegible] | [illegible] | 7 |
| Cork, Female, | [illegible] | — | — | [illegible] | — | — | — | [illegible] | [illegible] | — | — | [illegible] | 11 |
| Downpatrick, | [illegible] | — | [illegible] | [illegible] | [illegible] | — | — | [illegible] | [illegible] | [illegible] | [illegible] | [illegible] | 4 |
| Dundalk, | [illegible] | — | [illegible] | [illegible] | [illegible] | — | — | — | [illegible] | 1 | — | [illegible] | — |
| Galway, | [illegible] | — | [illegible] | [illegible] | [illegible] | [illegible] | — | [illegible] | [illegible] | [illegible] | — | [illegible] | 5 |
| Grangegorman, | [illegible] | [illegible] | [illegible] | [illegible] | [illegible] | [illegible] | [illegible] | [illegible] | [illegible] | [illegible] | [illegible] | [illegible] | 19 |
| Kilkenny, | [illegible] | — | [illegible] | [illegible] | [illegible] | — | — | [illegible] | [illegible] | — | — | [illegible] | 8 |
| Kilmainham, | [illegible] | — | [illegible] | [illegible] | [illegible] | [illegible] | — | — | [illegible] | [illegible] | — | [illegible] | — |
| Limerick, Male, | [illegible] | — | [illegible] | [illegible] | [illegible] | [illegible] | — | — | [illegible] | [illegible] | [illegible] | [illegible] | 7 |
| Limerick, Female, | [illegible] | — | — | [illegible] | [illegible] | — | — | [illegible] | [illegible] | — | — | [illegible] | 8 |
| Londonderry, | [illegible] | — | [illegible] | [illegible] | [illegible] | — | — | [illegible] | [illegible] | [illegible] | [illegible] | [illegible] | 5 |
| Maryborough, | [illegible] | — | [illegible] | [illegible] | [illegible] | [illegible] | — | — | [illegible] | — | — | [illegible] | — |
| Mullingar, | [illegible] | — | [illegible] | [illegible] | [illegible] | [illegible] | — | [illegible] | [illegible] | — | — | [illegible] | 8 |
| Naas, | [illegible] | — | [illegible] | [illegible] | [illegible] | [illegible] | — | [illegible] | [illegible] | — | — | [illegible] | 9 |
| Nenagh, | [illegible] | — | [illegible] | [illegible] | [illegible] | — | — | — | [illegible] | [illegible] | — | [illegible] | — |
| Omagh, | [illegible] | — | [illegible] | [illegible] | [illegible] | — | — | [illegible] | [illegible] | [illegible] | [illegible] | [illegible] | 4 |
| Richmond, | [illegible] | — | [illegible] | [illegible] | [illegible] | [illegible] | — | — | [illegible] | [illegible] | [illegible] | [illegible] | 1 |
| Sligo, | [illegible] | — | [illegible] | [illegible] | [illegible] | [illegible] | — | [illegible] | [illegible] | — | — | [illegible] | 8 |
| Tralee, | [illegible] | — | [illegible] | [illegible] | [illegible] | — | — | [illegible] | [illegible] | [illegible] | [illegible] | [illegible] | 6 |
| Tullamore, | [illegible] | — | [illegible] | [illegible] | [illegible] | [illegible] | — | [illegible] | [illegible] | [illegible] | [illegible] | [illegible] | 3 |
| Waterford, | [illegible] | — | [illegible] | [illegible] | [illegible] | — | — | [illegible] | [illegible] | [illegible] | [illegible] | [illegible] | 4 |
| Wexford, | [illegible] | — | [illegible] | [illegible] | [illegible] | — | — | [illegible] | [illegible] | [illegible] | [illegible] | [illegible] | 4 |
| Mountjoy, Male, | [illegible] | — | [illegible] | [illegible] | [illegible] | — | — | — | [illegible] | — | — | [illegible] | — |
| Mountjoy, Female, | — | [illegible] | — | [illegible] | [illegible] | — | — | [illegible] | — | — | — | — | [illegible] |

*continued.*

* Also surgeon to Female Prison.
† Duties performed by superior officers of General Prisons.
‡ Exclusive of officers employed with convicts.

TABLE XVII.—RETURN of the ACTUAL STAFF of the under-mentioned PRISONS on 31st March, 1883—*continued.*

| PRISONS. | Governors or Deputy Governors and Female Superintendents. | | Head or Chief Warders. | Chaplains. | Surgeons and Apothecaries. | Clerks, Schoolmasters, and Schoolmistresses. | | Matrons and Assistant Matrons. | Warders. | Other Subordinate Officers, including Bridewell Keepers, Messengers, &c. | | Total. | |
|---|---|---|---|---|---|---|---|---|---|---|---|---|---|
| SMALLER PRISONS. | M. | F. | | | | M. | F. | | | M. | F. | M. | F. |
| Carlow, . . . | – | – | 1 | – | – | – | – | 1 | 1 | – | – | [illegible] | 1 |
| Carrick-on-Shannon, | – | – | 1 | – | – | – | – | 1 | 1 | – | – | [illegible] | 1 |
| Cavan, . . . | – | – | 1 | – | – | – | – | 1 | 1 | – | – | [illegible] | 1 |
| Drogheda, . . | – | – | 1 | – | – | – | – | 1 | 1 | – | – | 2 | 1 |
| Ennis, . . . | – | – | 1 | – | – | – | – | 1 | 1 | – | – | [illegible] | 1 |
| Enniskillen, . . | – | – | 1 | – | – | – | – | 1 | 1 | – | – | 3 | 1 |
| Lifford, . . . | – | – | 1 | – | – | – | – | 1 | 1 | – | – | 2 | 1 |
| Longford, . . | – | – | 1 | – | – | – | – | 1 | 1 | – | – | [illegible] | 1 |
| Monaghan, . . | – | – | 1 | – | – | – | – | 1 | 1 | – | – | 2 | 1 |
| Roscommon, . . | – | – | 1 | – | – | – | – | 1 | 1 | – | – | 2 | 1 |
| Trim, . . . | – | – | 1 | – | – | – | – | 1 | 1 | – | – | 2 | 1 |
| Wicklow, . . | – | – | 1 | – | – | – | – | 1 | 1 | – | – | 2 | 1 |
| Total, 1882–83, | 30 | 1 | 38 | 80 | 77 | 19 | 1 | 90 | 278 | 47 | 84 | 478 | 159 |
| Total, 1881–82, | 30 | 1 | 40 | 63 | 39 | 27 | 8 | 84 | 300 | 18 | 40 | 610 | 129 |

TABLE XVIII.—WORKS of RECONSTRUCTION, REPAIRS, &c., during the Year ended 31st March, 1883, done by CONTRACT or other than PRISON LABOUR.

| LOCAL PRISONS. | Works. |
| --- | --- |
| **Belfast,** | Improvements in male hospital; improvements in female prison; new cooking boilers; construction of padded cell. |
| **Castlebar,** | Conversion of new female prison with all statutory requirements in old block. |
| **Clonmel,** | Fitting up, [illegible] partition, &c., in prison premises for persons confined under the Act for the Better Protection of Person and Property in Ireland; opening and cleaning out all the old sewers preparatory to laying new sewer pipes through the prison (the new pipes laid by prison labour); [illegible] and [illegible] new three engine [illegible] [illegible], with supply pipes to water tanks; supplying and fixing up ventilating pipes from closets, and drain pipes from gutters. |
| **Cork, Male,** | Heating with hot water No. 3 block; and erecting water closets and lavatories; raising and improving railings in two galleries in existing prison. |
| **Cork, Female,** | Formation of gravel channel for water outside wall; ventilating pipes for sewers; improvements in hospital baths; repairing warder's [illegible]; renewing [illegible] pipes. |
| **Dundalk,** | Erection of ventilating pipes from sewers; erection of [illegible] with [illegible] walls in stone breaking yard. |
| **Galway,** | Bringing water supply to chief warder's quarters; general repairs to gas fittings and closets through prison. |
| **Grangegorman,** | New cooking stove supplied; erecting new boilers in No. 1 and 2 Closets; new [illegible] [illegible] in [illegible] laundry drying closets; improving water supply; bath fitting for P. P. P. prisoners; extensive works in preparing part of prison for P. P. P. prisoners; rebuilding wall [illegible] in prison; [illegible] [illegible] in governor's quarters; new [illegible] for [illegible] [illegible]; improving gas fittings and supplying and fixing gas governors. |
| **Kilkenny,** | Relaying and cleansing main sewers; new closets; erecting [illegible] at heads of sewers; cleaning out pond; providing cistern [illegible]; ventilating sewers; repairing slating of roofs; new arrangement of [illegible] governor's house and part of old prison; [illegible] steam boiler; repairing pumps, &c.; new [illegible] governor's house; new lightning conductor; raising and strengthening gallery rails main wing; cleaning and repairing boilers; plumbing, &c. |
| **Kilmainham,** | Erection of iron railings in front of prison; improvement and repairs of warders' cottages and deputy-governor's house; extensive works rendered necessary by the detention of P. P. P. prisoners. |
| **Limerick, Male,** | Providing a new visiting room; altering cell doors with [illegible]; improvements in sanitary arrangements. |
| **Limerick, Female,** | Making new drying room for laundry; repairs, &c., to prison roofs. |
| **Londonderry,** | Heating with hot water reception block and erecting bath in [illegible] erection of visiting room and photographing room; extensive repairs of [illegible] [illegible]; improvements in governor's house. |

TABLE XVIII.—WORKS of RECONSTRUCTION, REPAIRS, &c.—*continued.*

| Larger Prisons. | Works. |
| --- | --- |
| Maryborough, . . | Supplying and erecting baths, cisterns, &c., and cooking apparatus in hospital; supplying and erecting water closets; putting up bells in new hospital; laying gas to medical officer's residence and to new hospital; laying and repairing water pipes; repairing [illegible] over entrance gate; erection of steam boiler for laundry. |
| Mountjoy, Male, . . | Roofs repaired. |
| Mountjoy, Female, . | Works and repairs in laundry; plumbing and mason work in laundry; repairs to saddle boiler; repairing fire-hose; painting, glazing, and whitewashing; repairing outer gate lodge and roof of central hall. |
| Mullingar, . . . | General repairs to roofs of prison, flooring officers' quarters, shelving for provision store; repairs to steam boiler; general repairs. |
| Naas, . . . . | Repairs and improvements in gas supply; repairs to crank pump; fitting up Protestant chapel; supplying and erecting new entrance gate and repairing iron check gate. |
| Nenagh, . . . . | Improvements in governor's house; repairs to water pump and valves; gas supply to officers' quarters. |
| Omagh, . . . . | Laying down new system of drainage all through the prison, new water-closets, flushing apparatus for sewers, &c.; kitchen range for governor's house; new eaves gutters; supplying copper circulating boiler for male hospital; repairing slating on prison roofs. |
| Richmond, . . . | Repairs to turret clock; repairs to [illegible]; new steam boilers. |
| Sligo, . . . . | Painting and repairing matron's apartments; fitting up gongs and bells, and inspection holes in doors, through prison; improvements in sanitary arrangements. |
| Spike Island, . . . | Nil. |
| Tralee, . . . . | Constructing visiting boxes for prisoners; repairing doors of male prison; repairs of heating boiler. Cahirciveen Bridewell—Repairs of roof and erection of turf shed. |
| Tullamore, . . . | Repairs to pumps; erecting cisterns and shower baths in male hospital; painting front wall of prison; erecting [illegible] in officers' quarters; supplying safety cranks with [illegible] to pumps; repairs to heating apparatus. |
| Waterford, . . . | Painting and repairing governor's house; new saddle boiler for heating female prison; new range for officers' mess room; boarding floors of cells in male prison; new stove for matron's room; supplying and putting up lamps; putting up down pipe from male prison; repairing hot water pipes for heating male prison; repairing crank pump; cementing end wall of governor's house; dashing portion of boundary wall. |
| Wexford, . . . | Erection of new water closets; erection of new saddle boiler for male prison; guttering; supplying new pump. |

TABLE XVIII.—WORKS of RECONSTRUCTION, REPAIRS, &c.—*continued.*

| SMALLER PRISONS. | Works. |
|---|---|
| Carlow, . . . | Repairing roofs. |
| Cavan, . . . | Sundry repairs to roofs, &c. |
| Ennis, . . . . | Fitting up new visiting room for prisoners. |
| Enniskillen, . . . | Repairs of boundary wall, roofs, &c. |
| Lifford, . . . . | Sundry repairs of roofs, &c. |
| Longford, . . . | Repairing and painting boundary wall of prison; repairing heating apparatus and pump. |
| Lusk, . . . . | Nil. |
| Monaghan, . . . | Sundry repairs. |
| Roscommon, . . | Painting front of prison; repairs to pump, to water-closet, to eaves-gutters, and lead gutters on roof; repairs to slating; supplying and putting up new cisterns. |
| Trim, . . . . | Renewing and painting the dome over the chapel. |
| Wicklow, . . . | General repairs of external walls; rough-casting, colouring, &c. |

TABLE XIX.—INDUSTRIAL and TRADES PURSUITS by

| PRISONS. | Upholstering. | [illegible] | [illegible] | Cotton and Flax [illegible] | Mat-making. | Brush-making. | Baskets and Wicker-work. | Whitewashing. | Weaving Linen, &c. | Sewing. | Knitting. | Tailoring. | Painting. | Carpentering. | Shoemaking and Shoemending. | Tailoring and [illegible] | Masons' and Smiths' Iron Work. | [illegible] | Picking Yarn. | Oakum-picking. |
|---|---|---|---|---|---|---|---|---|---|---|---|---|---|---|---|---|---|---|---|---|
| Armagh, | [illegible] | [illegible] | [illegible] | [illegible] | [illegible] | [illegible] | [illegible] | [illegible] | [illegible] | [illegible] | [illegible] | [illegible] | [illegible] | [illegible] | [illegible] | [illegible] | [illegible] | [illegible] | [illegible] | [illegible] |
| Belfast, | [illegible] | [illegible] | [illegible] | [illegible] | [illegible] | [illegible] | [illegible] | [illegible] | [illegible] | [illegible] | [illegible] | [illegible] | [illegible] | [illegible] | [illegible] | [illegible] | [illegible] | [illegible] | [illegible] | [illegible] |
| Carlow, | [illegible] | [illegible] | [illegible] | [illegible] | [illegible] | [illegible] | [illegible] | [illegible] | [illegible] | [illegible] | [illegible] | [illegible] | [illegible] | [illegible] | [illegible] | [illegible] | [illegible] | [illegible] | [illegible] | [illegible] |
| Carrick-on-Shannon, | [illegible] | [illegible] | [illegible] | [illegible] | [illegible] | [illegible] | [illegible] | [illegible] | [illegible] | [illegible] | [illegible] | [illegible] | [illegible] | [illegible] | [illegible] | [illegible] | [illegible] | [illegible] | [illegible] | [illegible] |
| Castlebar, | [illegible] | [illegible] | [illegible] | [illegible] | [illegible] | [illegible] | [illegible] | [illegible] | [illegible] | [illegible] | [illegible] | [illegible] | [illegible] | [illegible] | [illegible] | [illegible] | [illegible] | [illegible] | [illegible] | [illegible] |
| Cavan, | [illegible] | [illegible] | [illegible] | [illegible] | [illegible] | [illegible] | [illegible] | [illegible] | [illegible] | [illegible] | [illegible] | [illegible] | [illegible] | [illegible] | [illegible] | [illegible] | [illegible] | [illegible] | [illegible] | [illegible] |
| Clonmel, | [illegible] | [illegible] | [illegible] | [illegible] | [illegible] | [illegible] | [illegible] | [illegible] | [illegible] | [illegible] | [illegible] | [illegible] | [illegible] | [illegible] | [illegible] | [illegible] | [illegible] | [illegible] | [illegible] | [illegible] |
| Cork, Male, | [illegible] | [illegible] | [illegible] | [illegible] | [illegible] | [illegible] | [illegible] | [illegible] | [illegible] | [illegible] | [illegible] | [illegible] | [illegible] | [illegible] | [illegible] | [illegible] | [illegible] | [illegible] | [illegible] | [illegible] |
| Cork, Female, | [illegible] | [illegible] | [illegible] | [illegible] | [illegible] | [illegible] | [illegible] | [illegible] | [illegible] | [illegible] | [illegible] | [illegible] | [illegible] | [illegible] | [illegible] | [illegible] | [illegible] | [illegible] | [illegible] | [illegible] |
| Downpatrick, | [illegible] | [illegible] | [illegible] | [illegible] | [illegible] | [illegible] | [illegible] | [illegible] | [illegible] | [illegible] | [illegible] | [illegible] | [illegible] | [illegible] | [illegible] | [illegible] | [illegible] | [illegible] | [illegible] | [illegible] |
| Drogheda, | [illegible] | [illegible] | [illegible] | [illegible] | [illegible] | [illegible] | [illegible] | [illegible] | [illegible] | [illegible] | [illegible] | [illegible] | [illegible] | [illegible] | [illegible] | [illegible] | [illegible] | [illegible] | [illegible] | [illegible] |
| Dundalk, | [illegible] | [illegible] | [illegible] | [illegible] | [illegible] | [illegible] | [illegible] | [illegible] | [illegible] | [illegible] | [illegible] | [illegible] | [illegible] | [illegible] | [illegible] | [illegible] | [illegible] | [illegible] | [illegible] | [illegible] |
| Ennis, | [illegible] | [illegible] | [illegible] | [illegible] | [illegible] | [illegible] | [illegible] | [illegible] | [illegible] | [illegible] | [illegible] | [illegible] | [illegible] | [illegible] | [illegible] | [illegible] | [illegible] | [illegible] | [illegible] | [illegible] |
| Enniskillen, | [illegible] | [illegible] | [illegible] | [illegible] | [illegible] | [illegible] | [illegible] | [illegible] | [illegible] | [illegible] | [illegible] | [illegible] | [illegible] | [illegible] | [illegible] | [illegible] | [illegible] | [illegible] | [illegible] | [illegible] |
| Galway, | [illegible] | [illegible] | [illegible] | [illegible] | [illegible] | [illegible] | [illegible] | [illegible] | [illegible] | [illegible] | [illegible] | [illegible] | [illegible] | [illegible] | [illegible] | [illegible] | [illegible] | [illegible] | [illegible] | [illegible] |
| Grangegorman, | [illegible] | [illegible] | [illegible] | [illegible] | [illegible] | [illegible] | [illegible] | [illegible] | [illegible] | [illegible] | [illegible] | [illegible] | [illegible] | [illegible] | [illegible] | [illegible] | [illegible] | [illegible] | [illegible] | [illegible] |
| Kilkenny, | [illegible] | [illegible] | [illegible] | [illegible] | [illegible] | [illegible] | [illegible] | [illegible] | [illegible] | [illegible] | [illegible] | [illegible] | [illegible] | [illegible] | [illegible] | [illegible] | [illegible] | [illegible] | [illegible] | [illegible] |
| Kilmainham, | [illegible] | [illegible] | [illegible] | [illegible] | [illegible] | [illegible] | [illegible] | [illegible] | [illegible] | [illegible] | [illegible] | [illegible] | [illegible] | [illegible] | [illegible] | [illegible] | [illegible] | [illegible] | [illegible] | [illegible] |
| Lifford, | [illegible] | [illegible] | [illegible] | [illegible] | [illegible] | [illegible] | [illegible] | [illegible] | [illegible] | [illegible] | [illegible] | [illegible] | [illegible] | [illegible] | [illegible] | [illegible] | [illegible] | [illegible] | [illegible] | [illegible] |
| Limerick, Male, | [illegible] | [illegible] | [illegible] | [illegible] | [illegible] | [illegible] | [illegible] | [illegible] | [illegible] | [illegible] | [illegible] | [illegible] | [illegible] | [illegible] | [illegible] | [illegible] | [illegible] | [illegible] | [illegible] | [illegible] |
| Limerick, Female, | [illegible] | [illegible] | [illegible] | [illegible] | [illegible] | [illegible] | [illegible] | [illegible] | [illegible] | [illegible] | [illegible] | [illegible] | [illegible] | [illegible] | [illegible] | [illegible] | [illegible] | [illegible] | [illegible] | [illegible] |
| Londonderry, | [illegible] | [illegible] | [illegible] | [illegible] | [illegible] | [illegible] | [illegible] | [illegible] | [illegible] | [illegible] | [illegible] | [illegible] | [illegible] | [illegible] | [illegible] | [illegible] | [illegible] | [illegible] | [illegible] | [illegible] |
| Longford, | [illegible] | [illegible] | [illegible] | [illegible] | [illegible] | [illegible] | [illegible] | [illegible] | [illegible] | [illegible] | [illegible] | [illegible] | [illegible] | [illegible] | [illegible] | [illegible] | [illegible] | [illegible] | [illegible] | [illegible] |
| Maryborough, | [illegible] | [illegible] | [illegible] | [illegible] | [illegible] | [illegible] | [illegible] | [illegible] | [illegible] | [illegible] | [illegible] | [illegible] | [illegible] | [illegible] | [illegible] | [illegible] | [illegible] | [illegible] | [illegible] | [illegible] |
| Monaghan, | [illegible] | [illegible] | [illegible] | [illegible] | [illegible] | [illegible] | [illegible] | [illegible] | [illegible] | [illegible] | [illegible] | [illegible] | [illegible] | [illegible] | [illegible] | [illegible] | [illegible] | [illegible] | [illegible] | [illegible] |
| Mullingar, | [illegible] | [illegible] | [illegible] | [illegible] | [illegible] | [illegible] | [illegible] | [illegible] | [illegible] | [illegible] | [illegible] | [illegible] | [illegible] | [illegible] | [illegible] | [illegible] | [illegible] | [illegible] | [illegible] | [illegible] |
| Naas, | [illegible] | [illegible] | [illegible] | [illegible] | [illegible] | [illegible] | [illegible] | [illegible] | [illegible] | [illegible] | [illegible] | [illegible] | [illegible] | [illegible] | [illegible] | [illegible] | [illegible] | [illegible] | [illegible] | [illegible] |
| Nenagh, | [illegible] | [illegible] | [illegible] | [illegible] | [illegible] | [illegible] | [illegible] | [illegible] | [illegible] | [illegible] | [illegible] | [illegible] | [illegible] | [illegible] | [illegible] | [illegible] | [illegible] | [illegible] | [illegible] | [illegible] |
| Omagh, | [illegible] | [illegible] | [illegible] | [illegible] | [illegible] | [illegible] | [illegible] | [illegible] | [illegible] | [illegible] | [illegible] | [illegible] | [illegible] | [illegible] | [illegible] | [illegible] | [illegible] | [illegible] | [illegible] | [illegible] |
| Richmond, | [illegible] | [illegible] | [illegible] | [illegible] | [illegible] | [illegible] | [illegible] | [illegible] | [illegible] | [illegible] | [illegible] | [illegible] | [illegible] | [illegible] | [illegible] | [illegible] | [illegible] | [illegible] | [illegible] | [illegible] |
| Roscommon, | [illegible] | [illegible] | [illegible] | [illegible] | [illegible] | [illegible] | [illegible] | [illegible] | [illegible] | [illegible] | [illegible] | [illegible] | [illegible] | [illegible] | [illegible] | [illegible] | [illegible] | [illegible] | [illegible] | [illegible] |
| Sligo, | [illegible] | [illegible] | [illegible] | [illegible] | [illegible] | [illegible] | [illegible] | [illegible] | [illegible] | [illegible] | [illegible] | [illegible] | [illegible] | [illegible] | [illegible] | [illegible] | [illegible] | [illegible] | [illegible] | [illegible] |
| Tralee, | [illegible] | [illegible] | [illegible] | [illegible] | [illegible] | [illegible] | [illegible] | [illegible] | [illegible] | [illegible] | [illegible] | [illegible] | [illegible] | [illegible] | [illegible] | [illegible] | [illegible] | [illegible] | [illegible] | [illegible] |
| Trim, | [illegible] | [illegible] | [illegible] | [illegible] | [illegible] | [illegible] | [illegible] | [illegible] | [illegible] | [illegible] | [illegible] | [illegible] | [illegible] | [illegible] | [illegible] | [illegible] | [illegible] | [illegible] | [illegible] | [illegible] |
| Tullamore, | [illegible] | [illegible] | [illegible] | [illegible] | [illegible] | [illegible] | [illegible] | [illegible] | [illegible] | [illegible] | [illegible] | [illegible] | [illegible] | [illegible] | [illegible] | [illegible] | [illegible] | [illegible] | [illegible] | [illegible] |
| Waterford, | [illegible] | [illegible] | [illegible] | [illegible] | [illegible] | [illegible] | [illegible] | [illegible] | [illegible] | [illegible] | [illegible] | [illegible] | [illegible] | [illegible] | [illegible] | [illegible] | [illegible] | [illegible] | [illegible] | [illegible] |
| Wexford, | [illegible] | [illegible] | [illegible] | [illegible] | [illegible] | [illegible] | [illegible] | [illegible] | [illegible] | [illegible] | [illegible] | [illegible] | [illegible] | [illegible] | [illegible] | [illegible] | [illegible] | [illegible] | [illegible] | [illegible] |
| Wicklow, | [illegible] | [illegible] | [illegible] | [illegible] | [illegible] | [illegible] | [illegible] | [illegible] | [illegible] | [illegible] | [illegible] | [illegible] | [illegible] | [illegible] | [illegible] | [illegible] | [illegible] | [illegible] | [illegible] | [illegible] |
| Prisoners not Convicts— | | | | | | | | | | | | | | | | | | | | |
| Mountjoy, Male, | [illegible] | [illegible] | [illegible] | [illegible] | [illegible] | [illegible] | [illegible] | [illegible] | [illegible] | [illegible] | [illegible] | [illegible] | [illegible] | [illegible] | [illegible] | [illegible] | [illegible] | [illegible] | [illegible] | [illegible] |
| Mountjoy, Female, | [illegible] | [illegible] | [illegible] | [illegible] | [illegible] | [illegible] | [illegible] | [illegible] | [illegible] | [illegible] | [illegible] | [illegible] | [illegible] | [illegible] | [illegible] | [illegible] | [illegible] | [illegible] | [illegible] | [illegible] |

NOTE.—The asterisks placed opposite the name of each Prison denote that the [illegible] appear have been carried on by prisoners

Prisoners during the year ended 31st March, 1883.

| [illegible] | Smith Work. | [illegible] | [illegible] | [illegible] | [illegible] | [illegible] | [illegible] | [illegible] | [illegible] | [illegible] | Gardening. | [illegible] | [illegible] | [illegible] | [illegible] | Carpet Cleaning. | Making Firewood. | [illegible] | Prisons. |
|---|---|---|---|---|---|---|---|---|---|---|---|---|---|---|---|---|---|---|---|
| [illegible] | [illegible] | [illegible] | [illegible] | [illegible] | [illegible] | [illegible] | [illegible] | [illegible] | [illegible] | [illegible] | [illegible] | [illegible] | [illegible] | [illegible] | [illegible] | [illegible] | [illegible] | [illegible] | Armagh. |
| [illegible] | [illegible] | [illegible] | [illegible] | [illegible] | [illegible] | [illegible] | [illegible] | [illegible] | [illegible] | [illegible] | [illegible] | [illegible] | [illegible] | [illegible] | [illegible] | [illegible] | [illegible] | [illegible] | Belfast. |
| [illegible] | [illegible] | [illegible] | [illegible] | [illegible] | [illegible] | [illegible] | [illegible] | [illegible] | [illegible] | [illegible] | [illegible] | [illegible] | [illegible] | [illegible] | [illegible] | [illegible] | [illegible] | [illegible] | Carlow. |
| [illegible] | [illegible] | [illegible] | [illegible] | [illegible] | [illegible] | [illegible] | [illegible] | [illegible] | [illegible] | [illegible] | [illegible] | [illegible] | [illegible] | [illegible] | [illegible] | [illegible] | [illegible] | [illegible] | Carrick-on-Shannon. |
| [illegible] | [illegible] | [illegible] | [illegible] | [illegible] | [illegible] | [illegible] | [illegible] | [illegible] | [illegible] | [illegible] | [illegible] | [illegible] | [illegible] | [illegible] | [illegible] | [illegible] | [illegible] | [illegible] | Castlebar. |
| [illegible] | [illegible] | [illegible] | [illegible] | [illegible] | [illegible] | [illegible] | [illegible] | [illegible] | [illegible] | [illegible] | [illegible] | [illegible] | [illegible] | [illegible] | [illegible] | [illegible] | [illegible] | [illegible] | Cavan. |
| [illegible] | [illegible] | [illegible] | [illegible] | [illegible] | [illegible] | [illegible] | [illegible] | [illegible] | [illegible] | [illegible] | [illegible] | [illegible] | [illegible] | [illegible] | [illegible] | [illegible] | [illegible] | [illegible] | Clonmel. |
| [illegible] | [illegible] | [illegible] | [illegible] | [illegible] | [illegible] | [illegible] | [illegible] | [illegible] | [illegible] | [illegible] | [illegible] | [illegible] | [illegible] | [illegible] | [illegible] | [illegible] | [illegible] | [illegible] | Cork, Male. |
| [illegible] | [illegible] | [illegible] | [illegible] | [illegible] | [illegible] | [illegible] | [illegible] | [illegible] | [illegible] | [illegible] | [illegible] | [illegible] | [illegible] | [illegible] | [illegible] | [illegible] | [illegible] | [illegible] | Cork, Female. |
| [illegible] | [illegible] | [illegible] | [illegible] | [illegible] | [illegible] | [illegible] | [illegible] | [illegible] | [illegible] | [illegible] | [illegible] | [illegible] | [illegible] | [illegible] | [illegible] | [illegible] | [illegible] | [illegible] | Downpatrick. |
| [illegible] | [illegible] | [illegible] | [illegible] | [illegible] | [illegible] | [illegible] | [illegible] | [illegible] | [illegible] | [illegible] | [illegible] | [illegible] | [illegible] | [illegible] | [illegible] | [illegible] | [illegible] | [illegible] | Drogheda. |
| [illegible] | [illegible] | [illegible] | [illegible] | [illegible] | [illegible] | [illegible] | [illegible] | [illegible] | [illegible] | [illegible] | [illegible] | [illegible] | [illegible] | [illegible] | [illegible] | [illegible] | [illegible] | [illegible] | Dundalk. |
| [illegible] | [illegible] | [illegible] | [illegible] | [illegible] | [illegible] | [illegible] | [illegible] | [illegible] | [illegible] | [illegible] | [illegible] | [illegible] | [illegible] | [illegible] | [illegible] | [illegible] | [illegible] | [illegible] | Ennis. |
| [illegible] | [illegible] | [illegible] | [illegible] | [illegible] | [illegible] | [illegible] | [illegible] | [illegible] | [illegible] | [illegible] | [illegible] | [illegible] | [illegible] | [illegible] | [illegible] | [illegible] | [illegible] | [illegible] | Enniskillen. |
| [illegible] | [illegible] | [illegible] | [illegible] | [illegible] | [illegible] | [illegible] | [illegible] | [illegible] | [illegible] | [illegible] | [illegible] | [illegible] | [illegible] | [illegible] | [illegible] | [illegible] | [illegible] | [illegible] | Galway. |
| [illegible] | [illegible] | [illegible] | [illegible] | [illegible] | [illegible] | [illegible] | [illegible] | [illegible] | [illegible] | [illegible] | [illegible] | [illegible] | [illegible] | [illegible] | [illegible] | [illegible] | [illegible] | [illegible] | Grangegorman. |
| [illegible] | [illegible] | [illegible] | [illegible] | [illegible] | [illegible] | [illegible] | [illegible] | [illegible] | [illegible] | [illegible] | [illegible] | [illegible] | [illegible] | [illegible] | [illegible] | [illegible] | [illegible] | [illegible] | Kilkenny. |
| [illegible] | [illegible] | [illegible] | [illegible] | [illegible] | [illegible] | [illegible] | [illegible] | [illegible] | [illegible] | [illegible] | [illegible] | [illegible] | [illegible] | [illegible] | [illegible] | [illegible] | [illegible] | [illegible] | Kilmainham. |
| [illegible] | [illegible] | [illegible] | [illegible] | [illegible] | [illegible] | [illegible] | [illegible] | [illegible] | [illegible] | [illegible] | [illegible] | [illegible] | [illegible] | [illegible] | [illegible] | [illegible] | [illegible] | [illegible] | Lifford. |
| [illegible] | [illegible] | [illegible] | [illegible] | [illegible] | [illegible] | [illegible] | [illegible] | [illegible] | [illegible] | [illegible] | [illegible] | [illegible] | [illegible] | [illegible] | [illegible] | [illegible] | [illegible] | [illegible] | Limerick, Male. |
| [illegible] | [illegible] | [illegible] | [illegible] | [illegible] | [illegible] | [illegible] | [illegible] | [illegible] | [illegible] | [illegible] | [illegible] | [illegible] | [illegible] | [illegible] | [illegible] | [illegible] | [illegible] | [illegible] | Limerick, Female. |
| [illegible] | [illegible] | [illegible] | [illegible] | [illegible] | [illegible] | [illegible] | [illegible] | [illegible] | [illegible] | [illegible] | [illegible] | [illegible] | [illegible] | [illegible] | [illegible] | [illegible] | [illegible] | [illegible] | Londonderry. |
| [illegible] | [illegible] | [illegible] | [illegible] | [illegible] | [illegible] | [illegible] | [illegible] | [illegible] | [illegible] | [illegible] | [illegible] | [illegible] | [illegible] | [illegible] | [illegible] | [illegible] | [illegible] | [illegible] | Longford. |
| [illegible] | [illegible] | [illegible] | [illegible] | [illegible] | [illegible] | [illegible] | [illegible] | [illegible] | [illegible] | [illegible] | [illegible] | [illegible] | [illegible] | [illegible] | [illegible] | [illegible] | [illegible] | [illegible] | Maryborough. |
| [illegible] | [illegible] | [illegible] | [illegible] | [illegible] | [illegible] | [illegible] | [illegible] | [illegible] | [illegible] | [illegible] | [illegible] | [illegible] | [illegible] | [illegible] | [illegible] | [illegible] | [illegible] | [illegible] | Monaghan. |
| [illegible] | [illegible] | [illegible] | [illegible] | [illegible] | [illegible] | [illegible] | [illegible] | [illegible] | [illegible] | [illegible] | [illegible] | [illegible] | [illegible] | [illegible] | [illegible] | [illegible] | [illegible] | [illegible] | Mullingar. |
| [illegible] | [illegible] | [illegible] | [illegible] | [illegible] | [illegible] | [illegible] | [illegible] | [illegible] | [illegible] | [illegible] | [illegible] | [illegible] | [illegible] | [illegible] | [illegible] | [illegible] | [illegible] | [illegible] | Naas. |
| [illegible] | [illegible] | [illegible] | [illegible] | [illegible] | [illegible] | [illegible] | [illegible] | [illegible] | [illegible] | [illegible] | [illegible] | [illegible] | [illegible] | [illegible] | [illegible] | [illegible] | [illegible] | [illegible] | Nenagh. |
| [illegible] | [illegible] | [illegible] | [illegible] | [illegible] | [illegible] | [illegible] | [illegible] | [illegible] | [illegible] | [illegible] | [illegible] | [illegible] | [illegible] | [illegible] | [illegible] | [illegible] | [illegible] | [illegible] | Omagh. |
| [illegible] | [illegible] | [illegible] | [illegible] | [illegible] | [illegible] | [illegible] | [illegible] | [illegible] | [illegible] | [illegible] | [illegible] | [illegible] | [illegible] | [illegible] | [illegible] | [illegible] | [illegible] | [illegible] | Richmond. |
| [illegible] | [illegible] | [illegible] | [illegible] | [illegible] | [illegible] | [illegible] | [illegible] | [illegible] | [illegible] | [illegible] | [illegible] | [illegible] | [illegible] | [illegible] | [illegible] | [illegible] | [illegible] | [illegible] | Roscommon. |
| [illegible] | [illegible] | [illegible] | [illegible] | [illegible] | [illegible] | [illegible] | [illegible] | [illegible] | [illegible] | [illegible] | [illegible] | [illegible] | [illegible] | [illegible] | [illegible] | [illegible] | [illegible] | [illegible] | Sligo. |
| [illegible] | [illegible] | [illegible] | [illegible] | [illegible] | [illegible] | [illegible] | [illegible] | [illegible] | [illegible] | [illegible] | [illegible] | [illegible] | [illegible] | [illegible] | [illegible] | [illegible] | [illegible] | [illegible] | Tralee. |
| [illegible] | [illegible] | [illegible] | [illegible] | [illegible] | [illegible] | [illegible] | [illegible] | [illegible] | [illegible] | [illegible] | [illegible] | [illegible] | [illegible] | [illegible] | [illegible] | [illegible] | [illegible] | [illegible] | Trim. |
| [illegible] | [illegible] | [illegible] | [illegible] | [illegible] | [illegible] | [illegible] | [illegible] | [illegible] | [illegible] | [illegible] | [illegible] | [illegible] | [illegible] | [illegible] | [illegible] | [illegible] | [illegible] | [illegible] | Tullamore. |
| [illegible] | [illegible] | [illegible] | [illegible] | [illegible] | [illegible] | [illegible] | [illegible] | [illegible] | [illegible] | [illegible] | [illegible] | [illegible] | [illegible] | [illegible] | [illegible] | [illegible] | [illegible] | [illegible] | Waterford. |
| [illegible] | [illegible] | [illegible] | [illegible] | [illegible] | [illegible] | [illegible] | [illegible] | [illegible] | [illegible] | [illegible] | [illegible] | [illegible] | [illegible] | [illegible] | [illegible] | [illegible] | [illegible] | [illegible] | Wexford. |
| [illegible] | [illegible] | [illegible] | [illegible] | [illegible] | [illegible] | [illegible] | [illegible] | [illegible] | [illegible] | [illegible] | [illegible] | [illegible] | [illegible] | [illegible] | [illegible] | [illegible] | [illegible] | [illegible] | Wicklow. |
| | | | | | | | | | | | | | | | | | | | Prisoners and Convicts— |
| [illegible] | [illegible] | [illegible] | [illegible] | [illegible] | [illegible] | [illegible] | [illegible] | [illegible] | [illegible] | [illegible] | [illegible] | [illegible] | [illegible] | [illegible] | [illegible] | [illegible] | [illegible] | [illegible] | Mountjoy, Male. |
| [illegible] | [illegible] | [illegible] | [illegible] | [illegible] | [illegible] | [illegible] | [illegible] | [illegible] | [illegible] | [illegible] | [illegible] | [illegible] | [illegible] | [illegible] | [illegible] | [illegible] | [illegible] | [illegible] | Mountjoy, Female. |

trades or industrial work specified at head of the column in which these marks
in the year ended 31 March, 1883.

TABLE XX.—COMPARATIVE TABLE, showing the Number of Prisoners committed to Local Prisons from the 1st April, 1881, to 31st March, 1882, and from that date to the 31st March, 1883, distinguishing the Sexes and Classes.

| CLASS OF OFFENDERS. | To 31st March, 1882. | | | To 31st March, 1883. | | |
|---|---|---|---|---|---|---|
| | Males. | Females. | Total. | Males. | Females. | Total. |
| CONVICTED. | | | | | | |
| At Assizes and Quarter Sessions, | 1,632 | 285 | 1,917 | 1,429 | 321 | 1,730 |
| Criminal Lunatics, . . | 79 | 7 | 86 | 73 | 10 | 83 |
| Summarily :— | | | | | | |
| Offences under Prevention of Crime Act, . . . | - | - | - | 412 | 18 | 430 |
| Offenders under Larceny Acts, . | 1,381 | 492 | 1,873 | 1,384 | 486 | 1,870 |
| Misdemeanants, . . | 10,086 | 5,096 | 15,182 | 8,222 | 3,672 | 11,894 |
| Under Revenue Laws, . | 110 | 30 | 140 | 115 | 22 | 137 |
| Under Poor Law Acts, . | 200 | 54 | 254 | 300 | 60 | 360 |
| By Court-martial, . . | 548 | . | 548 | 654 | . | 660 |
| Deserters, . . . . | 171 | . | 171 | 118 | . | 118 |
| Under Vagrant Acts, . . | 485 | 351 | 836 | 424 | 222 | 746 |
| Drunkards, . . . | 8,183 | 8,274 | 16,457 | 8,009 | 5,294 | 13,303 |
| TOTAL, . . | 24,103 | 12,469 | 36,572 | 21,088 | 10,106 | 31,194 |
| NOT CONVICTED. | | | | | | |
| Acquitted, . . . .<br>No Bills, or no Prosecution, . | 597 | 161 | 758 | 474 | 107 | 581 |
| For further Examination and Discharged, . . . | 2,829 | 586 | 3,415 | 2,841 | 348 | 3,189 |
| TOTAL, . . | 3,426 | 747 | 4,173 | 3,315 | 455 | 3,770 |
| In Custody for Trial on 31st March, | 296 | 38 | 343 | 225 | 45 | 270 |
| GENERAL TOTAL, . | 27,824 | 13,254 | 41,088 | 24,628 | 10,606 | 35,484 |

[REPORTS.

# REPORTS BY THE GOVERNORS AND CHIEF-WARDERS ON EACH OF THE LOCAL PRISONS.

---

## ARMAGH PRISON.

**RETURN by the GOVERNOR, showing how Prisoners have been employed during the year ending 31st March, 1883, and the Earnings of those engaged in such Employments; also showing the average daily number of Unemployed from Sickness and other reasons.**

| Description of Employment. | Daily Average Number of Prisoners employed, unemployed, &c. Males. | Females. | Total. | Net profit on Work done by Prisoners. | Estimated Value of the Work done for the Prison. | Total. |
|---|---|---|---|---|---|---|
| | | | | £ s. d. | £ s. d. | £ s. d. |
| Gardening and Labouring, | [illegible] | — | [illegible] | — | [illegible] | [illegible] |
| Tailors, | [illegible] | — | [illegible] | — | [illegible] | [illegible] |
| Shoemakers, | [illegible] | — | [illegible] | — | [illegible] | [illegible] |
| Carpenters, | | | | — | [illegible] | [illegible] |
| Bricklayers, | | | | — | [illegible] | [illegible] |
| Painters and glaziers, | [illegible] | — | [illegible] | — | [illegible] | [illegible] |
| Tinsmiths, | | | | — | [illegible] | [illegible] |
| Whitewashers, | | | | — | [illegible] | [illegible] |
| Service of prison, | [illegible] | [illegible] | [illegible] | — | [illegible] | [illegible] |
| Washing clothing and bedding, | | | | [illegible] | [illegible] | [illegible] |
| Making bedding and clothing, | [illegible] | [illegible] | [illegible] | — | [illegible] | [illegible] |
| Repairing bedding and clothing, | | | | — | [illegible] | [illegible] |
| Stone-breaking, | | | | [illegible] | — | [illegible] |
| Weaving mats, | [illegible] | — | [illegible] | [illegible] | — | [illegible] |
| Cutting wood, | | | | [illegible] | — | [illegible] |
| Picking rope junk, | [illegible] | [illegible] | [illegible] | — | [illegible] | [illegible] |
| Knitting, | | | | [illegible] | [illegible] | [illegible] |
| Mangling, | — | [illegible] | [illegible] | [illegible] | [illegible] | [illegible] |
| Sick, | | | | — | — | — |
| Unemployed, | [illegible] | [illegible] | [illegible] | — | — | — |
| **Total,** | [illegible] | [illegible] | [illegible] | [illegible] | [illegible] | [illegible] |

RETURN by the GOVERNOR, showing how Prisoners have been employed during the year ending 31st March, 1883, and the Earnings of those engaged in such Employment; also showing the average daily number of Unemployed from Sickness and other reasons.

## BELFAST PRISON.

| Description of Employment. | Daily Average Number of Prisoners employed, unemployed, &c. | | | Net Profit on Work done by Prisoners. | Estimated Value of the Work done for the Prison. | Total. |
|---|---|---|---|---|---|---|
| | Males. | Females. | Total. | | | |
| | | | | £ s. d. | £ s. d. | £ s. d. |
| Scrub-brush and mat-making, picking coir and plaiting, | 21 | — | 21 | 46 8 1 | 8 10 9 | 57 10 5 |
| Gardening, | 3 | — | 3 | — | 36 14 4 | 36 14 4 |
| Tailors, | 10 | — | 10 | 0 7 9 | 243 7 0 | 243 15 9 |
| Shoemakers, | 7 | — | 7 | — | 169 15 0 | 169 15 0 |
| Carpenters, | 3 | — | 3 | — | 75 0 0 | 75 0 0 |
| Labourers, | 13 | — | 13 | — | 130 0 0 | 130 0 0 |
| Painters and glaziers, | 3 | — | 3 | — | 75 0 0 | 75 0 0 |
| Tinsmiths, gasfitters, and blacksmiths, | 3 | — | 3 | — | 75 0 0 | 75 0 0 |
| Whitewashers and bricklayers, | 7 | — | 7 | — | 40 0 0 | 40 0 0 |
| Weaving and winding, | 6 | — | 6 | — | 7 1 5 | 7 1 5 |
| Cleaning carpets, | 30 | — | 30 | 279 10 6 | — | 279 10 6 |
| Service of prison, | 15 | 6 | 21 | — | 157 10 0 | 157 10 0 |
| Cooking, | 5 | 1 | 6 | — | 90 0 0 | 90 0 0 |
| Washing clothing and bedding, | — | 15 | 15 | 17 1 0 | 270 0 0 | 287 10 0 |
| Making bedding and clothing, repairing bedding and clothing, knitting and sewing, | — | 75 | 75 | 74 0 9 | 300 19 10 | 375 0 0 |
| Stone-breaking, | 81 | — | 81 | 693 17 0 | 18 0 5 | 711 18 5 |
| Rope, hair and fibre-picking, | 46 | 48 | 94 | 30 19 9 | — | 30 19 9 |
| Linen cutting, | 1 | 3 | 4 | 74 16 11 | — | 74 16 11 |
| Making firewood, | 1 | — | 1 | 7 7 6 | — | 7 7 6 |
| Sick, Unemployed, | 43 | 70 | 83 | — | — | — |
| Total, | 273 | 160 | 433 | 944 5 4 | 1,679 16 8 | 2,574 4 0 |

*Trades, &c.*—Regular tradesmen are charged at one-half ordinary rates, learners, one-fourth, viz.:—2s. 6d. and 1s. 3d. per day, respectively. Whitewashers, 1s. 6d.; labourers and cooks, 1s.; cleaners, 6d.; females making and repairing clothing, knitting, and sewing, 4d.

Mat-making. The net profit on sales only is shown, no credit in this respect being taken for manufactured stock on hand.

Linen-weaving has not proved profitable. This is owing chiefly to causes which affect the trade generally.

Carpet cleaning still continues the most profitable industrial labour at this prison.

Shirt and drawers making for public has been further extended. The work has been so arranged as to afford instruction to those requiring it; while the more proficient are employed at finishing. This industry has the advantage of placing within the power of many of the female prisoners the means of earning an honest livelihood.

Stone-breaking shows a considerable increase in profit over former years, accounted for by somewhat better terms having been made and large deliveries.

Linen-cutting is a clean and fairly profitable industry; it is, however, limited in quantity, and local in character.

Firewood manufacture, owing to withdrawal of orders from Public Departments, has almost ceased. This is to be regretted, as it was both a profitable and desirable class of labour.

Such skilled labour as the prison afforded has been largely utilised in general repairs. A forge, and office in central hall have been erected. Disused part of laundry has been converted into reception and bath rooms for female prisoners.

A number of cells used as officers' quarters have been altered to original purpose.

Work done for other prisons is included in "estimated value" column.

The unemployed are represented by the untried, ball (unwilling to work), the physically unfit, and those discharged during labour hours.

Excepting in manufacture of material, the prison is generally self-supplying.

Calculations are made on year of 300 working days.

RETURN by the GOVERNORS, showing how Prisoners have been employed during the year ending 31st March, 1881, and the Earnings of those engaged in such Employments; also showing the average daily number of Unemployed from Sickness and other reasons.

## CASTLEBAR PRISON.

| Description of Employment. | Daily Average Number of Prisoners employed, unemployed, &c. Males. | Females. | Total. | Net Profit on Work done by Prisoners. | Estimated Value of the Work done for the Prison. | Total. |
|---|---|---|---|---|---|---|
| | | | | £ s. d. | £ s. d. | £ s. d. |
| Picking rope junk, | 12 | — | 12 | — | — | — |
| Tailors, Shoemakers, Carpenters, | 3 | — | 3 | — | 12 1 0 | 12 1 0 |
| Bricklayers and labourers, | 8 | — | 8 | — | 58 2 9 | [illegible] |
| Painters and glaziers, Tinsmiths, Blacksmiths, Whitewashers, | [illegible] | — | [illegible] | — | 7 10 6 | 7 10 6 |
| Pumping water, | 2 | — | 2 | — | 15 1 0 | 15 1 0 |
| Service of prison, | 1 | 2 | 3 | — | [illegible] | [illegible] |
| Washing clothing and bedding, | — | 3 | 3 | 8 4 4 | 10 16 8 | 18 1 0 |
| Stone-breaking, | 10 | — | 10 | 3 18 6 | [illegible] | 11 4 [illegible] |
| Knitting and sewing, | — | 3 | 3 | — | 15 [illegible] | 15 1 6 |
| Sick, | 1 | — | 1 | — | — | — |
| Unemployed, | 4 | 2 | 6 | — | — | — |
| Total, | [illegible] | 7 | [illegible] | 12 5 10 | 164 1 4 | [illegible] |

The employment of prisoners picking oakum in this prison is, in my opinion, a loss of their time, as there is a loss on this class of labour. Stone-breaking, which is easy to be pursued in winter, would be an industry much preferable. The ground attached to prison will, I hope this year, be made to yield a profit. I think instruction in making fishing-nets and gear might, under some circumstances, be usefully applied.

## CLONMEL PRISON.

| Description of Employment. | Males. | Females. | Total. | Net Profit on Work done by Prisoners. | Estimated Value of the Work done for the Prison. | Total. |
|---|---|---|---|---|---|---|
| | | | | £ s. d. | £ s. d. | £ s. d. |
| Mat-making, picking coir, &c., | — | — | — | [illegible] | — | [illegible] |
| Tailors, | 1 | — | 1 | — | [illegible] | [illegible] |
| Shoemakers, | [illegible] | — | [illegible] | — | [illegible] | [illegible] |
| Carpenters, | 2 | — | [illegible] | — | [illegible] | [illegible] |
| Bricklayers and labourers, | 10 | — | 10 | — | [illegible] | [illegible] |
| Painters and glaziers, | 1 | — | 1 | — | [illegible] | [illegible] |
| Blacksmiths, | 1 | — | 1 | — | [illegible] | [illegible] |
| Whitewashers, | 1 | — | 1 | — | [illegible] | [illegible] |
| Treadwheel, Pumping water, | 15 | — | 15 | — | [illegible] | [illegible] |
| Service of prison, | 6 | 1 | 7 | — | [illegible] | [illegible] |
| Washing clothing and bedding, | 10 | — | 10 | [illegible] | [illegible] | [illegible] |
| Repairing bedding and clothing, | 1 | — | 1 | — | [illegible] | [illegible] |
| Cutting timber, | [illegible] | — | [illegible] | [illegible] | [illegible] | [illegible] |
| Picking rope junk, | [illegible] | — | [illegible] | — | — | — |
| Tending gardens, | 1 | — | 1 | — | — | — |
| Cooking, | [illegible] | — | [illegible] | — | [illegible] | [illegible] |
| Sick, | [illegible] | — | [illegible] | — | — | — |
| Unemployed, | [illegible] | — | [illegible] | — | — | — |
| Total, | [illegible] | 1 | [illegible] | [illegible] | [illegible] | [illegible] |

This prison was open for reception of male prisoners only from April 1st, 1880, to February 1st, 1881.

The following works were carried out in the prison, by prison labour, during the year:— Wing of old prison partly taken down, 400 yards of sewers uncovered and filled, and 400 yards of 12-inch sewer pipes laid down and fixed, and two concrete flushing tanks in association halls, clothes store and laundry, with eight partitional compartments fitted up in female prison.

**Return by the Governor showing how Prisoners have been employed during the year ending 31st March, 1883, and the Earnings of those engaged in such Employment; also showing the average daily number of Unemployed from Sickness and other reasons.**

## CORK (MALE) PRISON.

| Description of Employment. | Daily Average Number of Prisoners employed, unemployed, &c. Males. | Females. | Total. | Net Profit on Work done by Prisoners. | Estimated Value of the Work done for the Prison. | Total. |
|---|---|---|---|---|---|---|
| | | | | £ s. d. | £ s. d. | £ s. d. |
| Mat-making, picking oakum, &c., | 4 | — | 4 | 31 8 11 | — | 31 8 11 |
| Stonecutting, | 1 | — | 1 | — | 36 8 3 | 36 8 3 |
| Gardening, | 1 | — | 1 | — | 22 14 8 | 22 14 8 |
| Tailors, | 3 | — | 3 | 7 16 6 | 88 8 3 | [illegible] 13 0 |
| Shoemakers, | 5 | — | 5 | 1 4 8 | 35 13 5 | [illegible] 18 5 |
| Carpenters, | 13 | — | 13 | — | 155 1 5 | 155 1 4 |
| Bricklayers and labourers, | 85 | — | 85 | — | 620 6 0 | 620 0 0 |
| Painters and glaziers, | 1 | — | 1 | — | 58 0 0 | 58 6 0 |
| Tinsmiths, | ½ | — | ½ | — | 15 5 6 | 15 5 6 |
| Blacksmiths, | 2 | — | 2 | — | 60 18 0 | 60 18 0 |
| Whitewashers, | ½ | — | ½ | — | 7 11 8 | 7 11 6 |
| Treadwheel, shot-drill, and oakum-picking, Pumping water, | 77 | — | 77 | *31 0 0 | †— | 31 0 0 |
| Service of prison, | 18 | — | 18 | — | 181 10 0 | 181 10 0 |
| Debtors, | 1 | — | 1 | — | — | — |
| Washing clothing and bedding, | 6 | — | 6 | — | 131 4 8 | 131 4 0 |
| Making bedding & clothing, Repairing bedding and clothing, | 1 | — | 1 | — | 13 5 0 | 13 5 0 |
| Stone-breaking, | ½ | — | ½ | 1 1 0 | 6 10 0 | 7 11 6 |
| Chopping wood, | 6 | — | 6 | 30 0 0 | 7 0 0 | 37 0 0 |
| Making wooden skewers, | 1 | — | 1 | 1 8 3 | — | 1 8 3 |
| Lime-burning, | 4½ | — | 4½ | 30 9 11 | 33 17 10 | 64 7 9 |
| Coopering, | ½ | — | ½ | 1 10 0 | 14 0 8 | 15 10 8 |
| Cooking, | 3 | — | 3 | — | 48 0 0 | 48 0 0 |
| Sick, | 1 | — | 1 | — | — | — |
| Unemployed, | 85 | — | 89 | — | — | — |
| **Total,** | 244 | — | 291 | 105 0 10 | 1,459 17 10 | 1,5[illegible] 18 8 |

* Profit on oakum sold. † Pending approval.

New and reconstructed buildings by prison labour:—

Built two retaining walls with coping, made and fixed on same ornamental iron railings. Erected five water closets.

Laid 700 feet of 9-inch sewer pipes, having to quarry in many places; provided same with numerous shafts and inspection holes. Erected large iron flushing tank at highest point of main sewer. Made another flushing tank in concrete for branch sewer. Fixed fourteen syphon traps. Reconstructed sewer of Governor's house and fixed ventilators. Made large timber gate for arch way. Flagged cook-house yard.

Reconstructed large chimney shaft, roof, and parapet walls of buildings at entrance gate.

Return by the Governors, showing how Prisoners have been employed during the year ending 31st March, 18[illegible], and the Earnings of those engaged in such Employment; also showing the average daily number of Unemployed from Sickness and other reasons.

## CORK (FEMALE) PRISON.

| Description of Employment. | Daily Average Number of Prisoners employed, unemployed, &c. — Males. | Females. | Total. | Net Profit on Work done by Prisoners. £ s. d. | Estimated Value of the Work done for the Prison. £ s. d. | Total. £ s. d. |
|---|---|---|---|---|---|---|
| Picking fibre, &c., Mat making, | — | 1 | 1 | — | [illegible] | [illegible] |
| Prison cleaning, | — | [illegible] | [illegible] | [illegible] | [illegible] | [illegible] |
| Shoemaking, repairs, | — | — | — | — | [illegible] | [illegible] |
| [illegible] | — | [illegible] | [illegible] | — | [illegible] | [illegible] |
| Cooking, | — | [illegible] | [illegible] | — | [illegible] | [illegible] |
| Whitewashing, Service of prison, | — | [illegible] | [illegible] | — | [illegible] | [illegible] |
| Washing clothing and bedding, | — | [illegible] | [illegible] | [illegible] | [illegible] | [illegible] |
| Making bedding & clothing, Repairing bedding and clothing, | — | [illegible] | [illegible] | — | [illegible] | [illegible] |
| Knitting, Quilting, | — | [illegible] | [illegible] | [illegible] | [illegible] | [illegible] |
| Sick, | — | [illegible] | [illegible] | — | — | — |
| Unemployed, | — | [illegible] | [illegible] | — | — | — |
| Total, | — | [illegible] | [illegible] | [illegible] | [illegible] | [illegible] |

*Farm and Garden.*—Under this head prisoners' work during exercise hours has supplied the prison with potatoes during the year, and vegetables the last nine months; also kept the yards and walks, &c., clean.

The value of prisoners' work for the prison is calculated at the following rates per day:—Shoe repairs, [illegible]; service of prison, cooking and cleaning, farm and gardening, 1s.; quilting, [illegible]; sewing and knitting, [illegible].

## DOWNPATRICK PRISON.

| | Males | Females | Total | £ s. d. | £ s. d. | £ s. d. |
|---|---|---|---|---|---|---|
| Tailors, | [illegible] | — | [illegible] | — | [illegible] | [illegible] |
| Shoemakers, | [illegible] | — | [illegible] | — | [illegible] | [illegible] |
| Carpenters, | [illegible] | — | [illegible] | — | [illegible] | [illegible] |
| Bricklayers and labourers, | [illegible] | — | [illegible] | — | [illegible] | [illegible] |
| Painters and glaziers, | [illegible] | — | [illegible] | — | [illegible] | [illegible] |
| Tinsmiths, | [illegible] | — | [illegible] | — | [illegible] | [illegible] |
| Whitewashers, | [illegible] | — | [illegible] | — | [illegible] | [illegible] |
| Pumping water, | [illegible] | — | [illegible] | — | [illegible] | [illegible] |
| Service of prison, | [illegible] | [illegible] | [illegible] | — | [illegible] | [illegible] |
| Washing clothing and bedding, | — | [illegible] | [illegible] | [illegible] | [illegible] | [illegible] |
| Repairing bedding and clothing, | — | [illegible] | [illegible] | — | [illegible] | [illegible] |
| Stone-breaking, | [illegible] | — | [illegible] | [illegible] | — | [illegible] |
| Picking oakum, | [illegible] | [illegible] | [illegible] | [illegible] | — | [illegible] |
| Knitting, | — | [illegible] | [illegible] | [illegible] | — | [illegible] |
| Cutting fibre, | — | [illegible] | [illegible] | [illegible] | — | [illegible] |
| Splitting wood, | [illegible] | — | [illegible] | [illegible] | — | [illegible] |
| Sick, | [illegible] | [illegible] | [illegible] | — | — | — |
| Unemployed, | [illegible] | [illegible] | [illegible] | — | — | — |
| Total, | [illegible] | [illegible] | [illegible] | [illegible] | [illegible] | [illegible] |

The split wood remains on hand.

**Return** by the **Governors** or **Chief Warders**, showing how Prisoners have been employed during the year ending 31st March, 1883, and the Earnings of those engaged in such Employment; also showing the average daily number of Unemployed from Sickness and other reasons.

## DROGHEDA PRISON.

| Description of Employment. | Daily Average Number of Prisoners employed, unemployed, &c. | | | Net Profit on Work done by Prisoners. | Estimated Value of the Work done for the Prison. | Total. |
|---|---|---|---|---|---|---|
| | Males. | Females. | Total. | | | |
| | | | | £ s. d. | £ s. d. | £ s. d. |
| Gardening, | — | — | — | — | 4 10 0 | 4 10 0 |
| Whitewashers, | — | — | — | — | 9 10 0 | [illegible] 10 0 |
| Service of prison, | — | 2 | 2 | — | [illegible] 0 0 | [illegible] 0 0 |
| Washing clothing and bedding, | — | 1 | 1 | 0 15 0 | 15 0 0 | 14 14 0 |
| Making bedding and clothing, Repairing bedding and clothing, | — | 5 | 5 | 1 11 6 | 25 0 0 | 26 11 0 |
| Rope picking, | *1 | 5 | 6 | 1 19 6 | — | 1 19 6 |
| Unemployed, | — | 2 | 2 | — | — | — |
| Total, | 1 | 15 | 16 | [illegible] | [illegible] | [illegible] |

* The average for Males only represents the three months ending 31st March, 1883; previous to which this prison had been exclusively Female.

## DUNDALK PRISON.

| Description of Employment. | Males. | Females. | Total. | Net Profit on Work done by Prisoners. | Estimated Value of the Work done for the Prison. | Total. |
|---|---|---|---|---|---|---|
| | | | | £ s. d. | £ s. d. | £ s. d. |
| Mat-making, picking oakum, &c., | 8 | — | 8 | 42 8 0 | — | 42 8 0 |
| Tailors, | 1 | — | 1 | — | 19 11 3 | 19 11 3 |
| Shoemakers, | 2 | — | 2 | — | 62 17 0 | 62 17 0 |
| Carpenters, | 1 | — | 1 | — | 36 10 0 | 36 10 0 |
| Bricklayers and labourers, | 15 | — | 15 | — | 155 0 4 | 155 0 4 |
| Painters and Glaziers, | 1 | — | 1 | — | 17 15 0 | 17 15 0 |
| Tinsmiths, | 1 | — | 1 | — | 11 14 3 | 11 14 3 |
| Whitewashers, | 1 | — | 1 | — | 17 13 0 | 17 13 0 |
| Pumping water, | 6 | — | 6 | — | 108 5 0 | 108 5 0 |
| Service of prison, | 5 | — | 5 | — | 65 12 0 | 65 12 0 |
| Washing clothing and bedding, | 4 | — | 4 | — | 73 0 8 | 73 0 8 |
| Repairing bedding and clothing, | 1 | — | 1 | — | 31 16 9 | 31 16 9 |
| Rope picking, | 28 | — | 28 | 15 9 2 | — | 15 9 2 |
| Stone-breaking, | 17 | — | 17 | 43 17 8 | — | 43 17 8 |
| Splitting wood, | 1 | — | 1 | 2 16 0 | — | 2 16 0 |
| Cooking, | 1 | — | 1 | — | 15 6 0 | 15 6 0 |
| Total, | 90 | — | 90 | 103 13 3 | [illegible] | [illegible] |

RETURN by the GOVERNORS, showing how Prisoners have been employed during the year ending 31st March, 18[illegible], and the Earnings of those engaged in each Employment; also showing the average daily number of Unemployed from Sickness and other reasons.

## GALWAY PRISON.

| Description of Employment. | Daily Average Number of Prisoners employed, unemployed, &c. | | | Net Profit on Work done by Prisoners. | Estimated Value of the Work done for the Prison. | Total. |
|---|---|---|---|---|---|---|
| | Males. | Females. | Total. | £ s. d. | £ s. d. | £ s. d. |
| Tailors, | [illegible] | — | [illegible] | — | [illegible] | [illegible] |
| Shoemakers, | [illegible] | — | [illegible] | — | [illegible] | [illegible] |
| Bricklayers and Labourers, | [illegible] | — | [illegible] | — | [illegible] | [illegible] |
| Whitewashers, | [illegible] | [illegible] | [illegible] | — | [illegible] | [illegible] |
| Service of prison, | [illegible] | [illegible] | [illegible] | — | [illegible] | [illegible] |
| Washing clothing and bedding, | — | [illegible] | [illegible] | — | [illegible] | [illegible] |
| Making bedding and clothing, | — | [illegible] | [illegible] | — | [illegible] | [illegible] |
| Repairing bedding and clothing, | — | [illegible] | [illegible] | — | [illegible] | [illegible] |
| Stone-breaking, | [illegible] | — | [illegible] | [illegible] | [illegible] | [illegible] |
| Firewood, | [illegible] | — | [illegible] | [illegible] | [illegible] | [illegible] |
| Oakum picking, | [illegible] | — | [illegible] | [illegible] | — | [illegible] |
| Knitting, | — | [illegible] | [illegible] | — | [illegible] | [illegible] |
| [illegible] | — | [illegible] | [illegible] | — | [illegible] | [illegible] |
| Sick, | [illegible] | — | [illegible] | — | — | — |
| Unemployed, | [illegible] | — | [illegible] | — | — | — |
| Total, | [illegible] | [illegible] | [illegible] | [illegible] | [illegible] | [illegible] |

## GRANGEGORMAN PRISON.

| Description of Employment. | Males. | Females. | Total. | Net Profit on Work done by Prisoners. | Estimated Value of the Work done for the Prison. | Total. |
|---|---|---|---|---|---|---|
| | | | | £ s. d. | £ s. d. | £ s. d. |
| Tailors, | [illegible] | — | [illegible] | — | [illegible] | [illegible] |
| Shoemakers, | [illegible] | — | [illegible] | — | [illegible] | [illegible] |
| Bricklayers and Labourers, | [illegible] | — | [illegible] | — | [illegible] | [illegible] |
| Painters and Glaziers, | [illegible] | — | [illegible] | — | [illegible] | [illegible] |
| Whitewashers, | [illegible] | — | [illegible] | — | [illegible] | [illegible] |
| Service of prison, | [illegible] | [illegible] | [illegible] | — | [illegible] | [illegible] |
| Washing clothing and bedding, | — | [illegible] | [illegible] | [illegible] | [illegible] | [illegible] |
| Making bedding and clothing, Repairing bedding and clothing, | — | [illegible] | [illegible] | [illegible] | [illegible] | [illegible] |
| Stone-breaking, | [illegible] | — | [illegible] | — | [illegible] | [illegible] |
| [illegible] | [illegible] | [illegible] | [illegible] | [illegible] | — | [illegible] |
| Nursing, | — | [illegible] | [illegible] | — | — | — |
| [illegible] | [illegible] | — | [illegible] | — | [illegible] | [illegible] |
| Splitting Wood, | [illegible] | — | [illegible] | — | [illegible] | [illegible] |
| Sick, | [illegible] | [illegible] | [illegible] | — | — | — |
| Unemployed, | [illegible] | [illegible] | [illegible] | — | — | — |
| Total, | [illegible] | [illegible] | [illegible] | [illegible] | [illegible] | [illegible] |

Prison clothing and bedding have been washed here during the year for Mountjoy Male, Richmond, and Kilmainham Prisons, and repairs done for the last two Prisons, but no profit shown, as only a nominal sum, sufficient to cover the expenditure in connexion therewith, is charged in the transfer accounts.

**Return by the Governors, showing how Prisoners have been employed during the year ending 31st March, 1883, and the Earnings of those engaged in such Employment; also showing the average daily number of Unemployed from Sickness and other reasons.**

## KILKENNY PRISON.

| Description of Employment. | Daily Average Number of Prisoners employed, unemployed, &c. | | | Net Profit on Work done by Prisoners. | Estimated Value of the Work done for the Prison. | Total. |
|---|---|---|---|---|---|---|
| | Males. | Females. | Total. | | | |
| | | | | £ s. d. | £ s. d. | £ s. d. |
| Mat-making, picking oakum, &c., | 6·0 | — | 6·0 | 0 1 0 | 10 0 0 | 34 11 0 |
| Shoemakers, | 1·0 | — | 1·0 | — | 22 10 0 | 22 10 0 |
| Bricklayers and labourers, | 3·0 | — | 3·0 | — | 30 0 0 | 30 0 0 |
| Painters and glaziers, | ·50 | — | ·50 | — | 11 5 0 | 11 5 0 |
| Pumping water, | 2·0 | — | 2·0 | — | 18 0 0 | 18 0 0 |
| Service of prison, | 5·0 | ·50 | 5·50 | — | 55 0 0 | 55 0 0 |
| Washing clothing and bedding, | 2·0 | ·50 | 2·50 | — | 37 10 0 | 37 10 0 |
| Making bedding and clothing, | — | 2·0 | 2·0 | — | 22 10 0 | 22 10 0 |
| Repairing bedding and clothing, | 1·0 | — | 1·0 | — | 7 10 0 | 7 10 0 |
| Rope picking, | 12·0 | 2·0 | 14·0 | — | — | — |
| Stone-breaking, | ·50 | — | ·50 | — | 5 0 0 | 5 0 0 |
| Wood for kindling, | 1·0 | — | 1·0 | 6 13 4 | 40 [illegible] 0 | 37 10 0 |
| Sick, Unemployed, | 24·0 | 1·0 | 25·0 | — | — | — |
| Total, | 56·0 | 6·0 | 62·0 | 15 13 4 | 226 12 6 | 242 5 6 |

Six tons of oakum sold for £96 16s. No profit.

## KILMAINHAM PRISON.

| | | | | | | |
|---|---|---|---|---|---|---|
| | | | | £ s. d. | £ s. d. | £ s. d. |
| Tailors, | 1 | — | 1 | 13 0 0 | 10 0 0 | 17 0 0 |
| Shoemakers, | 1 | — | 1 | 6 0 0 | 7 10 0 | 13 10 0 |
| Carpenters, Bricklayers and labourers, Painters and glaziers, | 1 | — | 1 | 24 0 0 | 54 0 0 | 80 0 0 |
| Whitewashers, | 1 | — | 1 | — | 30 0 0 | 30 0 0 |
| Service of prison, | 7 | — | 7 | — | 211 0 0 | 211 0 0 |
| Making oakum,* | 20 | — | 20 | 5 0 0 | 5 0 0 | 10 0 0 |
| Sick, | 3 | — | 3 | — | — | — |
| Unemployed, | 40 | — | 40 | — | — | — |
| Total, | 74 | — | 74 | 44 0 0 | 285 [illegible] 0 | 341 0 0 |

* Picked five tons at £1 per ton.

Tailors.—The average 1, is for 120 days total time worked in the year.
Shoemakers.— " 60 "
Carpenters, Bricklayers and Labourers, Painters and Glaziers.—The average 1, is for 210 days total time worked in the year.

**RETURN by the GOVERNORS, showing how Prisoners have been employed during the year ending 31st March, [illegible], and the Earnings of those engaged in such Employment; also showing the average daily number of Unemployed from Sickness and other reasons.**

## LIMERICK (MALE) PRISON.

| Description of Employment. | Daily Average Number of Prisoners employed, unemployed, &c. — Males. | Females. | Total. | Net Profit on Work done by Prisoners. | Estimated Value of the Work done in the Prison. | Total. |
|---|---|---|---|---|---|---|
| | | | | £ s. d. | £ s. d. | £ s. d. |
| Mat-making, net-making, picking oakum, &c., | 2 | — | 2 | 2 11 0 | — | 2 11 0 |
| Gardening and labouring, | 4 | — | 4 | — | 134 8 0 | 134 8 0 |
| Tailors, | 2 | — | 2 | — | 43 0 0 | 43 0 0 |
| Shoemakers, | 1 | — | 1 | — | 20 2 0 | 20 2 0 |
| Carpenters, | 3 | — | 3 | — | 82 17 8 | 82 17 8 |
| Bricklayers, | 3 | — | 3 | — | 39 17 0 | 39 17 0 |
| Painters and glaziers, | [illegible] | — | [illegible] | — | [illegible] 14 [illegible] | [illegible] 14 [illegible] |
| Whitewashers, | 3 | — | [illegible] | — | [illegible] | [illegible] |
| Pumping water, | 7 | — | 7 | — | [illegible] 0 10 | [illegible] 0 10 |
| Service of prison, | 7 | — | 7 | — | [illegible] | [illegible] |
| Cooking, | 2 | — | 2 | — | 43 8 0 | 43 8 0 |
| [illegible], | [illegible] | — | [illegible] | 14 19 11 | — | 14 19 11 |
| Stone-breaking, | 17 | — | 17 | [illegible] | — | [illegible] |
| Splitting wood, | 2 | — | 2 | 4 [illegible] 7 | — | [illegible] 7 |
| Sick, | 1 | — | 1 | — | — | — |
| Unemployed, | [illegible] | — | [illegible] | — | — | — |
| **Total,** | [illegible] | — | [illegible] | [illegible] | [illegible] | [illegible] |

## LIMERICK (FEMALE) PRISON.

| Description of Employment. | Males. | Females. | Total. | Net Profit on Work done by Prisoners. | Estimated Value of the Work done in the Prison. | Total. |
|---|---|---|---|---|---|---|
| | | | | £ s. d. | £ s. d. | £ s. d. |
| Painters and glaziers, | — | 2 | 2 | — | 25 0 0 | 25 0 0 |
| Whitewashers, | — | [illegible] | [illegible] | — | [illegible] | [illegible] 0 0 |
| Pumping water, | — | [illegible] | [illegible] | — | [illegible] | [illegible] 0 0 |
| Service of prison, | — | [illegible] | [illegible] | — | [illegible] | [illegible] 0 0 |
| Washing clothing and bedding, | — | 7 | 7 | — | [illegible] | [illegible] 0 0 |
| Making bedding and clothing, | — | 2 | [illegible] | — | [illegible] | [illegible] 0 0 |
| Repairing bedding and clothing, | — | 18 | 19 | — | [illegible] | [illegible] |
| Stocking making, | — | [illegible] | [illegible] | [illegible] | — | [illegible] |
| Quilt making, | — | 4 | 4 | [illegible] | — | [illegible] |
| Lace handkerchief making, | — | 1 | 1 | [illegible] | — | [illegible] |
| Sick, | — | [illegible] | [illegible] | — | — | — |
| Unemployed, | — | [illegible] | [illegible] | — | — | — |
| **Total,** | — | [illegible] | [illegible] | [illegible] | [illegible] | [illegible] |

The washing is much increased. **We are now doing for male and female prisons,**

| | £ s. d. |
|---|---|
| Some 1,500 or 1,600 pieces per week, estimated at £6 5s. per week, is for year, | 325 0 0 |
| Governors' washing—male and female prisons, | 40 0 0 |
| | 365 0 0 |

**Return by the Governors, showing how Prisoners have been employed during the year ending 31st March, 1883, and the Earnings of those engaged in such Employment; also showing the average daily number of Unemployed from Sickness and other reasons.**

## LONDONDERRY PRISON.

| Description of Employment. | Daily Average Number of Prisoners employed, unemployed, &c. | | | Net Profit on Work done by Prisoners. | Estimated Value of the Work done for the Prison. | Total. |
|---|---|---|---|---|---|---|
| | Males. | Females. | Total. | | | |
| | | | | £ s. d. | £ s. d. | £ s. d. |
| Mat-making, picking oakum, &c., | 10 | — | 10 | 100 3 0 | — | 230 [illegible] 0 |
| Tailors, | 1 | — | 1 | — | 34 10 0 | 33 12 0 |
| Shoemakers, | 1 | — | 1 | — | 34 10 0 | 36 11 0 |
| Carpenters, | 1 | — | 1 | — | 38 16 0 | 30 16 0 |
| Bricklayers and labourers, | 4 | — | 4 | — | 73 0 0 | 79 0 0 |
| Painters and glaziers, | 1 | — | 1 | — | 50 10 0 | 53 12 0 |
| Blacksmiths, | 1 | — | 1 | — | 31 10 0 | 30 10 0 |
| Whitewashers, | 1 | — | 1 | — | 34 10 0 | 34 10 0 |
| Service of prison, | 5 | 3 | 8 | — | 124 12 0 | 124 12 0 |
| Washing clothing and bedding, | — | 3 | 3 | — | 34 15 0 | 34 15 0 |
| Making bedding and clothing, | — | 4 | 4 | — | 32 0 0 | 32 0 0 |
| Repairing bedding and clothing, | — | 3 | 3 | — | 91 5 0 | 91 5 0 |
| Picking oakum, | 10 | 3 | 13 | 11 14 8 | — | 11 14 8 |
| Stone-breaking, | 10 | — | 10 | 45 15 8 | — | 45 15 8 |
| Sick, | 1 | — | 1 | — | — | — |
| Unemployed, | 7 | 1 | 8 | — | — | — |
| **Total,** | 63 | 22 | 75 | 157 7 4 | 630 12 0 | 882 19 0 |

## MARYBOROUGH PRISON.

| Description of Employment. | Males. | Females. | Total. | Net Profit on Work done by Prisoners. | Estimated Value of the Work done for the Prison. | Total. |
|---|---|---|---|---|---|---|
| | | | | £ s. d. | £ s. d. | £ s. d. |
| Mat-making, picking oakum, &c., | — | — | — | 2 0 0 | — | 2 0 0 |
| Tailors, | 3 | — | 3 | — | 86 0 0 | 86 0 0 |
| Shoemakers, | 3 | — | 3 | — | 93 0 0 | 93 0 0 |
| Carpenters, | 4 | — | 4 | — | 240 0 0 | 240 0 0 |
| Bricklayers and labourers, | 15 | — | 15 | — | 225 0 0 | 225 0 0 |
| Painters and glaziers, | 1 | — | 1 | — | 30 0 0 | 30 0 0 |
| Tinsmiths, | — | — | — | — | 6 0 0 | 6 0 0 |
| Blacksmiths, | 2 | — | 2 | — | 32 10 0 | 32 10 0 |
| Whitewashers, | 1 | — | 1 | — | 13 6 0 | 13 6 0 |
| Pensioners, | 4 | — | 4 | — | — | — |
| Service of prison, | 3 | — | 3 | — | 45 0 0 | 45 0 0 |
| Washing clothing and bedding, | 6 | — | 6 | — | 38 10 0 | 38 10 0 |
| Repairing bedding & clothing, | — | 1 | 1 | — | 15 1 1 | 15 1 1 |
| Mat-making, | 15 | — | 15 | 54 7 1 | — | 54 7 1 |
| Plastering, | 4 | — | 4 | — | 120 0 0 | 120 0 0 |
| Rope-picking, | 10 | — | 10 | — | — | — |
| Stone-breaking, | 2 | — | 2 | 1 0 0 | — | 1 0 0 |
| Chopping, | — | — | — | 6 7 0 | — | 6 7 0 |
| Stonecutting, | 3 | — | 3 | — | 90 0 0 | 90 0 0 |
| Sick, | 1 | — | 1 | — | — | — |
| Unemployed, | 10 | — | 10 | — | — | — |
| **Total,** | 82 | 1 | 83 | 63 14 1 | 1,009 14 8 | 1,073 8 1 |

*New work.*—A residence for the medical officer is now almost completed; it has been nearly all executed by prison labour.

*Reconstruction.*—Matron's residence has been converted into an hospital, the ceilings sheeted with iron, and a waterclosit built and fitted up in it.

A spacious room in the Governor's late residence has been fitted up as a Protestant church; the R.C. chapel is now complete and has been suitably fitted up. An iron railing 100 feet long and 14 feet high has been erected in convict exercise yard. Extensive walls have been removed from the late hospital, which has been converted into officers' quarters.

**Return by the Governors, showing how Prisoners have been employed during the year ending 31st March, 18[illegible], and the Earnings of those engaged in such Employment; also showing the average daily number of Unemployed from Sickness and other reasons.**

## MULLINGAR PRISON.

| Description of Employment. | Daily Average Number of Prisoners employed, unemployed, &c. Males. | Females. | Total. | Net Profit on Workshops by Prisoners. £ s. d. | Estimated Value of the Work done for the Prison. £ s. d. | Total. £ s. d. |
|---|---|---|---|---|---|---|
| Grinding corn, | [illegible] | — | [illegible] | [illegible] | — | [illegible] |
| Gardening, | [illegible] | — | [illegible] | [illegible] | [illegible] | [illegible] |
| Tailors, | [illegible] | — | [illegible] | — | [illegible] | [illegible] |
| Shoemakers, | [illegible] | — | [illegible] | — | [illegible] | [illegible] |
| Carpenters, | [illegible] | — | [illegible] | — | [illegible] | [illegible] |
| Bricklayers and labourers, | [illegible] | — | [illegible] | — | [illegible] | [illegible] |
| Painters and glaziers, | [illegible] | — | [illegible] | — | [illegible] | [illegible] |
| Tinsmiths, Blacksmiths, | [illegible] | — | [illegible] | — | [illegible] | [illegible] |
| Whitewashers, | [illegible] | — | [illegible] | — | [illegible] | [illegible] |
| Service of prison, | [illegible] | [illegible] | [illegible] | — | [illegible] | [illegible] |
| Washing clothing and bedding, | — | [illegible] | [illegible] | [illegible] | [illegible] | [illegible] |
| Making bedding and clothing, Repairing bedding and clothing, | — | [illegible] | [illegible] | — | [illegible] | [illegible] |
| Oakum-picking, | [illegible] | — | [illegible] | — | [illegible] | [illegible] |
| Sewing sacks, | [illegible] | — | [illegible] | [illegible] | — | 147 5 10 |
| Cooking, | [illegible] | — | [illegible] | — | [illegible] | [illegible] |
| Stone-breaking, | [illegible] | — | [illegible] | [illegible] | — | [illegible] |
| Knitting, | — | [illegible] | [illegible] | [illegible] | [illegible] | [illegible] |
| Sick, | [illegible] | [illegible] | [illegible] | — | — | — |
| Unemployed, | [illegible] | [illegible] | [illegible] | — | — | — |
| **Total,** | [illegible] | [illegible] | [illegible] | [illegible] | [illegible] | [illegible] |

## NAAS PRISON.

| Description of Employment. | Males. | Females. | Total. | Net Profit. £ s. d. | Estimated Value. £ s. d. | Total. £ s. d. |
|---|---|---|---|---|---|---|
| Mat-making, picking coir, &c., Picking, picking oakum, upholstering, brush-filling, | [illegible] | [illegible] | [illegible] | [illegible] | — | [illegible] |
| Tailors, | [illegible] | — | [illegible] | — | [illegible] | [illegible] |
| Shoemakers, | [illegible] | — | [illegible] | — | [illegible] | [illegible] |
| Carpenters, Bricklayers and labourers, Painters and glaziers, | [illegible] | — | [illegible] | — | [illegible] | [illegible] |
| Tinsmiths, Blacksmiths, | [illegible] | — | [illegible] | — | [illegible] | [illegible] |
| Whitewashers and cleaners, | [illegible] | [illegible] | [illegible] | — | [illegible] | [illegible] |
| Pumping water, | [illegible] | — | [illegible] | — | [illegible] | [illegible] |
| Washing clothing and bedding, | [illegible] | — | [illegible] | — | [illegible] | [illegible] |
| Making bedding and clothing, Repairing bedding and clothing, | — | [illegible] | [illegible] | — | [illegible] | [illegible] |
| Sack-making, | [illegible] | [illegible] | [illegible] | [illegible] | — | [illegible] |
| Stone-breaking, | [illegible] | — | [illegible] | — | [illegible] | [illegible] |
| Cooking, | [illegible] | — | [illegible] | — | [illegible] | [illegible] |
| Sick and unemployed, | [illegible] | — | [illegible] | — | — | — |
| **Total,** | [illegible] | [illegible] | [illegible] | [illegible] | [illegible] | [illegible] |

RETURN by the GOVERNORS, showing how Prisoners have been employed during the year ending 31st March, 1883, and the Earnings of those engaged in such Employment; also showing the average daily number of Unemployed from Sickness and other reasons.

## NENAGH PRISON.

| Description of Employment. | Daily Average Number of Prisoners employed, unemployed, &c. | | | Net Profit on Work done by Prisoners. | Estimated Value of the Work done for the Prison. | Total. |
|---|---|---|---|---|---|---|
| | Males. | Females. | Total. | | | |
| | | | | £ s. d. | £ s. d. | £ s. d. |
| Mat-making, picking coir, &c., | 2 | — | 2 | 1 4 0 | — | 1 4 0 |
| Gardening, | 2 | — | 2 | 8 11 10 | 6 11 3 | 15 3 1 |
| Tailors, | 1 | — | 1 | — | 30 4 0 | 30 4 0 |
| Carpenters, | 1 | — | 1 | — | 30 4 0 | 30 4 0 |
| Bricklayers and labourers, | 6 | — | 6 | — | 203 10 0 | 203 10 0 |
| Painters and Glaziers, | 1 | — | 1 | — | 30 4 0 | 30 4 0 |
| Pumping water, | 1 | — | 1 | — | 18 2 0 | 18 2 0 |
| Washing clothing and bedding, | 3 | — | 3 | — | 23 10 0 | 27 10 0 |
| Stone-breaking, | 7 | — | 7 | 20 2 0 | 5 10 0 | 75 15 0 |
| Picking oakum, | 7 | — | 7 | — | — | — |
| Cooking, | 1 | — | 1 | — | 15 2 0 | 15 1 0 |
| Messengers, | 1 | — | 1 | — | 30 4 0 | 30 4 0 |
| Splitting wood, | 2 | — | 2 | 1 12 0 | 1 6 0 | 2 18 0 |
| Sick, | 1 | — | 1 | — | — | — |
| Unemployed, | 6 | — | 6 | — | — | — |
| **Total,** | 44 | — | 44 | 31 0 7 | 396 1 3 | 427 10 10 |

## OMAGH PRISON.

| Description of Employment. | Males. | Females. | Total. | Net Profit on Work done by Prisoners. | Estimated Value of the Work done for the Prison. | Total. |
|---|---|---|---|---|---|---|
| | | | | £ s. d. | £ s. d. | £ s. d. |
| Mat-making, picking coir, &c., | 3 | — | 3 | 20 16 0 | 0 10 0 | 21 6 0 |
| Tailors, | 1 | — | 1 | — | 18 15 0 | 18 15 0 |
| Shoemakers, | 1 | — | 1 | — | 23 10 0 | 23 10 0 |
| Carpenters, | 2/3 | — | 2/3 | — | 15 0 0 | 15 0 0 |
| Bricklayers and labourers, | 3 | — | 3 | 1 0 0 | 46 0 0 | 47 0 0 |
| Painters and glaziers, | 1 | — | 1 | — | 18 15 0 | 18 15 0 |
| Tinsmiths, Blacksmiths, and Plumbers, | 1 | — | 1 | — | 16 0 0 | 16 0 0 |
| Whitewashers, | 1 | — | 1 | — | 16 0 0 | 16 0 0 |
| Treadwheel, | 10 | — | 10 | — | — | — |
| Pumping water, | 5 | — | 5 | — | 30 0 0 | 30 0 0 |
| Service of prison, | 3 | 2 | 5 | — | 30 5 0 | 35 5 0 |
| Washing clothing and bedding, | 3 | 1 | 4 | — | 30 0 0 | 30 0 0 |
| Making bedding and clothing, Repairing bedding and clothing, | — | 1 | 1 | — | 7 10 0 | 7 10 0 |
| Stone-breaking, | 3 | — | 3 | — | 10 0 0 | 10 0 0 |
| Picking oakum, | 1 | 1 | 2 | 2 13 6 | — | 2 13 6 |
| Wood-splitting and bundling, | 1 | — | 1 | 1 15 0 | 5 0 0 | 6 15 0 |
| Knitting, | — | 1 | 1 | — | 5 0 0 | 5 0 0 |
| Sick, | 0·5 | 0·5 | 1 | — | — | — |
| Unemployed, | 1 | 0·8 | 1·8 | — | — | — |
| **Total,** | 38 | 7 | 45 | 24 17 8 | 306 5 0 | 330 2 8 |

RETURN by the Governors, showing how Prisoners have been employed during the year ending 31st March, 1883, and the Earnings of those engaged in such Employment; also showing the average daily number of Unemployed from Sickness and other reasons.

## RICHMOND PRISON.

| Description of Employment. | Daily Average Number of Prisoners employed, unemployed, &c. Males. | Females. | Total. | Net Profit on Work done by Prisoners.* | Estimated Value of the Work done for the Prison. | Total. |
|---|---|---|---|---|---|---|
| | | | | £ s. d. | £ s. d. | £ s. d. |
| Mat-making, | 14·73 | | | | | |
| Weaving mats, | 4·17 | | | | | |
| Picking yarn, | 15·63 | | 46·[illegible] | 133 10 9 | — | 133 10 9 |
| Weaving matting, | 7·16 | | | | | |
| Warping and winding, | 5·03 | | | | | |
| [illegible] | 3·61 | — | 3·61 | 53 10 9 | — | 53 10 9 |
| Tailoring, | 9·15 | — | 9·15 | 168 5 6 | — | 168 5 6 |
| Shoemaking, | 7·94 | — | 7·94 | 86 10 2 | — | 86 10 2 |
| Carpentering and slating, | 3·31 | | | | | |
| Bricklayers and labourers, | 28·06 | — | 31·37 | — | 449 10 0 | 449 10 0 |
| Painting and glazing, | 8·17 | — | 8·17 | — | 41 10 0 | 41 10 0 |
| Tinsmithing, | ·37 | — | ·37 | 4 10 6 | — | 4 10 6 |
| Plumbing, | 5·12 | — | 5·12 | — | 50 0 0 | 50 0 0 |
| Whitewashing, | 8·10 | — | 8·10 | — | 46 10 0 | 46 10 0 |
| [illegible] | 20·16 | — | 20·16 | — | — | — |
| Cooking, | 4· | — | 4· | — | 46 0 0 | 46 0 0 |
| Cleaning prison, | 17·[illegible] | — | 11·[illegible] | — | 166 0 0 | 166 0 0 |
| Mattress-making, | 6·03 | — | 6·03 | 36 3 6 | — | 36 3 6 |
| Weaving frieze, | 7·69 | | | | | |
| Winding [illegible], | 9·05 | — | 16·[illegible] | 441 17 0 | — | 441 17 0 |
| [illegible] | 4·16 | — | 4·16 | 10 10 7 | — | 10 10 7 |
| Oakum-picking, | 15·63 | — | 15·63 | 16 0 0 | — | 16 0 0 |
| Stone-breaking, | 25·16 | — | 25·16 | 0 1 0 | — | 0 1 0 |
| [illegible] | 7·70 | — | 7·70 | 154 5 3 | — | 154 5 3 |
| Sick, | [illegible] | — | [illegible] | — | — | — |
| Unemployed, | [illegible] | — | [illegible] | — | — | — |
| Total, | [illegible] | — | [illegible] | 1,109 0 4 | 762 10 0 | 1,871 10 4 |

* Net profit as per "Productive Ledger" under several heads of manufacture.

## SLIGO PRISON.

| | | | | | | |
|---|---|---|---|---|---|---|
| | | | | £ s. d. | £ s. d. | £ s. d. |
| Tailors, | [illegible] | — | [illegible] | — | [illegible] | [illegible] |
| Shoemakers, | [illegible] | — | [illegible] | — | [illegible] | [illegible] |
| Carpenters, | [illegible] | — | [illegible] | — | [illegible] | [illegible] |
| Painters and glaziers, | [illegible] | — | [illegible] | — | [illegible] | [illegible] |
| Whitewashers, | [illegible] | [illegible] | [illegible] | — | [illegible] | [illegible] |
| [illegible] | [illegible] | — | [illegible] | — | — | — |
| Pumping water, | [illegible] | — | [illegible] | — | [illegible] | [illegible] |
| Service of prison, | [illegible] | [illegible] | [illegible] | — | [illegible] | [illegible] |
| Washing clothing and bedding, | — | [illegible] | [illegible] | — | [illegible] | [illegible] |
| Making bedding and clothing, | — | — | — | — | [illegible] | [illegible] |
| Repairing bedding and clothing, | — | [illegible] | [illegible] | — | [illegible] | [illegible] |
| Rag-picking, | [illegible] | [illegible] | [illegible] | [illegible] | — | [illegible] |
| Stone-breaking, | [illegible] | — | [illegible] | [illegible] | — | [illegible] |
| Splitting wood, | [illegible] | — | [illegible] | [illegible] | [illegible] | [illegible] |
| Knitting, | — | [illegible] | [illegible] | [illegible] | [illegible] | [illegible] |
| Sick, | [illegible] | [illegible] | [illegible] | — | — | — |
| Unemployed, | [illegible] | [illegible] | [illegible] | — | — | — |
| Total, | [illegible] | [illegible] | [illegible] | [illegible] | [illegible] | [illegible] |

RETURN by the GOVERNORS, showing how Prisoners have been employed during the year ending 31st March, 1883, and the Earnings of those engaged in such Employment; also showing the average daily number of Unemployed from Sickness and other reasons.

## TRALEE PRISON.

| Description of Employment. | Daily Average Number of Prisoners employed, Unemployed, &c. | | | Net Profit on Work done by Prisoners. | Estimated Value of the Work done for the Prison. | Total. |
|---|---|---|---|---|---|---|
| | Males. | Females. | Total. | £ s. d. | £ s. d. | £ s. d. |
| Mat-making, picking coir, &c., | 1·91 | — | 1·91 | 0 19 [illegible] | — | [illegible] |
| Tailors, | ·27 | — | ·27 | — | [illegible] | [illegible] |
| Shoemakers, | ·40 | — | ·40 | — | [illegible] | [illegible] |
| Carpenters, | ·48 | — | ·48 | — | [illegible] | [illegible] |
| Bricklayers and labourers, | 3·71 | — | 3·71 | — | [illegible] | [illegible] |
| Painters and glaziers, | ·84 | — | ·84 | — | [illegible] | [illegible] |
| Tinsmiths, | ·26 | — | ·26 | — | [illegible] | [illegible] |
| Whitewashers, | ·05 | ·31 | ·36 | — | 0 19 0 | [illegible] |
| Crank Pump, | 1·35 | — | 1·35 | — | — | — |
| Service of prison, | 1·86 | ·28 | 2·14 | — | [illegible] | [illegible] |
| Washing clothing and bedding, | — | 1·84 | 1·84 | — | [illegible] | [illegible] |
| Repairing bedding and clothing, | — | ·94 | ·94 | — | [illegible] | [illegible] |
| Stone-breaking, | 11·10 | — | 11·10 | [illegible] | [illegible] | [illegible] |
| Picking oakum, | 8·77 | — | 8·77 | — | — | — |
| Knitting, | — | ·78 | ·78 | — | [illegible] | [illegible] |
| Cooking, | — | 2 | 2 | — | [illegible] | [illegible] |
| Sick, | ·35 | ·78 | 1·13 | — | — | — |
| Unemployed, | 10·73 | [illegible] | [illegible] | — | — | — |
| Total, | [illegible] | [illegible] | [illegible] | [illegible] | [illegible] | [illegible] |

## TULLAMORE PRISON.

| Description of Employment. | Males. | Females. | Total. | Net Profit on Work done by Prisoners. | Estimated Value of the Work done for the Prison. | Total. |
|---|---|---|---|---|---|---|
| | | | | £ s. d. | £ s. d. | £ s. d. |
| Tailors, | 1 | — | 1 | — | [illegible] | [illegible] |
| Shoemakers, | 1 | — | 1 | — | [illegible] | [illegible] |
| Carpenters, | 1 | — | 1 | — | [illegible] | [illegible] |
| Bricklayers and labourers, | 3 | — | 3 | — | [illegible] | [illegible] |
| Painters and glaziers, | ·23 | — | ·23 | — | [illegible] | [illegible] |
| Tinsmiths, Blacksmiths, | ·4 | — | ·4 | — | [illegible] | [illegible] |
| Whitewashers, | ·23 | — | ·23 | — | [illegible] | [illegible] |
| Pumping water, | 6 | — | 6 | — | [illegible] | [illegible] |
| Service of prison, | 8 | — | 8 | — | [illegible] | [illegible] |
| Washing clothing and bedding, | — | [illegible] | [illegible] | [illegible] | [illegible] | [illegible] |
| Making bedding and clothing, Repairing bedding and clothing, | — | [illegible] | [illegible] | — | [illegible] | [illegible] |
| Picking oakum, | 2 | — | 2 | [illegible] | — | [illegible] |
| Cooking, | 2 | — | 2 | — | [illegible] | [illegible] |
| Sack-making, | 31 | — | 31 | [illegible] | — | [illegible] |
| Sick, | 1·3 | — | 1·3 | — | — | — |
| Unemployed, | [illegible] | 1 | [illegible] | — | — | — |
| Total, | [illegible] | [illegible] | 64 | [illegible] | [illegible] | [illegible] |

Sack-making has been carried on well during the past year. The officers have been most attentive in giving the necessary instructions, and the prisoners worked well with a few exceptions.

RETURN by the GOVERNORS, showing how Prisoners have been employed during the year ending 31st March, 18[illegible], and the Earnings of those engaged in such Employments; also showing the average daily number of Unemployed from Sickness and other reasons.

## WATERFORD PRISON.

| Description of Employment. | Daily Average Number of Prisoners employed, unemployed, etc. — Males. | Females. | Total. | Net Profit on Work done by Prisoners. £ s. d. | Estimated Value of the Work done for the Prison. £ s. d. | Total. £ s. d. |
|---|---|---|---|---|---|---|
| Mat-making, picking coir, hair, &c., | [illegible] | — | [illegible] | [illegible] | — | [illegible] |
| Tailors, | [illegible] | — | [illegible] | — | [illegible] | [illegible] |
| Shoemakers, | | | | | [illegible] | [illegible] |
| Carpenters, | | | | | [illegible] | [illegible] |
| Bricklayers and labourers, | [illegible] | — | [illegible] | — | [illegible] | [illegible] |
| Blacksmiths, | [illegible] | — | [illegible] | — | [illegible] | [illegible] |
| Whitewashers, | | | | | [illegible] | [illegible] |
| Pumping water and stoking, | [illegible] | — | [illegible] | — | [illegible] | [illegible] |
| Service of prison, | [illegible] | [illegible] | [illegible] | — | [illegible] | [illegible] |
| Washing clothing and bedding, | [illegible] | [illegible] | [illegible] | [illegible] | [illegible] | [illegible] |
| Repairing bedding & clothing, | — | [illegible] | [illegible] | — | [illegible] | [illegible] |
| Knitting, | — | [illegible] | [illegible] | [illegible] | [illegible] | [illegible] |
| Wood-cutting, | [illegible] | — | [illegible] | [illegible] | [illegible] | [illegible] |
| Picking, packing, and sorting oakum, | [illegible] | [illegible] | [illegible] | [illegible] | — | [illegible] |
| Cooking, | [illegible] | — | [illegible] | — | [illegible] | [illegible] |
| [illegible], | [illegible] | — | [illegible] | [illegible] | — | [illegible] |
| Sick, | [illegible] | [illegible] | [illegible] | — | — | — |
| Unemployed, | [illegible] | [illegible] | [illegible] | — | — | — |
| Total, | [illegible] | [illegible] | [illegible] | [illegible] | [illegible] | [illegible] |

The averages are computed according to the number of working days, and those in brackets could not be given separately unless in fractional parts.
The net profit is on articles actually disposed of and paid for.

## WEXFORD PRISON.

| | | | | £ s. d. | £ s. d. | £ s. d. |
|---|---|---|---|---|---|---|
| Mat-making, picking coir, &c., | [illegible] | — | [illegible] | [illegible] | — | [illegible] |
| Tailors, | [illegible] | — | [illegible] | — | [illegible] | [illegible] |
| Carpenters, | [illegible] | — | [illegible] | — | [illegible] | [illegible] |
| Bricklayers and labourers, | [illegible] | — | [illegible] | — | [illegible] | [illegible] |
| Painters and glaziers, | [illegible] | — | [illegible] | — | [illegible] | [illegible] |
| Whitewashers, | [illegible] | — | [illegible] | — | [illegible] | [illegible] |
| Service of prison, | [illegible] | [illegible] | [illegible] | — | [illegible] | [illegible] |
| Washing clothing and bedding, | — | [illegible] | [illegible] | — | [illegible] | [illegible] |
| Picking oakum, | [illegible] | — | [illegible] | [illegible] | — | [illegible] |
| Shoemaking, | [illegible] | — | [illegible] | [illegible] | — | [illegible] |
| Sewing, | — | [illegible] | [illegible] | — | [illegible] | [illegible] |
| Knitting, | — | [illegible] | [illegible] | — | [illegible] | [illegible] |
| Cutting wood, | [illegible] | — | [illegible] | [illegible] | — | [illegible] |
| Unemployed, | [illegible] | — | [illegible] | — | — | — |
| Total, | 63 | 4 | [illegible] | [illegible] | [illegible] | [illegible] |

Return by the Governor and Superintendent, showing how Prisoners (not Convicts) have been employed during the year ending 31st March, 1883, and the Earnings of those engaged in such Employment; also showing the average daily number of Unemployed from Sickness and other reasons.

## MOUNTJOY (MALE) PRISON. [LOCAL PRISONERS.]

| Description of Employment. | Daily Average Number of Prisoners employed, unemployed, &c. Males. | Females. | Total. | Net Profit on Work done by Prisoners. | Estimated Value of the Work done for the Prison. | Total. |
|---|---|---|---|---|---|---|
| | | | | £ s. d. | £ s. d. | £ s. d. |
| Mat making, picking coir, &c., | 73·77 | — | 73·77 | 968 17 3 | — | 964 17 3 |
| Brushes, | 1·20 | — | 1·20 | 6 7 6 | — | 6 7 6 |
| Tailors, | 29·07 | — | 29·07 | 571 14 9 | — | 571 14 9 |
| Shoemakers, | 29·75 | — | 29·75 | 271 2 9 | — | 271 2 9 |
| Carpenters, | 6·1 | — | 6·1 | — | 606 12 0 | 606 12 9 |
| Tinsmiths, | 1·84 | — | 1·84 | 10 8 6 | — | 19 0 4 |
| [illegible], | 6·16 | — | 6·16 | [illegible] 8 9 | — | 75 5 0 |
| Whitewashers, | ·20 | — | ·20 | — | 16 13 1 | 14 13 1 |
| Service of prison, | 7·84 | — | 7·84 | — | 150 16 1 | 150 16 1 |
| Repairing bedding and clothing, | ·21 | — | ·21 | — | 8 11 6 | 8 11 6 |
| Net making, | ·40 | — | ·40 | 6 11 1 | — | 6 11 1 |
| Weavers, | 7·62 | — | 7·62 | 49 5 7 | — | 49 5 7 |
| Oakum picking, | 10·10 | — | 10·10 | 9 0 3 | — | 9 0 3 |
| Firewood, | 11·18 | — | 11·18 | 211 9 9 | — | 211 9 0 |
| Sick, | 9·5 | — | 9·5 | — | — | — |
| Unemployed, | 7·37 | — | 7·37 | — | — | — |
| Total, | 199·66 | — | 199·66 | 1,[illegible] 17 10 | [illegible] 17 9 | 1,867 14 1 |

## MOUNTJOY (FEMALE) PRISON. [LOCAL PRISONERS.]

| | | | | | | |
|---|---|---|---|---|---|---|
| | | | | £ s. d. | £ s. d. | £ s. d. |
| Mat-making, picking coir, &c., | — | ·11 | ·16 | — | 1 10 6 | 1 10 6 |
| Service of prison, | — | 12·99 | 12·64 | — | 137 13 10 | 137 13 10 |
| Washing clothing and bedding, | — | 37·47 | 37·47 | — | 1,515 17 6 | 1,515 17 6 |
| Making bedding and clothing, | — | 11·93 | 11·93 | — | 65 17 9 | 65 17 9 |
| Sick, | — | 2·64 | 2·64 | — | — | — |
| Unemployed, | — | ·85 | ·85 | — | — | — |
| Total, | — | 65·65 | 65·65 | — | 1,[illegible] 5 6 | 1,[illegible] 5 6 |

RETURN by the CHIEF WARDERS, showing how Prisoners have been employed during the year ending 31st March, 1883, and the Earnings of those engaged in each Employment; also showing the average daily number of Unemployed from Sickness and other reasons.

## CARLOW PRISON.

| Description of Employment. | Daily average Number of Prisoners employed, unemployed, &c. Males. | Females. | Total. | Net Profit on Work done by Prisoners. | Estimated Value of the Work done for the Prison. | Total. |
|---|---|---|---|---|---|---|
| | | | | £ s. d. | £ s. d. | £ s. d. |
| Gardening, | 4 | — | 4 | — | — | — |
| Whitewashers, | 4 | — | 4 | — | — | — |
| Service of prison, | 23 | 8 | 31 | — | — | — |
| Washing clothing and bedding, | — | 21 | 21 | — | — | — |
| Picking oakum, | 265 | 9 | 272 | — | — | — |
| Knitting, | — | 10 | 10 | — | — | — |
| Nursing, | — | 14 | 14 | — | — | — |
| Punishment, | 24 | 1 | 25 | — | — | — |
| Sick, | 3 | 10 | 13 | — | — | — |
| Unemployed, | 216 | [illegible] | [illegible] | — | — | — |
| Total, | [illegible] | [illegible] | [illegible] | — | — | — |

In the above table I have given the total numbers of days employed, &c., under each heading, the numbers being so small I could not give a daily average. Net profits unknown.

## CARRICK-ON-SHANNON PRISON.

| | | | | | | |
|---|---|---|---|---|---|---|
| | | | | £ s. d. | £ s. d. | £ s. d. |
| Whitewashers, | ·84 | ·04 | ·88 | — | 6 17 8 | 6 17 8 |
| Pumping water, | ·15 | — | ·15 | — | 5 5 0 | 5 5 0 |
| Service of prison, | 1·[illegible] | ·16 | 1·[illegible] | — | 53 14 0 | 53 14 0 |
| Washing clothing and bedding, | ·13 | ·[illegible] | ·71 | — | 3 5 4 | 3 5 4 |
| Repairing bedding and clothing, | ·[illegible] | ·[illegible] | ·74 | — | 2 7 0 | 2 7 0 |
| Unemployed, | ·74 | ·1[illegible] | ·[illegible] | — | — | — |
| Total, | 2·79 | ·4[illegible] | 3·1[illegible] | — | 67 4 10 | 67 4 10 |

All prisoners employed as opposite their numbers. No profits can be counted on as it requires all prisoners committed here to keep the prison and yards clean, &c.

RETURN by the CHIEF WARDERS, showing how Prisoners have been employed during the year ending 31st March, 1883, and the Earnings of those engaged in each Employment; also showing the average daily number of Unemployed from Sickness and other reasons.

## CAVAN PRISON.

| Description of Employment. | Daily Average Number of Prisoners employed, unemployed, &c. | | | Net Profit on Work done by Prisoners. | Estimated Value of the Work done for the Prison. | Total. |
|---|---|---|---|---|---|---|
| | Males. | Females. | Total. | | | |
| | | | | £ s. d. | £ s. d. | £ s. d. |
| Gardening and labouring, | 1· | — | 1· | — | 7 11 0 | 7 11 0 |
| Whitewashers, | 0·11 | — | 0·11 | — | 7 8 10 | 7 8 10 |
| Pumping water and picking oakum, | 1· | — | 1· | — | [illegible] | [illegible] |
| Service of prison, | 1· | 0·10 | 1·10 | — | [illegible] | [illegible] |
| Washing, clothing, and bedding, | — | 0·30 | 0·30 | — | 11 0 0 | 11 0 0 |
| Knitting and mending, | — | 0·17 | 0·17 | [illegible] | [illegible] | [illegible] |
| Stone-breaking, | 0·22 | — | 0·22 | 0 13 0 | [illegible] | [illegible] |
| Sick, | 0·23 | — | 0·23 | — | — | — |
| Unemployed, | 1· | 0·10 | 1·10 | — | — | — |
| Total, | 4·38 | [illegible] | [illegible] | [illegible] | [illegible] | [illegible] |

The above calculations are on 302 working days at the following rates:—Labourers, 6d.; whitewashers, 1s. 6d.; washers (female), 1s. 6d.; cleaners, 6d.; knitting and mending, 4d.

## ENNIS PRISON.

| | | | | £ s. d. | £ s. d. | £ s. d. |
|---|---|---|---|---|---|---|
| Tailors, | 0·07 | — | 0·07 | — | 3 0 0 | 3 0 0 |
| Shoemakers, | 0·01 | — | 0·01 | — | 0 4 0 | 0 4 0 |
| Carpenters, | 0·04 | — | 0·04 | — | 0 10 0 | 0 10 0 |
| Bricklayers and labourers, | 0·24 | — | 0·24 | — | 4 7 0 | 4 7 0 |
| Painters and glaziers, | 0·04 | — | 0·04 | — | 0 19 0 | 0 19 0 |
| Whitewashers, | 0·11 | — | 0·11 | — | 3 0 0 | 3 0 0 |
| Pumping water, | 0·44 | — | 0·44 | — | 0 14 0 | 0 14 0 |
| Service of prison, | 0·49 | — | 0·49 | — | 0 16 10 | 0 16 10 |
| Washing clothing and bedding, | 0·10 | 0·16 | 0·26 | — | [illegible] | [illegible] |
| Making bedding and clothing, | — | 0·05 | 0·05 | — | 1 5 4 | 1 5 4 |
| Stone-breaking, | [illegible] | — | [illegible] | [illegible] | — | [illegible] |
| Splitting wood, | 0·12 | — | 0·12 | — | 1 16 0 | 1 16 0 |
| Picking oakum, | 0·12 | — | 0·12 | 0 3 6 | — | [illegible] |
| Sick, Unemployed, | 4·24 | 0·01 | 4·25 | — | — | — |
| Total, | [illegible] | [illegible] | [illegible] | [illegible] | [illegible] | [illegible] |

**Return by the Chief Warders, showing how Prisoners have been employed during the year ending 31st March, 1883, and the Earnings of those engaged in such Employment; also showing the average daily number of Unemployed from Sickness and other reasons.**

## ENNISKILLEN PRISON.

| Description of Employment. | Daily Average Number of Prisoners employed, unemployed, &c. Males. | Females. | Total. | Net Profit on Work done by Prisoners. | Estimated Value of the Work done for the Prison. | Total. |
|---|---|---|---|---|---|---|
| | | | | £ s. d. | £ s. d. | £ s. d. |
| Gardening, Tailors, Shoemakers, | 1 | — | 1 | [illegible] | [illegible] | 10 13 6 |
| Service of prison, | [illegible] | — | 3 | [illegible] | [illegible] | [illegible] |
| Washing, clothing, and bedding, | 1 | — | 1 | [illegible] | [illegible] | [illegible] |
| Repairing bedding and clothing, Knitting and sewing, | — | 1 | 1 | [illegible] | [illegible] | [illegible] |
| Cooking, | 1 | — | 1 | [illegible] | [illegible] | [illegible] |
| Splitting wood and whitewashing, | 1 | — | 1 | [illegible] | [illegible] | [illegible] |
| Sick,* | — | — | — | — | — | — |
| Total, | [illegible] | 1 | [illegible] | [illegible] | [illegible] | [illegible] |

* For 105 days, one sick.

Had not males enough to average one daily for each employment. Had not females to average one daily.

## LIFFORD PRISON.

| | | | | | | |
|---|---|---|---|---|---|---|
| | | | | £ s. d. | £ s. d. | £ s. d. |
| Service of prison, | 1 | — | 1 | — | 7 16 6 | 7 16 6 |
| Total, | 1 | — | 1 | — | 7 16 6 | 7 16 6 |

I calculated on 313 days at 6d. per day for all work done by prisoners such as whitewashing, splitting wood, and cleaning prison.

## LONGFORD PRISON.

| | | | | | | |
|---|---|---|---|---|---|---|
| | | | | £ s. d. | £ s. d. | £ s. d. |
| Gardening, | ·52 | — | ·52 | 5 0 0 | 2 0 0 | 7 0 0 |
| Whitewashers, | ·07 | — | ·07 | — | 1 [illegible] 0 | 1 [illegible] [illegible] |
| Service of prison, | ·96 | ·19 | 1·15 | — | 18 7 0 | [illegible] 7 0 |
| Washing clothing and bedding, | — | ·14 | ·14 | — | 1 11 10 | 1 11 10 |
| Repairing bedding and clothing, | — | ·10 | ·10 | — | [illegible] | [illegible] |
| Picking oakum, | ·85 | — | ·85 | — | [illegible] | [illegible] |
| Sick, | ·01 | — | ·01 | — | — | — |
| Unemployed, | ·56 | ·23 | ·79 | — | — | — |
| Total, | [illegible] | ·71 | [illegible] | 5 0 0 | [illegible] | [illegible] |

**Return** by the **Chief Warders**, showing how Prisoners have been employed during the year ending 31st March, 1882, and the Earnings of those engaged in each Employment; also showing the average daily number of Unemployed from Sickness and other reasons.

### MONAGHAN PRISON.

| Description of Employment. | Daily Average Number of Prisoners employed, unemployed, &c. – Males. | Females. | Total. | Net Profit on Work done by Prisoners. £ s. d. | Estimated Value of the Work done for the Prison. £ s. d. | Total. £ s. d. |
|---|---|---|---|---|---|---|
| Gardening, Tailors, Shoemakers, Carpenters, Bricklayers and Labourers, | 1 | — | 1 | — | 20 10 0 | 20 10 0 |
| Whitewashers, | 3 | — | 3 | — | 30 [illegible] 0 | 30 [illegible] 0 |
| Pumping water, | 1 | — | 1 | — | 13 [illegible] 0 | 13 [illegible] 0 |
| Service of prison, | 3 | — | 3 | 7 0 10* | 30 10 0 | 37 10 10 |
| Washing clothing and bedding, Making bedding and clothing, Repairing bedding and clothing, | — | 1 | 1 | — | 15 0 0 | 15 0 0 |
| Sick, | 1 | — | 1 | — | — | — |
| Unemployed, | 7 | — | 7 | — | — | — |
| **Total**, | 14 | 1 | 15 | 7 0 10 | 117 5 0 | 124 5 10 |

* This was money paid by the P.P.P. Prisoners for the cleaning of their cells, &c.

This prison was closed immediately after the P.P.P. Prisoners were transferred from this prison on the 14th June, 1882.

The unemployed were P.P.P. Prisoners.

### ROSCOMMON PRISON.

| Description of Employment. | Males. | Females. | Total. | Net Profit on Work done by Prisoners. £ s. d. | Estimated Value of the Work done for the Prison. £ s. d. | Total. £ s. d. |
|---|---|---|---|---|---|---|
| Gardening, | 0·2 | — | 0·2 | 3 3 3 | 6 16 0 | 9 1 [illegible] |
| Tailors, | 0·07 | — | 0·07 | — | 4 [illegible] 0 | [illegible] |
| Shoemakers, | | | | — | 0 13 0 | 0 13 0 |
| Labourers, | 0·4 | — | 0·4 | — | 2 18 0 | 2 18 0 |
| Painters, | 0·1 | — | 0·1 | — | 1 [illegible] 0 | 1 4 0 |
| Whitewashers, | | | | — | 0 [illegible] 0 | [illegible] |
| Pumping water, | 1·2 | 0·2 | 1·4 | — | 1 12 0 | 1 12 0 |
| Service of prison, | | | | — | 0 11 0 | 0 11 0 |
| Washing clothing and bedding, Making bedding and clothing, Repairing bedding and clothing, | — | 0·2 | 0·2 | — | 3 18 0 | 3 18 0 |
| Sick, | 0·22 | 0·04 | 0·26 | — | — | — |
| Unemployed, | 0·58 | 0·2 | 0·78 | — | — | — |
| **Total**, | 2·7[illegible] | 0·[illegible]4 | 3·81 | 3 3 3 | [illegible] 4 0 | [illegible] |

**Return by the Chief Warder, showing how Prisoners have been Employed during the year ending 31st March, 1883, and the Earnings of those engaged in such Employment; also showing the average daily number of Unemployed from Sickness and other reasons.**

## TRIM PRISON.

| Description of Employment. | Daily Average Number of Prisoners employed, unemployed, &c. | | | Net Earnings of Work done by Prisoners. | Estimated Value of the Work done for the Prison. | Total. |
|---|---|---|---|---|---|---|
| | Males. | Females. | Total. | | | |
| | | | | £ s. d. | £ s. d. | £ s. d. |
| Gardening, | 2 | — | 2 | [illegible] 9 0 | 1 8 0 | 10 5 6 |
| Service of prison, | ·24 | ·0041 | ·3041 | — | 2 13 6 | 2 10 0 |
| Washing clothing and bedding. Making bedding and clothing. Repairing bedding and clothing. | — | ·5041 | ·5041 | — | 2 10 0 | 2 10 0 |
| Stone-breaking, &c., | 4 | — | 4 | — | 2 15 0 | 2 15 0 |
| Unemployed, | ·24 | — | ·25 | — | — | — |
| Total, | 3 | ·9082 | [illegible] | 24 1 0 | 6 3 6 | 31 1 0 |

I had the stones raised from the garden for breaking, which is also making the ground arable.

## WICKLOW PRISON.

| | | | | | | |
|---|---|---|---|---|---|---|
| | | | | £ s. d. | £ s. d. | £ s. d. |
| Tailors, | [illegible] | — | [illegible] | — | [illegible] | [illegible] |
| Carpenters and glaziers, | [illegible] | — | [illegible] | — | [illegible] | [illegible] |
| Whitewashers, | [illegible] | — | [illegible] | — | [illegible] | [illegible] |
| Pumping water, | ·128 | — | [illegible] | — | [illegible] | [illegible] |
| Service of prison, | [illegible] | [illegible] | [illegible] | — | [illegible] | [illegible] |
| Washing clothing and bedding, | — | [illegible] | [illegible] | — | [illegible] | [illegible] |
| Picking oakum, | [illegible] | — | [illegible] | — | — | — |
| Knitting, | — | [illegible] | [illegible] | — | — | — |
| Knitting, | — | [illegible] | [illegible] | — | [illegible] | [illegible] |
| Sick, Unemployed, | [illegible] | [illegible] | [illegible] | — | — | — |
| Total, | [illegible] | [illegible] | [illegible] | — | [illegible] | [illegible] |

# B.—CONVICT PRISONS.

## 1.—MOUNTJOY MALE CONVICT PRISON.

### GOVERNOR'S REPORT.

Mountjoy Male Convict Prison,
June, 1883.

GENTLEMEN,—I have the honour to forward herewith the statistical returns for this prison for the year ending 31st March, 1883.

As the Mountjoy Prison is being now re-organized, I beg merely to report that the rules laid down for the management of the prison have been strictly complied with, with the exception of such particular cases as have been reported and brought under the notice of the General Prison Board.

I have the honour to be, gentlemen,
Your obedient servant,
P. W. HACKETT, Governor.

The General Prisons Board (Ireland),
Dublin Castle.

CLASSIFIED STATEMENT of the NUMBER of OFFENCES committed by the Convicts during the year ended 31st March, 1883.

| Offences. | No. | Offences. | No. |
|---|---|---|---|
| Assaults on Officers, - - - | 3 | Insubordination, - - - - | 6 |
| Assaults on convicts, - - - | 21 | Insolence, - - - - - | 1 |
| Attempts to escape, - - - | 1 | Idleness, - - - - - | 6 |
| Attempt at suicide, feigned, - - | 1 | Injuring prison property, - - | 15 |
| Disobedience, - - - - | 30 | Prohibited articles, - - - | 9 |
| Disobedience and insolence, - - | 4 | Theft, - - - - - | 1 |
| Disorderly conduct, - - - | 8 | Other offences, - - - - | 113 |
| Fighting, - - - - - | 4 | | |
| Gross insubordination, - - - | [illegible] | Total, - - - | 265 |

CLASSIFICATION of CRIMES for which those Convicts have been sentenced who were received during the year ended 31st March, 1883.

| Crimes. | No. | Crimes. | No. |
|---|---|---|---|
| Abduction, - - - - - | 1 | Burglary, - - - - - - | 9 |
| Assault, - - - - - | 4 | Burglary in a Roman Catholic chapel and in a school-room and former conviction, - - - - | 1 |
| Assault with intent to commit robbery, - - - - - | 1 | Burglary and previous conviction, - | 6 |
| Assault with intent to rob, - - | 2 | Breaking and entering counting-house, - - - - - | 2 |
| Assault on police, - - - - | 4 | Breaking into church and larceny, | 2 |
| Assault, bodily harm, - - - | 3 | Breaking and entering shop and previous conviction, - - - | 1 |
| Assault, grievous bodily harm, - | 1 | Bigamy, - - - - - - | 3 |
| Assault and robbery, - - - | 3 | Cattle stealing, - - - - | 4 |
| Attack and fire shots into house, - | 1 | Coining, - - - - - - | 1 |
| Arson, - - - - - - | 3 | Conspiracy to murder, - - - | 1 |
| Attempt to do grievous bodily harm, | 1 | | |
| Breaking and entering a dwelling-house with intent, - - - | 1 | | |

MOUNTJOY MALE CONVICT PRISON.

Governor's Report.

CLASSIFICATION of CRIMES for which those Convicts have been sentenced who were received during the year ended 31st March, 1883—*continued.*

| Crimes. | No. | Crimes. | No. |
|---|---|---|---|
| Felony, - - - - - | 2 | Manslaughter on the high seas, - | 3 |
| Felonious assault with intent to rob, | 1 | Malicious wounding, - - - | 1 |
| Felony of money [?], - - - - | 1 | Military offences, - - - - | 43 |
| Firing at with intent to kill and murder, - - - - - | 4 | Obtaining money under false pretences, - - - - - | 2 |
| Felony of a gun [?], - - - - | 1 | Occasioning actual bodily harm with intent, - - - - | 1 |
| Feloniously wounding [?], - - - | 1 | Robbery, person, - - - - | 6 |
| Forming a disguised party, threatening, and carry away arms, - | 2 | Robbery with violence, - - - | 16 |
| Forgery and uttering cheques, | 1 | Robbery, - - - - - | 1 |
| Forgery, - - - - - | 3 | Rape, - - - - - | 5 |
| Having implements of coining, | 1 | Receiving stolen goods, - - - | 3 |
| Having implements of housebreaking, - - - - - | 2 | Stealing sheep, - - - - | 2 |
| Housebreaking, - - - - - | 13 | Stabbing and endangering life, - | 1 |
| Housebreaking and larceny, - - | 4 | Shooting at with intent to do grievous bodily harm, - - | 1 |
| Housebreaking and former conviction, - - - - - | 3 | Stealing [illegible], - - - - | 1 |
| Housebreaking and robbery, - | 6 | Threatening a witness to prevent her giving evidence, - - - | 1 |
| Horse stealing, - - - - | 1 | Unlawful assembly and breaking into house, - - - - - | 8 |
| Indecent assault, - - - - - | 1 | Uttering base coin, - - - - | 2 |
| Larceny, - - - - - | 31 | Uttering forged certificate of death, | 1 |
| Larceny after previous conviction for felony, - - - - - | 1 | Unlawful assembly by night being armed, and assaulting dwelling-house, - - - - - | 1 |
| Larceny with violence, - - - | 1 | Wounding, - - - - - | 3 |
| Larceny from the person, - - | 18 | Whiteboy offences, - - - - | 6 |
| Larceny [illegible] and previous convictions, - - - - - | 1 | Wounding to maim, - - - - | 1 |
| Larceny, exhib. - - - - - | 1 | Wounding with intent to maim, - | 1 |
| Larceny and previous conviction, - | 52 | Wounding with intent to murder, - | 5 |
| Larceny and receiving, - - - | 1 | Writing and publishing threatening notices, - - - - - | 1 |
| Larceny from the person and previous conviction, - - - | 4 | | |
| Murder, - - - - - | 8 | | |
| Manslaughter, - - - - - | 15 | Total, - - - | 320 |

NUMBER of CONVICTS admitted in association during the year ended 31st March, 1883.

| Trades. | No. | Trades. | No. |
|---|---|---|---|
| Received:— | | Removed, viz.:— | |
| Carpenters, - - - - - | 3 | Carpenters, - - - - - | 3 |
| Coopers, - - - - - | 1 | Labourers - - - - - | 27 |
| Labourers, - - - - - | 31 | Masons, - - - - - | 4 |
| Painters, - - - - - | 3 | Plasterers, - - - - - | 8 |
| Smiths, - - - - - | 3 | Painters, - - - - - | 1 |
| Shoemakers, - - - - - | 4 | Plumbers, - - - - - | 1 |
| Tailors, - - - - - | 10 | Shoemakers, - - - - - | 14 |
| Tinsmiths, - - - - - | 1 | Tailors, - - - - - | 16 |
| Remaining on 31st March, 1882, - | 63 | Tinsmiths, - - - - - | 5 |
| | | Weavers, - - - - - | 1 |
| | | Remaining on 31st March, 1883, - | 33 |

MOUNTJOY MALE CONVICT PRISON.

*Governor's Report.*

RETURN showing how CONVICTS have been Employed during the year ended 31st March, 1863, and the Earnings of those engaged in each employment; also showing the average daily number of Unemployed from sickness and other reasons.

| Description of Employment. | Daily Average Number of Prisoners employed, unemployed, &c. | Net Profit on Work done by Prisoners. | Estimated Value of the Work done for the Prison. | Total. |
|---|---|---|---|---|
| | | £ s. d. | £ s. d. | £ s. d. |
| Mat-making, &c., | 38·3 | 166 14 5 | — | 166 14 5 |
| Labourers, gardening, &c., | 25·5 | — | 487 3 1 | 487 3 1 |
| Tailors, | 30·47 | 411 14 0 | — | 411 14 0 |
| Shoemakers, | 35·40 | 261 18 8 | — | 261 18 8 |
| Carpenters, | 1·47 | — | 183 4 0 | 183 4 0 |
| Smiths and tinsmiths, | 2·48 | 24 13 0 | — | 24 13 0 |
| Masons, | 1·31 | — | 67 8 11 | 67 8 11 |
| Coopers, | ·21 | — | 7 19 1 | 7 19 1 |
| Painters, | 1·47 | — | 40 16 0 | 40 16 0 |
| Picking oakum, | 57·36 | 9 0 7 | — | 9 0 7 |
| Chopping firewood, | 8·40 | 46 1 3 | — | 46 1 3 |
| Service of prison, | 13·58 | — | 884 3 10 | 884 3 10 |
| Picking fibre, &c., | 33·34 | — | 872 19 8 | 872 19 8 |
| Making bedding, | 3·11 | — | 104 15 4 | 104 15 4 |
| Not employed—Punishment, | 1·12 | — | — | — |
| " Sick, &c., | 1·37 | — | — | — |
| " Lodged,* | ·66 | — | — | — |
| Total, | 253·76 | 940 13 3 | 2,042 3 3 | 2,996 18 6 |

* Received from Spike Island Prison for removal to Lusk Prison, or for discharge on completion of sentence.

## RETURN of WORK for the year ended 31st March, 1863.

### SHOEMAKING DEPARTMENT.

*Making.*

| | | |
|---|---|---|
| Blucher boots, | pairs | 725 |
| Navy " | " | 46 |
| Women's " | " | 6 |
| Men's shoes, | " | 1,460 |
| Women's shoes, | " | 467 |
| Warders' slippers, | " | 74 |
| Matrons " | " | 61 |
| Frieze " | " | 318 |
| Canvas " | " | 460 |
| Shoe laces, | doz. | 130 |
| Strait jacket, | | 1 |
| Warders' belts, | | 145 |

*Repairing.*

| | | |
|---|---|---|
| Men's shoes, | pairs | 1,083 |
| Warders' boots, | " | 138 |
| " slippers, | " | 17 |
| Hammocks, | | 44 |

### TAILORING DEPARTMENT.

*Making.*

| | |
|---|---|
| Warders' tunics, | 417 |
| " trousers, | 584 |
| " capes, | 484 |
| " top coats, | 268 |
| " tweed suits, | 38 |
| Serge suits, | 168 |
| Frieze jackets, | 2,000 |
| " trousers, | 2,513 |
| " vests, | 1,156 |
| " caps, | 2,227 |
| " braces, pairs | 2,280 |
| Satin P. O. frieze, | 54 |
| Canvas suits, | 112 |
| Hospital suits, | 70 |
| Cord trousers, | 54 |
| Barragon vests, | 98 |
| Women's canvas dresses, | 6 |
| Badges lined, | 218 |

*Repairing.*

| | | |
|---|---|---|
| Warders' uniforms, | pieces | 115 |
| Prisoners' clothing, | " | 1,769 |

### MAT, MATTING, &c., DEPARTMENT.

3,239 Brush mats, 60,661 lbs.
1,864 Chain mats, 6,493 lbs.
1,485 Bordered mats, 5,070 super. feet.
44 Wool mats.
102 Hearth rugs.
1,077 Square yards matting.
300 Feed-offs.
79 Coir scrubs.
1,412 Cell brushes.
144½ cwt. oakum picked.
1,349 Nets made.
2,537 gross firewood (fine).
185½ cwt. " (coarse).

MOUNTJOY MALE CONVICT PRISON.

Governor's Report.

RETURN OF WORK for the year ended 31st March, 1883—*continued.*

TINSMITHS, &c.

*Making.*

| | | | |
|---|---|---|---|
| Gallon measures, | 11 | Tin plates, | 183 |
| Pint „ | 16 | „ cans, | 10 |
| ½ „ „ | 62 | „ scoops, | 309 |
| ¼ „ „ | 30 | „ cases, | 6 |
| Pint tins, | 165 | Zinc chambers, | 783 |
| ½ „ „ | 225 | „ basins, | 73 |
| Quart „ | 2,047 | | |

*Repairing.*

| | |
|---|---|
| Tin vessels, | 1,187 |
| Zinc „ | 103 |

STATEMENT of the NUMBER of CONVICTS committed and disposed of, from 1st April, 1882, to 31st March, 1883.

| Received— | No. | Removed— | No. |
|---|---|---|---|
| Convict depôts, | 133 | Convict depôts, | 139 |
| Local prisons, | 200 | Discharged, | 65 |
| Licence revoked cases, | 18 | Died, | 1 |
| Military barracks, | 50 | Dundrum Lunatic Asylum, | 3 |
| Dundrum Lunatic Asylum, | 1 | Commutation of sentence, | 1 |
| Gosport Prison, | 1 | Local Prisons, | 7 |
| In custody on 31st March, 1882, | 243 | Convict Prisons, England, | 46 |
| | | Remaining in custody on 31st March, 1883, | 216 |
| | 646 | | 646 |

TABLE showing the reported PREVIOUS IMPRISONMENTS of the Convicts received during the year ended 31st March, 1883.

| | | | |
|---|---|---|---|
| Not reported to have been in prison before, | 93 | Seven times, | 6 |
| Once, | 41 | Eight „ | 6 |
| Twice, | 43 | Nine „ | 5 |
| Three times, | 28 | Ten and under fifteen times, | 10 |
| Four „ | 35 | Fifteen times and over, | 10 |
| Five „ | 20 | Antecedents not known, | 74 |
| Six „ | 13 | Total, | 330 |

AGES of CONVICTS on CONVICTION, received during the year ended 31st March, 1883.

| | | | |
|---|---|---|---|
| Fifteen and under twenty years of age, | 44 | Fifty and under sixty, | 5 |
| Twenty and under twenty-five, | 134 | Sixty and over, | 11 |
| Twenty-five and under thirty, | 67 | | |
| Thirty and under forty, | 60 | Total, | 330 |
| Forty and under fifty, | 27 | | |

SENTENCES of the CONVICTS committed to the Prison during the year ended 31st March, 1883.

| | | | |
|---|---|---|---|
| Five years' penal servitude, | 214 | Twenty years' penal servitude, | 4 |
| Seven „ „ | 68 | Thirty „ „ | 1 |
| Eight „ „ | 1 | Life, „ „ | 14 |
| Ten „ „ | 21 | | |
| Fourteen „ „ | 2 | Total, | 330 |
| Fifteen, „ „ | 5 | | |

Single, 256. Married, 74.

Roman Catholics, 233. Protestants, 84. Presbyterians, 13.

NUMBER of CONVICT PRISONERS on the 1st day of each month during the year ended 31st March, 1883.

| | | | |
|---|---|---|---|
| 1st April, 1882, | 242 | 1st October, 1882, | 229 |
| „ May, „ | 243 | „ November, „ | 241 |
| „ June, „ | 253 | „ December, „ | 270 |
| „ July, „ | 248 | „ January, 1883, | 240 |
| „ August, „ | 246 | „ February, „ | 241 |
| „ September, „ | 224 | „ March, „ | 233 |

MOUNTJOY MALE CONVICT PRISON.
—
Governor's Report.

STATISTICAL RETURN of Mountjoy Male Prison School for the year ending 31st March, 1883.

| | Convicts. | Local Prisoners. |
|---|---|---|
| Number on the rolls on the 31st March, 1882, | 169 | 43 |
| Number admitted during the year, | 234 | 96 |
| Number transferred from this school to other prisons, | 171 | 3 |
| Number on the rolls on the 31st March, 1883, | 116 | 43 |

Promotions during the year.

| | Convicts. | Local Prisoners. |
|---|---|---|
| Advanced from First to Second Book, | 62 | 19 |
| " Second to Third Book, | 64 | 30 |
| " Third to higher Books, | 17 | – |
| Totals of promotions, | 143 | 49 |

TABLE showing the proficiency attained by the Prisoners who passed through the School during the above year.

| Subjects examined in and Proficiency attained. | Numbers. | | | | Percentage. | | | |
|---|---|---|---|---|---|---|---|---|
| | On Admission. | | On Removal. | | On Admission. | | On Removal. | |
| | Convicts. | Local Prisoners. | Convicts. | Local Prisoners. | Convicts. | Local Prisoners. | Convicts. | Local Prisoners. |
| **Reading:** | | | | | | | | |
| Not able, | 55 | 41 | 9 | 1 | 24·8 | 43·2 | 5·3 | 33·3 |
| Badly, | 70 | 40 | 35 | 1 | 29·9 | 42·1 | 21·1 | 33·3 |
| Fairly, | 108 | 14 | 128 | 1 | 45·3 | 14·7 | 73·6 | 33·3 |
| Totals, | 234 | 95 | 171 | 3 | 100·0 | 100·0 | 100·0 | 100·0 |
| **Writing:** | | | | | | | | |
| Not able, | 56 | 41 | 9 | 1 | 24·8 | 43·2 | 5·3 | 33·3 |
| Badly, | 70 | 40 | 34 | 1 | 29·9 | 42·1 | 21·1 | 33·3 |
| Fairly, | 109 | 14 | 127 | 1 | 45·3 | 14·7 | 73·6 | 33·3 |
| Totals, | 234 | 95 | 171 | 3 | 100·0 | 100·0 | 100·0 | 100·0 |
| **Arithmetic:** | | | | | | | | |
| Perfectly ignorant of, | 55 | 41 | 9 | 1 | 24·8 | 43·2 | 5·3 | 33·3 |
| Simple Rules, | 70 | 40 | 35 | 1 | 29·9 | 42·1 | 21·1 | 33·3 |
| Compound Rules, | 71 | 14 | 10 | 1 | 30·3 | 14·7 | 40·9 | 33·3 |
| Above Compound Rules, | 38 | – | 58 | – | 15·0 | – | 33·7 | – |
| Totals, | 234 | 95 | 171 | 3 | 100·0 | 100·0 | 100·0 | 100·0 |

## MEDICAL OFFICER'S REPORT.

*Mountjoy Male Convict Prison. — Medical Officer's Report.*

Mountjoy Male Prison,
April, 1883.

SIR,—I have the honour to submit the annual report on the state of health of the officers and prisoners, as well as the usual medical statistics for the year ending 31st March, 1883.

Thirty-seven officers were on the sick list at intervals during the year, and three were discharged on the ground of ill-health.

Of the forty-six prisoners admitted to hospital the cases were not of a very grave character with one exception which terminated fatally from pulmonary consumption.

Seven prisoners from the Lusk establishment were treated in hospital, but they are not included in the medical statistics.

Three cases of mania occurred, which were sent to the Central Asylum.

I am happy to say there has not been any outbreak of infectious or contagious disease during the year.

I have to acknowledge the prompt and efficient aid rendered to me by all the officers in the execution of my duties.

I have the honour to be, sir,

Your obedient servant,

J. W. YOUNG, M.D., Medical Officer.

The Chairman, General Prisons Board, Dublin Castle.

---

TABLE I.—HOSPITAL RETURN for the year ending 31st March, 1883.

| | | | |
|---|---|---|---|
| Number of patients in hospital, 1st April, 1882, | - | 2 | 48 |
| admitted during the year, | - | 46 | |
| discharged | - | 41 | 48 |
| sent to Lunatic Asylum, | - | 3 | |
| died in hospital, | - | 1 | |
| in hospital, 1st April, 1883, | - | 3 | |
| Daily average in hospital, | - | | 5 |
| Extras prescribed for, | - | | 1,913 |
| Daily average prescribed for, | - | | 5·31 |

TABLE II.—DISEASES of those admitted to HOSPITAL.

| | | | |
|---|---|---|---|
| Pulmonic, | 6 | Mania, | 3 |
| Stricture, | 1 | Syphilis, | 1 |
| Heart, | 3 | Piles, | 1 |
| Observation, | 2 | Abscess, | 6 |
| Scrofula, | 3 | Wounds, | 3 |
| Hernia, | 1 | Diarrhœa, | 1 |
| Podagra, | 1 | Jaundice, | 1 |
| Ulcer, | 2 | Otalgia, | 2 |
| Tape Worm, | 1 | Burns, | 1 |
| Ophthalmia, | 1 | Dyspepsia, | 1 |
| Febrile, | 2 | Gastric, | 3 |
| Debility, | 5 | Scald, | 1 |

*MOUNTJOY MALE CONVICT PRISON. — Medical Officer's Report.*

TABLE III.—DEATHS during the year.

| Register No. | Initials of Name. | Received in Prison. | Admitted to Hospital. | Died. | Cause of Death. |
|---|---|---|---|---|---|
| A 530 | W. O'B. | 24 July, 1882, | 11 Sep., 1882, | 26 Oct., 1882, | Phthisis. |

TABLE IV.—CONVICTS sent to Central Lunatic Asylum.

| Register No. | Initials of Name. | Where Convicted. | Date of Conviction. | Removal to Prison. | Transferred to Asylum. |
|---|---|---|---|---|---|
| A 432 | M. B. | Limerick, . | 9 Mar., 1882, | 16 Mar., 1882, | 6 April, 1882, |
| A 348 | P. G. | Wicklow, . | 1 Nov., 1881, | 8 Nov., 1881, | 14 July, ,, |
| A 537 | L. M. | Cork, . . | 23 July, 1882, | 14 Aug., 1882, | 30 October, ,, |

*Protestant Chaplain's Report.*

## PROTESTANT CHAPLAIN'S REPORT.

H.M. Prison, Mountjoy, Dublin,
May, 1883.

SIR,—I have to state, as heretofore, that during the past year the services of the Church have been held, religious instruction given, and the prisoners visited in their cells. The demeanour of the prisoners at Divine service was orderly and attentive, and to me personally, as I visited them, was most respectful and gratifying. There has been, however, more than ordinary breach of Prison rules, and consequently more than usual punishment inflicted upon prisoners, to be accounted for by the fact that a large class of habitually ill-conducted men has been sent here for special treatment and supervision. Beyond this, I have nothing special to remark.

I am, sir, your faithful servant,

ROBERT FLEMING, M.A.,

Chaplain, Irish Church.

The Chairman, General Prisons Board, Dublin Castle.

---

*Roman Catholic Chaplain's Report.*

## ROMAN CATHOLIC CHAPLAIN'S REPORT.

Mountjoy Male Prison,
9th May, 1883.

The Chairman, Prisons Board.

SIR,—I beg to submit my report for the year commencing 1st April, 1882, and ending 31st March, 1883.

The conduct of the prisoners entrusted to my care has, all the circumstances considered, been as good as might be expected. I have been satisfied with the docility of the prisoners in receiving religious instruction, as also with their good will and earnest desire in availing themselves of the other services of my ministry.

Individuals in the class of prisoners, sent here for misconduct from Spike Island, have done some mischief by occasionally breaking forth

Mountjoy Male Convict Prison. — Roman Catholic Chaplain's Report.

into stormy outbursts of passion and the use of improper language, especially during dinner hours. Men of this kind are, in my opinion, as far from being incorrigible as almost any other class of convicts when properly treated; because they have deep down in the heart the true Catholic faith, and most firmly believe the great truths of religion, death, judgment, eternal happiness, and eternal misery in the next world. I do not remember meeting any prisoner, whose faith had not been tampered with, whom I believed absolutely incorrigible. I am persuaded that a fairly good, I will not say the best, prison system, worked by men really qualified to work it, prudent, patient, kind, having sympathy with the prisoners under them, and firm when necessary, would be successful in reforming no small number of those who are imprisoned. Very much for good or evil depends upon the men selected and employed in working the prison machinery. With them it rest, in a great measure, to prevent prison offences and prison crimes, or to create and nurture them.

I have no doubt whatever that the best persons to be employed in disposing R.C. prisoners for moral reformation are fit and proper R.C. officers. The constant and close relations existing between R.C. prisoners and warders of a different persuasion is calculated, more or less, to induce a certain indifference to all religion, and so far tends to destroy or weaken the hope of moral improvement.

In making these observations I have in view, solely, the general good; private interests are of very little importance compared with the interest the State has in the reclamation of its criminal population.

I beg to express my grateful sense of the ready and obliging manner and willing services which I experienced from all the officials of the Prison, and to add, in conclusion, that every facility was given me in the exercise of my ministry during the year.

I have the honour to be, sir,

Your most obedient servant,

MICHAEL CODY, R.C. Chaplain.

---

## PRESBYTERIAN CHAPLAIN'S REPORT.

Presbyterian Chaplain's Report.

Mountjoy Government Prison,
May, 1883.

SIR,—In reviewing the entries in my journal, I find nothing of special importance, or exceptional, to report. All the duties of my chaplaincy have been regularly performed. Divine service has been conducted every Sabbath day; religious instruction imparted to the convicts every Thursday, and cellular visits paid to prisoners on each Tuesday.

I have been enabled to attend to these exercises generally myself, and in my necessary or permitted absence, by one of the ministers whose names were submitted to, and sanctioned by the Board.

Marked attention has been always given to my ministrations; and, I think, with considerable pleasing results.

As hitherto, every facility has been rendered to me by all the officers for the satisfactory discharge of my duties.

I am, sir, your obedient servant,

S. G. MORRISON,

Presbyterian Chaplain.

The Chairman, General Prisons Board, Dublin Castle.

*Mountjoy Female Convict Prison.*

*Superintendent's Report.*

## MOUNTJOY FEMALE CONVICT PRISON.

### SUPERINTENDENT'S REPORT.

Mountjoy Female Prison,
5th June, 1883.

Sir,—I have the honour to submit my report on this Prison for the year ended 31st March, 1883, with usual statistical returns.

The conduct of the officers has been satisfactory, and the prisoners, with few exceptions, were well behaved and industrious.

No change has taken place in the routine of this Prison during the year.

I certify that the rules laid down for the government of the prison have been complied with.

I have the honour to be, sir,
Your obedient servant,
Anne Sheeran, Superintendent.

The Chairman, General Prisons Board, Dublin Castle.

---

Return of the Number of Convicts received and disposed of from 1st April, 1882, to 31st March, 1883.

| | Convicts. | Children. |
|---|---|---|
| In confinement 1st April, 1882, | 108 | – |
| Received during the year, | 36 | 2 |
| Born, | – | 2 |
| Total, | 144 | 4 |
| Discharged, sentence completed, | 8 | – |
| Discharged on license, | 10 | – |
| Transferred to Lunatic asylum, | 3 | – |
| Transferred to Refuges, viz.:—Protestant, 1; Roman Catholics, 15, | 16 | – |
| Died, | 2 | 1 |
| Sent to Nurse, | – | 1 |
| Total disposed of, | 43 | 2 |
| Remaining in custody 31st March, 1883, | 101 | 2 |

AGES (ON CONVICTION) OF CONVICTS NOW IN CUSTODY.

| | |
|---|---|
| 16 years and under 20 years, | 8 |
| 20 " 25 " | 10 |
| 25 " 30 " | 17 |
| 30 " 35 " | 18 |
| 35 " 40 " | 5 |
| 40 " 45 " | 16 |
| 45 years and upwards, | 27 |
| Total, | 101 |

Age of oldest prisoner on conviction, 70 years.

Age of youngest prisoner on conviction, 16 years.

NUMBER OF CONVICTS NOW IN CUSTODY WHO WERE CONVICTED IN THE FOLLOWING YEARS.

| | |
|---|---|
| In the year 1864, | 1 |
| " 1866, | 1 |
| " 1871, | 1 |
| " 1872, | 3 |
| " 1873, | 1 |
| " 1874, | 1 |
| " 1875, | 4 |
| " 1876, | 5 |
| " 1877, | 6 |
| " 1878, | 5 |
| " 1879, | 9 |
| " 1880, | 13 |
| " 1881, | 19 |
| " 1882, | 24 |
| " 1883, | 2 |
| Total, | 101 |

MOUNTJOY FEMALE CONVICT PRISON.

*Superintendent's Report.*

SENTENCES of PRISONERS now in CUSTODY.

| | | | |
|---|---|---|---|
| Penal Servitude for Life, | 19 | Penal Servitude for 7 years, | [illegible] |
| " 20 years, | 9 | " 5 " | 60 |
| " 10 " | 4 | | |
| " 8 " | 1 | Total, | 101 |

CRIMES of PRISONERS now in CUSTODY.

| | | | |
|---|---|---|---|
| Administering poison, | 1 | Manslaughter, | 9 |
| Assault and robbery, | 4 | Murder, | 16 |
| Arson, | 1 | Receiving stolen goods, and previous conviction, | 1 |
| Bigamy, | 2 | Stealing money from person, | 3 |
| Child stealing, | 1 | Stabbing and endangering life, | 1 |
| Feloniously receiving stolen goods, | 2 | Theft and robbery, | 1 |
| Felony, | 3 | | |
| Felony, and previous conviction, | 4 | | |
| Larceny, | 38 | Total, | 101 |
| Larceny, and previous conviction, | 23 | | |

Number of CONVICTS in CUSTODY on the first day of each month during the year ended 31st March, 1883.

| | | | |
|---|---|---|---|
| April, | 109 | October, | 110 |
| May, | 103 | November, | 108 |
| June, | 108 | December, | 108 |
| July, | 109 | January, | 105 |
| August, | 118 | February, | 104 |
| September, | 116 | March, | 103 |

SCHOOL.

*School.*

| | |
|---|---|
| Number of days on which prisoners were taught, | 307 |
| Average on rolls for the year, | 99 |
| Average daily attendance, | 83 |
| Newly admitted, | 29 |

Those received during the year were examined on reception, and classified as under:—

| | |
|---|---|
| First Book, wholly illiterate, | 15 |
| Able to read badly, | 5 |
| " fairly, | 9 |
| Total, | 29 |

The annexed table shows the advances in the several classes:—

Advanced during the year:—

| | |
|---|---|
| From First to Second Book, | 10 |
| " Second to Third " | 16 |
| " Third to Fourth " | 18 |
| Learned to write, | 19 |
| " to make figures, | 17 |
| Advanced from Simple Addition to Simple Subtraction, | 13 |
| " to Compound Rules, | 9 |

RETURN by the SUPERINTENDENT, showing how Convicts have been Employed during the year ending 31st March, 1883, and the Earnings of those engaged in such Employment; also showing the average daily number of Unemployed from Sickness and other causes.

| Description of Employment. | Daily Average Number of Prisoners employed, unemployed, &c. | | | Net Profit on Work done by Prisoners. | Estimated Value of the Work done for the Prison. | Total. |
|---|---|---|---|---|---|---|
| | Males. | Females. | Total. | £ s. d. | £ s. d. | £ s. d. |
| Tailors, | — | [illegible] | [illegible] | — | 12 14 4 | 12 14 4 |
| Service of prison, | — | [illegible] | [illegible] | — | 252 9 3 | 252 9 3 |
| Washing clothing & bedding, | — | [illegible] | [illegible] | — | 1,417 9 11 | 1,417 9 11 |
| Making bedding and clothing, | — | [illegible] | [illegible] | — | 142 15 2 | 142 15 2 |
| Sick, | — | [illegible] | [illegible] | — | — | — |
| Unemployed, | — | [illegible] | [illegible] | — | — | — |
| Total, | — | [illegible] | [illegible] | — | 1,824 9 8 | 1,824 9 8 |

MOUNTJOY FEMALE CONVICT PRISON.

Superintendent's Report.

ESTIMATED VALUE of CONVICT PRISONERS' LABOUR for the year ended 31st March, 1883.

| How employed. | Average No. of Prisoners employed daily. | Estimated Value of the Work performed. £ | s. | d. |
|---|---|---|---|---|
| Sewing and knitting prison materials, | 38·97 | 123 | 3 | 11 |
| Sewing for customers, | | 17 | 3 | 4 |
| Knitting for officers, | | 1 | 8 | 0 |
| Tailoring, | ·73 | 12 | 16 | 6 |
| Washing prison clothing, bedding, &c., | 33·31 | 60 | 11 | 5 |
| " for Mountjoy Male Prison, | | 3 | 6 | 7 |
| " for Lusk Prison, | | 4 | 12 | 5 |
| " for General Prisons Board, | | 8 | 1 | 4 |
| " for prison officers, | | 14 | 5 | 3 |
| " for Royal Irish Constabulary Depot, | | 65 | 16 | 9 |
| " for Department of National Education, | | 315 | 11 | 6 |
| " for Royal Hospital, | | 170 | 16 | 1 |
| " for Royal Hibernian Military School, | | 151 | 7 | 3 |
| " for Mountjoy Barracks, | | 8 | 1 | 5 |
| Cooking, nursing, cleaning for 304 working days, at 4d. per day, | 21·07 | 262 | [illegible] | [illegible] |
| Total, | — | 1,[illegible] | [illegible] | [illegible] |

| | |
|---|---|
| Daily average number of convict prisoners in custody during the year, | 108·34 |
| Per-centage on prison population working, | 90·73 |
| " " in punishment, | 1·[illegible] |
| " " sick or infirm, | 7·67 |

Medical Officer's Report.

## MEDICAL OFFICER'S REPORT.

Mountjoy Female Prison,
April, 1883.

SIR,—I have the honour to submit the usual report of the sanitary condition of this prison during the past year.

The amount of sickness among the officers and prisoners has been light; two deaths occurred, and three cases of mania were transferred to the Central Asylum.

Twenty-six of the officers were at intervals on the sick list, two were discharged on medical grounds, and one death occurred.

The condition of the prison is most satisfactory in a sanitary point of view, and no cases of infectious or contagious disease occurred.

I thankfully acknowledge the very great assistance and co-operation I obtain from the Superintendent and all the Officers in the discharge of my duties.

I have the honour to be, sir,
Your obedient servant,
J. W. YOUNG, M.D., Medical Officer.

The Chairman, General Prisons Board,
Dublin Castle.

MOUNTJOY FEMALE CONVICT PRISON.

Medical Officer's Report.

TABLE I.—HOSPITAL RETURN for the year ending 31st March, 1883.

| | | |
|---|---|---|
| Number of patients in hospital, 1st April, 1882, | 9 | 73 |
| „ admitted during the year, | 64 | |
| „ discharged, | 64 | 73 |
| „ sent to lunatic asylum, | 3 | |
| „ died in hospital, | 2 | |
| „ remaining in hospital 1st April, 1883, | 4 | |
| Daily average of sick in hospital, | | 3·14 |
| Extras prescribed for, | | 300 |
| Daily average prescribed for, | | 1 |

TABLE II.—DISEASES of those admitted to Hospital.

| | | | |
|---|---|---|---|
| Colds and Catarrhal Affections, | 16 | Bilious, | 1 |
| Bronchitis, | 5 | Strumous, | 1 |
| Debility, | 7 | Mania, | 1 |
| Febrile attacks, | 3 | Ophthalmia, | 1 |
| Paralysis, | 3 | Gastric, | 3 |
| Necrosis, | 1 | Uterine, | 2 |
| Ulceration, | 8 | Boil, | 1 |
| Quinsy, | 1 | Heart, | 1 |
| Neuralgia, | 2 | Colic, | 1 |
| Varicella, | 1 | Knee joints, | 1 |
| Anaemia, | 1 | Tonsillitis, | 1 |
| Whitlow, | 1 | Lumbago, | 1 |
| Parturition, | 2 | Eczema, | 1 |

TABLE III.—DEATHS during the year.

| Register No. | Initials of Name. | Received in Prison. | Admitted to Hospital. | Died. | Cause of Death. |
|---|---|---|---|---|---|
| B. 46 | M. L. | 27 Jan., 1880. | 16 Jan., 1882, | 24 Feb., 1882, | Phthisis. |
| B. 19 | R. A. M. | 16 Jan., 1880, | 18 Jan., 1882, | 27 Aug., „ | Chronic Bronchitis. |

TABLE IV.—CONVICTS sent to Central Lunatic Asylum.

| Register No. | Initials of Name. | Where convicted. | Date of Conviction. | Removal to Prison. | Transferred to Asylum. |
|---|---|---|---|---|---|
| 3487 | C. M. | Dublin, | 5 Jan., 1878. | 16 Jan., 1878, | 4 Apr., 1882. |
| 2289 | R. M. | Clonmel, | 6 Oct., 1875. | 21 Oct., 1878, | 10 July, „ |
| B. 6 | M. D. | Kilkenny, | 31 Mar., 1879, | 6 Apr., 1879. | 24 Jan., 1883. |

## PROTESTANT CHAPLAIN'S REPORT.

*Protestant Chaplain's Report.*

Mountjoy Female Prison,
April 28th, 1883.

SIR,—In furnishing my report for the year ending March 31st, 1883, I have the pleasure of stating that the prisoners under my care have been well conducted and submissive to the prison discipline. Again I have also the pleasure of attesting the mild but firm rule of the Superintendent.

*Mountjoy Female Convict Prison.*

*Protestant Chaplain's Report.*

The industry of the women in the school-room, work-room, laundry, and in the cleaning and cooking occupations, has been satisfactory to the officers in these departments.

The Sunday and week-day services in the Church have been celebrated without an omission. The Holy Communion has been statedly administered, and I must say that the attention and earnestness with which the prisoners engage in these services is most gratifying to me.

Prisoners who have been in hospital have received reasonably considerate treatment.

Our lady visitors make mention of the pleasing welcome with which they are received, and the matrons have most willingly given to me such assistance as I have required from them.

I am, sir, your obedient servant,

DAVID STUART, Protestant Chaplain.

To the Chairman of the General Prisons Board,
Dublin Castle.

---

*Roman Catholic Chaplains' Report.*

## ROMAN CATHOLIC CHAPLAINS' REPORT.

Mountjoy Female Convict Prison,
June, 1883.

SIR,—We beg to submit to you our report for the year ending March, 1883.

The Catholic prisoners under our care were well conducted, docile and attentive to their religious duties.

It is gratifying to know that real and solid work has been done in the reformation of these outcasts, many of whom got into bad habits through ignorance and evil example rather than through malice. If the more ill-conditioned and wicked of them could be kept apart from the rest the results would be still more satisfactory.

We return sincere thanks to the officers of the prison for the aid they so cheerfully gave us, and especially to the Superintendent under whose wise and steady administration Mountjoy Female Prison has been so successful.

We have the honour to be, sir,
Your obedient servants,

MICHAEL WALSH, R.C.C.
THOMAS O'DONNELL, A.R.C.C.

To the Chairman, General Prisons Board.

---

*Presbyterian Chaplain's Report.*

## PRESBYTERIAN CHAPLAIN'S REPORT.

Mountjoy Female Convict Prison,
April, 1883.

SIR,—There have been during the past year, and are at present, but three Presbyterian convicts in this prison.

Their conduct has been unexceptionably all that could be desired.

They have closely attended to my weekly ministrations; and I have reason to believe have in measure profited by [illegible] visitations which are paid every Tuesday, and to the religious instruction given in the class generally on Thursdays. Mountjoy Female Convict Prison. — Presbyterian Chaplain's Report.

All the duties of the chaplaincy have been regularly performed during the year, either by myself, or, in my unavoidable absence, by one of the ministers authorised by the Board.

I have nothing of a special nature to report. As usual I have received all the attention from the matron of the prison, so necessary, and so helpful to me in the satisfactory discharge of my duties.

I am, sir, your obedient servant,
S. G. Morrison, Presbyterian Chaplain.

The Chairman of the General Prisons Board,
Dublin Castle.

---

## 3.—SPIKE ISLAND CONVICT PRISON.

Spike Island Convict Prison. — Governor's Report.

### GOVERNOR'S REPORT.

Spike Island Government Prison,
May, 1883.

Sir,—I have the honour to submit my Annual Report for the year ended 31st March, 1883.

The conduct of the subordinate officers has been generally satisfactory. Any reports involving serious neglect or inattention to strict discipline were referred to and dealt with by your Board, while minor offences were disposed of in accordance with the approved scale of fines. Several transfers, both to and from local gaols, were made during the year, and six resigned the service.

No change took place in the employment of the prisoners, and the usual daily routine has been strictly adhered to. All prisoners available for the public works were regularly employed on the Dock labour at Haulbowline. The Ordnance Department had also a party of ten prisoners daily employed. The several trades were carried on as usual, both at Haulbowline and Spike Island, according to the requirements of the respective departments. About fifty prisoners were also employed by the Royal Engineer Department on Spike Island.

I regret having to state that some disturbances occurred on the works at Haulbowline on the 27th and 31st January last. That of the 27th was in no way premeditated or concerted, but arose simply out of a fight between two prisoners, and on the warders interfering to stop it they were set upon, both by the men actually fighting and some of their friends, all of whom were very badly conducted prisoners generally, and who had only recently been sent on the public works, as having no other way or means of employing them. The Deputy Governor, who was present at the time, seeing the few warders likely to be roughly handled, called on the assistance of the police and military forming the guard, thinking this would deter any further resort to resistance; but, in place of having the desired effect, their presence became the signal for others to join in the disturbance, and thus for a time there was a

*Spike Island Convict Prison. — Governor's Report.*

good deal of insubordination and violence among a portion of the prisoners employed in the Dock basin, but in which the stonecutters or other tradesmen present did not join, and the only person injured on either side was the head-constable of police, who got a cut on the head with a shovel. The occurrence of the 31st January was an outcome of that of the 27th, being a case of insubordination at the dinner hour by a considerable number of the prisoners refusing to take their dinner milk on the ground that it was bad; but no threat or violence of any kind was offered on this occasion. It was, however, to some extent premeditated and concocted by one or two very bad prisoners, who were on the point of going to their liberty, and expected to escape the consequences; the object mainly in view being to bring about a change of diet, and on this ground they all the more easily gained the sympathy of their fellow-prisoners. The milk complained of was subsequently analysed by the county analyst, and certified to be good. The instigators and principal offenders on both occasions were removed from association, and placed in strict probation, and six of the ringleaders received corporal punishment. Since the removal from their midst of the badly-disposed class, a marked change has taken place in the tone and conduct of the prisoners generally, and none of them have shown any disposition to renew the disturbance or give any trouble. This fact clearly demonstrates that it is very unsafe to allow very badly-conducted prisoners to associate with well-disposed on the public works.

Some few prisoners from here, with a proportion of warders, are still employed on buildings and repairs at Cork and Maryborough gaols.

Twenty-nine invalid prisoners were sent from here to Maryborough in the month of March, on the opening of that prison as an invalid depôt.

The returns show the number of prisoners received during the year, and their disposal.

| | |
|---|---|
| Daily average number employed, . . | 406 |
| Not employed (in cells and hospital), . . | 30 |
| Total daily average, . . | 436 |

Eight convicts received corporal punishment.

There was one unsuccessful attempt at escape.

A great loss was sustained by the death of the Rev. Dr. Collis, Protestant Chaplain, and he was very much regretted by officers and prisoners.

In view of the early closing of Spike Island as a convict depôt, it is unnecessary to refer to the condition of the buildings, or any other matter connected with the prison arrangements.

The school has been carried on as usual; but having only one schoolmaster, the teaching power is very limited.

I have not seen or received intimation of any abuse or abuses not reported by me; and I hereby certify that the rules laid down for the government of the prison have been complied with during the past year, except in such cases as have been reported to or brought under the notice of the Board.

I have the honour to be, sir,

Your most obedient servant,

P. Hay, Governor.

The Chairman, General Prisons Board,
Dublin Castle.

SPIKE ISLAND CONVICT PRISON.

Governor's Report.

ABSTRACT ACCOUNT showing the ESTIMATED VALUE of the PRODUCTIVE LABOUR of the Prisoners, and the NUMBER EMPLOYED during the Year ended 31st March, 1883.

| How Employed. | Daily Average Number Employed for 312 days. | | Estimated Value of Work performed. | Total. |
|---|---|---|---|---|
| | | | £ s. d. | £ s. d. |
| PRISON WORKS. | | | | |
| Tailors, - - - - | 24 | | 598 10 0 | |
| Shoemakers, - - - - | 8 | | 359 10 0 | |
| Carpenters, - - - - | 3 | | 153 8 0 | |
| Smiths and Nailers, - - - | 2 | | 90 19 0 | |
| Painters, - - - - | 1 | | 31 18 0 | |
| Masons, - - - - | 1 | | 45 6 0 | |
| Bakers, - - - - | 6 | | 371 10 0 | |
| Coopers and Tinmen, - - | 3 | | 150 8 0 | |
| Repairing Beds, Socks, &c., - - | 9 | | 159 18 0 | |
| Labourers in Prison Garden and on Prison Works generally, - - | 97 | | 409 13 8 | |
| Washing in Laundry, - - | 7 | | 211 0 0 | |
| Cooks, - - - - | 8 | | 73 10 0 | |
| Fatigue work, Cleaning, and Messing, | 18 | | 280 10 0 | |
| Hospital, - - - - | 4 | | 90 12 0 | |
| Oakum picking (on wet days and penal class), - - - | 15 | | 56 12 6 | |
| Do. (invalids), - - | 12 | | 14 2 0 | |
| | | 148 | | 2,820 1 [illegible] |
| ROYAL ENGINEER WORKS. | | | | |
| Labourers, - - - - | 80 | | 785 0 0 | |
| | | 80 | | 785 0 0 |
| WAR DEPARTMENT (HAULBOWLINE). | | | | |
| Labourers, - - - - | 9 | | 203 17 0 | |
| | | 9 | | 203 17 0 |
| ADMIRALTY WORKS. | | | | |
| Masons and Stonecutters, - - | 39 | | 1,870 8 0 | |
| Do. do. beginners, | 14 | | 261 17 4 | |
| Carpenters, - - - - | 5 | | 201 8 8 | |
| Do. beginners, - - | 0 | | 67 16 0 | |
| Smiths, - - - - | 3 | | 159 16 0 | |
| Do. beginners, - - - | 7 | | 188 11 0 | |
| Labourers, - - - - | 186 | | 2,877 1 4 | |
| | | 169 | | 4,917 19 4 |
| Total, - - - | | 406 | | 8,730 17 [illegible] |

| | |
|---|---|
| Daily average number employed, - - - | 406 |
| " " not employed (in cells and hospital), - | 30 |
| Total daily average, - - - | 436 |

Spike Island Convict Prison. — Governor's Report.

RETURN showing the CRIMES of 425 CONVICTS in CUSTODY, 31st March, 1863.

| | | | |
|---|---|---|---|
| Murder, | 16 | Having implements of housebreaking, | 8 |
| Assault with intent to murder, | 1 | Stealing from the person, | 63 |
| Attempting to kill and murder one Owen M'Fadden, | 1 | Larceny and previous conviction, | 77 |
| Manslaughter, | 18 | Cattle stealing, | 6 |
| Stabbing, cutting, and wounding, | 14 | Horse stealing, | 3 |
| Felonious, grievous, malicious, and other assaults, | 20 | Sheep stealing, | 4 |
| Assault to do grievous bodily harm, | 1 | Receiving stolen goods, | 15 |
| Felonious cheating, | 9 | Obtaining goods and money by false pretences, | 8 |
| Assault and robbery, | 18 | Sodomy, | 8 |
| Assault with intent to rob, | 8 | Buggery, | 1 |
| Riot and Assault, | 1 | Carnal knowledge of females under 12 years of age, | 6 |
| Highway robbery, | 8 | Rape and abduction, | 24 |
| Burglary and robbery, and previous conviction, | 18 | Arson, | 9 |
| Robbery, | 4 | Perjury, | 1 |
| Attempt to rob, | 1 | Placing obstruction on a railway, | 3 |
| Housebreaking and robbery, | 46 | Malicious injury, | 1 |
| Felony and previous conviction, | 8 | Military offences, | 18 |
| Forgery, | 3 | Whiteboy offence, | 9 |
| Uttering forged bank-notes, | 2 | Misdemeanour, | 1 |
| Coining, | 2 | | |
| Having base coin in possession, | 9 | **Total,** | 425 |
| Having instruments for coining, | 1 | | |

RETURN showing the NUMBER of CONVICTS in CUSTODY, committed and disposed of during the Year ended 31st March, 1863.

| | | How disposed of. | |
|---|---|---|---|
| 1st April, 1862— | | 31st March, 1863— | |
| In custody, | 279 | Remaining in custody, | 425 |
| Committed from— | | Removed during the year to— | |
| Mountjoy Male Prison, | 246 | Mountjoy Male Prison, | 34 |
| Cork Male Prison, | 14 | Mountjoy for Lusk, | 26 |
| Maryborough Prison, | 14 | Mountjoy for release on licence, | 31 |
| | | Mountjoy for discharge, | 7 |
| | | Cork Male Prison, | 44 |
| | | Maryborough Prison, | 40 |
| | | Dundrum Lunatic Asylum, | 3 |
| | | Released on licence (four of them on Medical Grounds), | 10 |
| | | Discharged on expiration of sentence, | 6 |
| | | Discharged on commutation of sentence on Medical Grounds, | 2 |
| | | Died, | 5 |
| Total, | 553 | Total, | 553 |

RETURN showing the SENTENCES and the AGES on CONVICTION of 425 CONVICTS in CUSTODY, 31st March, 1863.

SENTENCES.

| | | | |
|---|---|---|---|
| Five Years' Penal Servitude, | 198 | Life penal servitude, | 22 |
| Seven " " | 112 | | |
| Ten " " | 81 | | |
| Twelve " " | 3 | | |
| Fourteen " " | 10 | | |
| Fifteen " " | 13 | | |
| Twenty " " | 16 | | |
| Twenty-five " " | 1 | | |
| | 403 | | 22 |

Total, 425.

AGES ON CONVICTION.

| | | | |
|---|---|---|---|
| Under Twenty Years, | 45 | Fifty and under Sixty, | 20 |
| Twenty and under Twenty-five, | 117 | Sixty and under Seventy, | 8 |
| Twenty-five and under Thirty, | 81 | Seventy and under Eighty, | 6 |
| Thirty and under Thirty-five, | 67 | | |
| Thirty-five and under Forty, | 34 | **Total,** | 425 |
| Forty and under Fifty, | 36 | | |

Return by the Governor, showing how Prisoners have been Employed during the year ending 31st March, 1883, and the Earnings of those engaged in each Employment; also showing the average daily number of Unemployed from Sickness and other reasons. SPIKE ISLAND CONVICT PRISON. Governor's Report.

| How Employed. | Daily Average Number of Prisoners employed, unemployed, &c. | | | Net Profit on Work done by Prisoners. | Estimated Value of the Work done in the Prison. | Total. |
|---|---|---|---|---|---|---|
| | Males. | Females. | Total. | | | |
| | | | | £ s. d. | £ s. d. | £ s. d. |
| Gardening, | 14 | — | 14 | 149 13 9 | — | 149 13 [illegible] |
| Tailors, | 13 | — | 13 | — | 348 15 6 | 348 15 [illegible] |
| Shoemakers, | 17 | — | 17 | — | [illegible] | [illegible] |
| Carpenters, | 13 | — | 13 | — | 126 [illegible] | [illegible] |
| Bricklayers, masons, and labourers, | 214 | — | 214 | — | 4,094 17 [illegible] | 4,094 17 [illegible] |
| Painters and glaziers, | [illegible] | — | [illegible] | — | [illegible] | [illegible] |
| Tinsmiths and coopers, | [illegible] | — | [illegible] | — | [illegible] | [illegible] |
| Blacksmiths and nailers, | [illegible] | — | [illegible] | — | [illegible] | [illegible] |
| Pumping water, | [illegible] | — | [illegible] | — | [illegible] | [illegible] |
| Service of prison, | [illegible] | — | [illegible] | — | [illegible] | [illegible] |
| Washing clothing and bedding, | [illegible] | — | [illegible] | — | [illegible] | [illegible] |
| Repairing bedding & clothing, | [illegible] | — | [illegible] | — | [illegible] | [illegible] |
| Scavengers, | [illegible] | — | [illegible] | — | [illegible] | [illegible] |
| Bakers, | [illegible] | — | [illegible] | — | [illegible] | [illegible] |
| Cooks, | [illegible] | — | [illegible] | — | [illegible] | [illegible] |
| Boatmen, | [illegible] | — | [illegible] | — | [illegible] | [illegible] |
| Plasterers, | [illegible] | — | [illegible] | — | [illegible] | [illegible] |
| Picking oakum, | [illegible] | — | [illegible] | [illegible] | [illegible] | [illegible] |
| Sick, | [illegible] | — | [illegible] | — | — | — |
| Unemployed, | [illegible] | — | [illegible] | — | — | — |
| **Total,** | [illegible] | — | [illegible] | 164 18 11 | 5,543 16 4 | 5,708 15 3 |

* £[illegible] 12s. 8d. of this sum is the estimated value of the labour of the convicts belonging to Spike Island Prison, and temporarily employed at Cork and Maryborough Prisons.

Return of the several Industrial and Useful pursuits in which Prisoners were employed during the year ended 31st March, 1883, viz.:—

Tailoring.
Shoemaking.
Carpentering.
Bricklaying and masoning.
Painting.
Tinsmith work.
Blacksmith work.
Coopering.
Nail making.
Washing in laundry.
Repairing bedding and clothing.
Scavengering.
Baking.
Cooking.
Boatmen.
Plastering.
Picking oakum.
Fatigue work, cleaning and mowing.
Gardening.

## MEDICAL OFFICER'S REPORT.

*Medical Officer's Report.*

Spike Island Convict Prison,
19th May, 1883.

SIR,—I have the honour to submit the annual report on the state of health of the officers and prisoners, and on the general sanitary condition of this prison, with the usual medical statistics for the year ended 31st March last.

There were fifty-seven warders treated in hospital during the year, chiefly for ordinary ailments. No death occurred. The steward and

*Spike Island Convict Prison.* — *Medical Officer's Report.*

one warder were discharged the service on medical grounds; the latter having been rendered permanently unfitted for his duties, owing to injuries he sustained in an assault by a convict.

During the year there were 240 prisoners received from Mountjoy Prison, ten of whom having been found unfit for the ordinary labour of this prison, were placed at employment best suited to the conditions of their health.

There were 210 convicts admitted into hospital during the year principally for diseases of the respiratory and the digestive systems, febrile affections, wounds and contusions, rheumatism and debility. There were five deaths; one from dropsy, one from gangrene of the lungs, one from pneumonia, one from liver disease, and one from old age and debility.

During the year there were six convicts released from prison on medical grounds, three of whom were found to be delicate, and three in good health, on reception here. There were three prisoners transferred to Dundrum Criminal Lunatic Asylum during the year; in none of whom was there a previous history of insanity.

The opening of Maryborough Prison for invalids relieved this establishment of a number of delicate and weak-minded convicts, who were always a source of great anxiety in this—a public works—prison.

Nothing of particular importance in a medical point of view occurred during the year, and I am happy to be able to record, that the general favourable sanitary condition, of past years, of this prison, has been fairly maintained.

The governor and the other prison officers always afforded me active assistance, and promptly gave effect to any recommendations I found it necessary to make. The Resident Apothecary performed his duty in the most satisfactory manner, and received well-merited promotion in being appointed Resident Medical Officer, Maryborough Prison.

I have the honour to be, sir,

Your most obedient servant,

P. O'Keeffe, M.D., Medical Officer.

The Chairman, General Prisons Board,
Dublin Castle.

---

**Medical Statistics for the Year ended 31st March, 1893.**

| | |
|---|---|
| Number of sick remaining in hospital on the 1st April, 18[illegible], | 25 |
| „ admitted during the year, | 210 |
| Total, | 235 |
| Of these were discharged from hospital, | 214 |
| Died during the year, | 5 |
| Remaining in hospital on the 1st April, 1893, | 16 |
| Total, | 235 |
| Daily average number of sick treated in hospital during the year, | [illegible] |
| Number of externs treated during the year, | [illegible] |
| Daily average number of externs treated during the year, | [illegible] |
| Number of Prisoners released from Prison on medical grounds, | 6 |
| Number of Prisoners transferred to Dundrum Lunatic Asylum, during the year, | 3 |
| Number of Warders treated in hospital during the year, | 57 |
| Number of Warders who died during the year, | – |
| Number of Warders discharged the service on medical grounds during the year, | 1 |

Spike Island Convict Prison.

Medical Officer's Report.

## Number of Diseases treated in Hospital during the Year.

| | | | |
|---|---|---|---|
| Bronchitis, pneumonia, and other diseases of the respiratory organs, | 43 | Tonsillitis, | [illegible] |
| Dyspepsia, diarrhoea, constipation, and other diseases of the digestive organs, | 35 | Observation, | [illegible] |
| Wounds, contusions, and ulcers, | 33 | Haemoptysis, | 3 |
| Febrile affections, | 21 | Ophthalmia, | [illegible] |
| Rheumatism, | 12 | Haemorrhoids, | [illegible] |
| Epilepsy, paraplegia, and other diseases of the nervous system, | 8 | [illegible] | [illegible] |
| Debility, | 6 | Hepatitis and dropsy, | 1 |
| Abscesses, | 5 | Tumours, | [illegible] |
| Heart disease, | 5 | Fracture, | 1 |
| | | Scrofula, | 1 |
| | | Herpes, | 1 |
| | | Total, | [illegible] |

## Mortality Table.

| Register Number. | Initials of Name. | Date of Admission into Hospital. | Date of Death. | Cause of Death. |
|---|---|---|---|---|
| 14,[illegible] | W. B. | 6 Feb., 1882, | 15 April, 1882, | Dropsy. |
| 15,[illegible] | M. M. | 16 March, " | 25 April, " | Gangrene of lungs. |
| A 197 | W. M. | 11 April, " | 25 April, " | Pneumonia. |
| A 188 | J. K. | 15 March, " | 6 May, " | Liver disease and general debility. |
| 14,[illegible] | T. F. | 30 Jan., " | 25 Aug., " | Old age and debility. |

## List of Prisoners transferred to Dundrum Criminal Lunatic Asylum.

| Register No. | Initials of Name. | Date of reception at Spike Island. | Where convicted. | Crime. | Date of removal to Asylum. |
|---|---|---|---|---|---|
| A 159 | J. L. | 21 Sep., 1880, | Belfast, | Intent to commit felony. | 6th May, 1882. |
| A 226 | W. H. | 24 Apr., 1882, | Dublin, | Larceny, | 17 Oct., 1882. |
| 14,611 | S. H. | 7 Mar., 1879, | Dublin, | Larceny from person. | 24 Nov., 1882. |

## List of Prisoners released from Prison on Medical Grounds.

| Register No. | Initials of Name. | Date of reception at Spike Island. | Where convicted. | Crime. | Disease. |
|---|---|---|---|---|---|
| A 134 | J. K. | 8 June, 1880, | Dublin, | Larceny from the person. | Debility. |
| A 162 | T. L. | 23 Jan., 188[illegible], | Dublin, | Larceny. | Phthisis. |
| 14,[illegible] | T. C. | 8 Dec., 18[illegible], | Belfast, | Larceny. | Heart disease. |
| 14,[illegible] | G. K. | 4 Mar., 18[illegible], | Dublin, | Highway robbery. | Debility and partial paralysis. |
| A 182 | J. B. | 28 Nov., 1880, | Cork, | Fraudulent embezzlement. | Abdominal tumours. |
| A 237 | H. E. | 3 Dec., 1880, | Dublin, | Obtaining money by false pretences. | Asthma & bronchitis. |

Spike Island Convict Prison.

Protestant Chaplain's Report.

## PROTESTANT CHAPLAIN'S REPORT.

Queenstown, July 2nd, 1883.

Sir,—I beg to present my report for the term of the years 1882 and 1883, during which I held the office of Protestant Chaplain to the Convict Settlement at Spike Island.

I visited (either myself or my assistant) the Prison—both hospital and cells—and gave the usual religious instructions, three times each week at least; and it gives me much pleasure to be able to state that I always found the prisoners most respectful and quiet in my intercourse with them. They were always very ready to listen to any advice or instruction I had to give, and seemed anxious to follow it.

An addition of some useful books was made to the Sunday library early in the year 1883, which the men fully appreciated. In fact, from the anxious wish of the prisoners to have the privilege of reading these books, as they are passed in by the men who have used them, I am of opinion that a good Sunday library would be most useful as a means of moral and intellectual improvement among the prisoners.

I have to acknowledge gratefully the kindness and consideration of the Governor, and all under him in the government of Spike Island, for affording me every facility for the discharge of my duties.

I beg to remain, sir,

Your faithful servant,

William Dauft, M.A.

The Chairman, General Prisons Board,
Dublin Castle.

---

Roman Catholic Chaplain's Report.

## ROMAN CATHOLIC CHAPLAIN'S REPORT.

Spike Island, May, 1883.

Sir,—I beg leave to send you my report for the year ending 31st March, 1883, which is my 34th Annual Report as the Roman Catholic Chaplain of Spike Island Convict Prison.

In doing so, I beg to state that the several duties prescribed for the Roman Catholic Chaplains by the prison rules were duly performed during the year. A large number of the prisoners availed themselves of the religious opportunities thus afforded them, and prepared themselves, in all appearance, earnestly and piously, to receive the sacrament of penance and the holy eucharist at Easter, and several have done so more frequently during the year. And I think it right to state that the prisoners who had been concerned in the refractory conduct which took place at Haulbowline in January last have since repeatedly expressed their sorrow and repentance for any part they had taken in it, and have since made amends by very improved conduct; and I am glad to be able to state that it was the only instance of such an occurrence here during the last thirty-five years, while Spike Island was used as a convict prison, notwithstanding the very unsuitableness and circumstances of the prison.

I have the honour to be, sir,

Your very obedient servant,

T. F. Lyons, R.C. Chaplain.

The Chairman of the General Prisons Board,
Dublin Castle.

Spike Island Convict Prison.

Assistant Roman Catholic Chaplain's Report.

## ASSISTANT ROMAN CATHOLIC CHAPLAIN'S REPORT.

Spike Island, May, 1883.

SIR,—I have the honour to submit my report for the year ending 31st March, 1883.

I am pleased to be able to state that the moral and religious condition of the Roman Catholic prisoners has been, generally, satisfactory.

The great body of them have been very attentive to their religious duties, a considerable number approaching the sacraments once a month. Their demeanour in the chapel during mass, prayer, and religious instruction, has been, as a rule, edifying.

I regret, however, to be compelled to repeat, what I have mentioned in former reports, viz.—that the evils resulting from the defective cellular construction of the prison, as well as the want of proper classification, still continue. It is however, to be hoped that these great impediments to the thorough reformation of the criminal population, will be soon removed, and that a happier state of things will obtain elsewhere in the near future.

I have, as usual, celebrated mass for the warders and prisoners twice a week, with few exceptions, and paid daily visits to the sick in hospital, and the defaulters in the separate cells.

In conclusion, I beg to say how grateful I feel to the Governor, and the entire prison staff, for the cordial support and uniform courtesy I have received from them on all occasions.

I have the honour to be, sir,

Your most obedient servant,

JOHN O'CONNOR, A.R.C.C.

The Chairman, General Prisons Board,
Dublin Castle.

---

Presbyterian Chaplain's Report.

## PRESBYTERIAN CHAPLAIN'S REPORT.

Spike Island, 4th May, 1883.

SIR,—I have the honour to present to you my report for the year ending the 31st of March, 1883.

As it is the last, I suppose, that I shall be called on to lay before you, I may be allowed to say, that the feelings of sorrow, pity, or hope, which arose as I reported on the prisoners from year to year, now crowd upon the retrospect of duties so soon to close. The side of the prisoners' character which opens itself to the view of one acting in my relation towards them is so different from that presented to the discipline officers, that the way I have spoken of them may appear more professional than just. But the view of them my calling leads me to take, is a true one in itself, and I know instances in which it did not mislead me. I had a letter not long ago from a former prisoner, who is now filling a very responsible situation in England, and leading a Christian life, and he said to me, that it was well for him he had been in Spike Island.

That the authorities share in this higher view of the question, is evinced by the regulations they from time to time make, such as the segregation of prisoners for first offences, from the more hardened criminals. I hope the day will come, when they will see their way to having warders trained from youth for the discharge of their important duties, just as nurses are now trained for hospitals. There are, I believe, warders who have a gift for managing prisoners in such a way as to do them good, as there have always been women who had a gift for tending the sick and wounded. What was the gift of one woman is now made

Spike Island Convict Prison.

*Presbyterian Chaplain's Report.*

the accomplishment of a hundred. The same might be done with warders.

Among the prisoners under my charge nothing has occurred during the bygone year worthy of a place in this report. I have regularly fulfilled my duties to them. There have been very few of them sick, and, with one exception, I think their prison conduct has been good.

I look back over my twenty years of service in Spike Island with a grateful memory of the kindness I have received from the Governor in all our intercourse, the amity and good feeling shown to me by those of a like vocation to my own, and the co-operation and ready aid afforded me by the other officers of every rank.

Whatever may be the remaining days given me on earth, I shall ever remember my residence in Queenstown, and my duties in the Island, as covering the happiest portion of the happiest part of my life.

I have the honour to be, sir,

Your very obedient servant,

Wm. J. Kirkland, LL.D., Presbyterian Chaplain.

The Chairman, General Prisons Board, Dublin Castle.

---

## 4.—LUSK CONVICT PRISON.

Lusk Convict Prison.

*Superintendent's Report.*

### SUPERINTENDENT'S REPORT.

Lusk Convict Prison, May, 1883.

Sir,—I beg to submit my annual report on the Lusk Convict Prison for the year ending 31st March, 1883.

The duties of the prison and farm have been performed same as in former years. Two of the officers have been removed to Mountjoy Male Prison for temporary duty—this is the only change on the staff. On the 1st April, 1882, in custody at Lusk 29 convicts; received during the year, 47 convicts, making a total of 76 in full. They have been disposed of :—released on licence, 51; removed to Mountjoy Prison Hospital, 2; removed to Mountjoy for misconduct, 1; removed to Mountjoy for mason work, 1; removed to Mountjoy for attempting to escape, 1; remaining in custody, 31st March, 1883, 20. The daily average number in custody, 24·7. The employment of the convicts at farmwork has been useful, and to improve them. The new stables have been slated and fitted up, and building kept in good repair. Some very handy men at mason and slating, were received during the year, and the conduct and industry were very good. One attempted to abscond, but was overtaken and brought back, being only a short time absent; he was only received here the day before. One was removed to Mountjoy Male Prison for slight misconduct. It is satisfactory to be able to report that fully two-thirds of the released convicts have sought new fields of employment, leaving bad homes and companions. This is a good step in their effort to do well, and is both hopeful and encouraging. The chaplains have used their influence to good advantage, and the Prisoners' Aid Society has in some few cases assisted the men after release. The medical officer, assisted by Dr. Davys, have attended the sick, and the school instructor has attended the men at school each evening, and he reports fair progress.

Mr. Dowdy, the agent for released convicts, has done all he could in making arrangement and finding out employers for the released men.

It is only just to state that the officers have done their best in striving to get the works on the farm done, and have worked well themselves to encourage the small number here through a very wet and severe season. The usual statistics are annexed. I certify that the rules have been complied with to the best of my ability, and any infringement that came to my knowledge reported.

I have the honour to be, sir,

Your most obedient servant,

R. Gunning, Superintendent.

The Chairman, General Prisons Board.

Lusk Convict Prison. — Superintendent's Report.

---

RETURN showing the Number of Convicts in custody during the year ended 31st March, 1883, and how they have been disposed of.

| | |
|---|---|
| In custody 1st April, 1882, | [illegible] |
| Received from Mountjoy Male Convict Prison, | 7 |
| " Spike Island *via* Mountjoy " | 30 |
| " Cork Male " | 3 |
| " Maryborough " | 3 |
| **Total,** | 75 |
| **Released on licence,** | 31 |
| **Removed to Mountjoy Male Prison—hospital,** | 6 |
| " " " misconduct, | 1 |
| " " " for mason work, | 1 |
| " " " attempting to escape, | 1 |
| **Remaining in custody, 31st March, 1883,** | 39 |
| Total, | 78 |
| Daily average number in custody, | 36·7 |

CRIMES of 47 Prisoners received during the year ended 31st March, 1883.

| | |
|---|---|
| Army offences, | 1 |
| Arson, | 2 |
| Burglary, | 1 |
| " and robbery, | 1 |
| Breaking and entering warehouse, and larceny and previous conviction, | 1 |
| Cattle stealing, | 2 |
| Assault and robbery, | 2 |
| " with intent to rob, | 1 |
| Felony, | 1 |
| Feloniously passing base coin, | 1 |
| Highway robbery with violence, | 1 |
| Housebreaking, | 1 |
| " and robbery, | 1 |
| Killing a sheep with intent to steal the skin, | 1 |
| Larceny, | 3 |
| " from the person, | 6 |
| " and previous conviction, | 7 |
| " from person with violence, | 3 |
| Manslaughter, | 2 |
| Obtaining money by false pretences, | 1 |
| Placing wood and iron bar on railway, | 1 |
| Robbery, | 3 |
| " from person and previous conviction, | 1 |
| Receiving stolen goods, | 2 |
| Sheep stealing, | 2 |
| Stealing [illegible] and previous conviction, | 2 |
| Shooting at with intent to do grievous bodily harm, | 1 |
| Total, | 47 |

Of the 47 Convicts received during the year ended 31st March, 1883,

6 were convicted in Dublin City.
8 " Cork "
3 " Belfast.
30 " other towns in Ireland.

SENTENCES of 47 Convicts received during the year ended 31st March, 1883.

| | |
|---|---|
| 5 years' penal servitude, | 29 |
| 7 " " | 16 |
| 10 " " | 2 |
| Total, | 47 |

AGES on reception of 47 Convicts received during the year ended 31st March, 1883.

| | |
|---|---|
| 20 years and under 30, | 18 |
| 30 " " 40, | 19 |
| 40 " " 50, | 6 |
| 50 " " 60, | 4 |
| 60 years and upwards, | – |
| Total, | 47 |

RETURN showing the reported Previous Convictions of 47 Convicts received in this Prison during the year ended 31st March, 1883.

| | | | |
|---|---|---|---|
| Not reported to have been previously convicted, | 4 | Ten times, | 2 |
| Once, | 13 | Eleven " | 1 |
| Twice, | 8 | Twelve " | 3 |
| Three times, | 3 | Fifteen " | 1 |
| Four " | 3 | Nineteen " | 1 |
| Five " | 1 | Twenty-nine " | 1 |
| Six " | 3 | Total, | 47 |
| Nine " | 1 | | |

ACCOUNT showing the value of Productive Labour of Prisoners at Lusk for the year ended 31st March, 1883.

| Trades. | Amount. £ s. d. | Observations. |
|---|---|---|
| Masons, | 34 18 0 | |
| Carpenters, | 39 14 0 | |
| Smiths, | 5 18 0 | Daily average number, 24·7 |
| Shoemakers, | 18 14 5 | Less sick, ·5 |
| Tailors, | 9 7 8 | 24·2 |
| | 120 6 7 | |
| 20·9 prisoners employed at general farm works, for 52 weeks, at 11s per week per prisoner, | 597 14 0 | Average earnings of each effective prisoner, £29 13s. 5d. |
| Total, | 718 0 7 | |

## MEDICAL OFFICER'S REPORT.

Lusk Prison, 30th April, 1883.

SIR,—I beg to submit the usual annual report of the sanitary condition of this prison for the year ending the 31st of March, last.

The health of the officers and prisoners was excellent during that period. There was no death; nor in fact any illness of a serious character. I attribute this very satisfactory state of things to the good order of the buildings in which the prisoners are lodged, and to the attention paid by the officers to clothing and diet. The various character of the works enables the prisoners to be kept always employed—and, during severe weather, without unnecessary exposure or hardship.

I am, sir, your obedient servant,

F. J. B. QUINLAN, M.D., F.C.P.,
Medical Superintendent.

## PROTESTANT CHAPLAIN'S REPORT.

Lusk Reformatory Prison. Protestant Chaplain's Report.

Lusk Prison,
April, 1883.

SIR,—In making my report for the year past, I am happy to say the prisoners under my spiritual care have been uniformly attentive and respectful in their conduct both in church and during weekly religious instruction.

Several young and promising men have emigrated, apparently with a fixed desire to do better for the future.

The prisoners for the last twelve months have been, for the most part, very intelligent men, and I hope may become useful members of society.

I remain, sir, faithfully yours,

A. D. POMEROY, Chaplain.

The Chairman, General Prisons Board, Dublin Castle.

---

## ROMAN CATHOLIC CHAPLAIN'S REPORT.

Roman Catholic Chaplain's Report.

The Presbytery, Lusk,
May 11th, 1883.

SIR,—I beg leave to forward to you my report for the year ending the 31st March, 1883, as R. C. Chaplain of Lusk Reformatory Prison.

It affords me great pleasure to be able to state that the religious and moral tone pervading the R. C. prisoners here has been, and is, all that I could desire. The prisoners have been very docile and respectful. They have been also fairly attentive to their religious duties during the year, and really edifying in their demeanour whilst assisting at Mass on Sundays and Holidays in our parochial church. A large number of R. C. Prisoners were discharged during the year, and I have every confidence their conduct in after life will give satisfaction.

In conclusion I have only to add that every facility, the prison rules would admit, has been afforded me in the discharge of my duty by your worthy Superintendent and the other officials of the prison.

I am, gentlemen, faithfully yours,

M. J. GIBNEY.

To the Chairman of the General Prisons Board.

**Table I.—Return showing the Proportion of Sick and Deaths to the Number of Convicts, in the Irish Convict Prisons for the years 1854, 1855, 1856, 1857, 1858, and 1859.**

| — | 1854. | | | | | 1855. | | | | |
|---|---|---|---|---|---|---|---|---|---|---|
| | Spike Island and Philipstown. | Cork and Grangegorman. | Newgate and Smithfield. | Mountjoy. | Totals, 1854. | Spike Island and Philipstown. | Cork and Grangegorman. | Newgate and Smithfield. | Mountjoy. | Totals, 1855. |
| No. of Convicts, | 2,280 | 339 | 556 | 443 | 3,628 | 1,777 | 498 | 430 | 462 | 3,167 |
| Average daily No. of Sick, | 276 | 23 | 46 | 23 | 368 | 333 | 26 | 48 | 17 | [illegible] |
| No. of Deaths, | 241 | 6 | 33 | 6 | 289 | 101 | 6 | 31 | 8 | 149 |
| Per-centage of Deaths on prison population, | 10·6 | 1·8 | 5·9 | 2· | 8· | 5·7 | 1·6 | 7·9 | 2· | 4·7 |

| — | 1856. | | | | | 1857. | | | | |
|---|---|---|---|---|---|---|---|---|---|---|
| | Spike Island and Philipstown. | Cork and Grangegorman. | Newgate and Smithfield. | Mountjoy. | Totals, 1856. | Spike Island and Philipstown. | Cork and Grangegorman. | Smithfield and Lusk. | Mountjoy. | Totals, 1857. |
| No. of Convicts, | 1,608 | 613 | 130 | 431 | 2,832 | 1,623 | 466 | 79 | 457 | 2,542 |
| Average daily No. of Sick, | 105 | 43 | 36 | 18 | 194 | 67 | 32 | 6 | 16 | 128 |
| No. of Deaths, | 35 | 11 | 5 | 3 | 54 | 34 | 4 | 2 | 3 | 43 |
| Per-centage of Deaths on prison population, | 2·1 | 1·8 | 3·9 | ·7 | 1·8 | 2·1 | · | 2·9 | ·6 | 1·6 |

| — | 1858. | | | | | 1859. | | | | |
|---|---|---|---|---|---|---|---|---|---|---|
| | Spike Island and Philipstown. | Female Prisons. | Smithfield and Lusk. | Mountjoy Male. | Totals, 1858. | Spike Island and Philipstown. | Mountjoy Female. | Smithfield and Lusk. | Mountjoy Male. | Totals, 1859. |
| No. of Convicts, | 1,093 | 580 | 67 | 826 | 2,013 | 237 | 454 | 99 | 269 | 1,079 |
| Average daily No. of Sick, | 43 | 41 | 4 | 12 | 98 | 32 | 14 | 3 | 13 | 67 |
| No. of Deaths, | 15 | 11 | 2 | 3 | 30 | 13 | 9 | · | 1 | 25 |
| Per-centage of Deaths on prison population, | 1·3 | 2· | 3·6 | 0·3 | 1·4 | 1·5 | 0·6 | · | 0·3 | 0·9 |

RETURN showing the PROPORTION of SICK and DEATHS to the Number of Convicts in the Irish Convict Prisons for the years 1860, 1861, 1862, 1863, 1864, and 1865.

| — | 1860. | | | | | 1861. | | | | |
|---|---|---|---|---|---|---|---|---|---|---|
| | Spike Island and Philipstown.* | Mountjoy Female Prison. | Smithfield and Lusk. | Mountjoy Male. | Totals, 1860. | Spike Island and Philipstown. | Mountjoy Female Prison. | Smithfield and Lusk. | Mountjoy Male. | Totals, 1861. |
| No. of Convicts, . | 763 | 423 | 186 | 301 | 1,343 | 676 | 334 | 64 | 306 | 1,[illegible] |
| Average daily No. of Sick, . . | 27 | 17 | 4 | 11 | 54 | 15 | 26 | 4 | 11 | 56 |
| No. of Deaths, . | 8 | 11 | — | 1 | 13 | 1 | 6 | 1 | 3 | 11 |
| Per-centage of Deaths on Prison population, . | ·5 | 2·6 | — | ·4 | ·[illegible] | ·1 | 1·8 | 1·1 | 1·6 | ·60 |

| — | 1862. | | | | | 1863. | | | | |
|---|---|---|---|---|---|---|---|---|---|---|
| | Spike Island and Philipstown. | Mountjoy Female Prison. | Smithfield and Lusk. | Mountjoy Male. | Totals, 1862. | Spike Island. | Mountjoy Female Prison. | Smithfield and Lusk. | Mountjoy Male. | Totals, 1863. |
| No. of Convicts, . | 768 | 416 | 79 | 616 | 1,819 | 763 | 469 | 73 | 370 | 1,[illegible] |
| Average daily No. of Sick, . . | 14 | 27 | 4 | 17 | 62 | 9 | 30 | 4 | 17 | 56 |
| No. of Deaths, . | 8 | 10 | — | 5 | 23 | 10 | 4 | — | 5 | 19 |
| Per-centage of Deaths on Prison population, . | 1·1 | 2·4 | — | 1·5 | 1·5 | 1·3 | ·8 | — | 1·3 | 1·1 |

| — | 1864. | | | | | 1865. | | | | |
|---|---|---|---|---|---|---|---|---|---|---|
| | Spike Island. | Mountjoy Female Prison. | Smithfield and Lusk. | Mountjoy Male. | Totals, 1864. | Spike Island. | Mountjoy Female Prison. | Smithfield and Lusk. | Mountjoy Male. | Totals, 1865. |
| No. of Convicts, . | 919 | 439 | 89 | 370 | 1,[illegible] | 861 | 465 | 108 | 221 | 1,712 |
| Average daily No. of Sick, . . | 6 | 30 | 8 | 16 | 62 | 8 | 28 | 3 | 19 | 60 |
| No. of Deaths, . | 7 | 13 | 2 | 10 | 32 | 10 | 10 | 2 | 2 | 24 |
| Per-centage of Deaths on Prison population, . | ·7 | 3· | 2·0 | 2·4 | 1·7 | 1·1 | ·2 | 1·9 | ·9 | 1· |

* Philipstown Prison was closed on the 31st March, 1862.

**Return showing the Proportion of Sick and Deaths to the Number of Convicts in the Irish Convict Prisons for the years 1866, 1867, 1868, and 1869.**

1866.

| — | Spike Island. | Mountjoy Female. | Smithfield and Lusk. | Mountjoy Male. | Total, 1866. |
|---|---|---|---|---|---|
| No. of Convicts, | 799 | 482 | 96 | 161 | 1,548 |
| Average daily No. of Sick, | 11 | 14 | 3 | 16 | 44 |
| No. of Deaths, | 12 | 3 | – | 4 | 22 |
| Per-centage of Deaths on prison population, | 1·5 | 1· | – | 2·1 | 1·4 |

1867.

| — | Spike Island. | Mountjoy Female. | Smithfield and Lusk. | Mountjoy Male. | Total, 1867. |
|---|---|---|---|---|---|
| No. of Convicts, | 772 | 420 | 80 | 150 | 1,427 |
| Average daily No. of Sick, | 13 | 24 | 4 | 2 | 47 |
| No. of Deaths, | 9 | 3 | – | 1 | 13 |
| Per-centage of Deaths on prison population, | 1·2 | ·7 | – | ·6 | ·9 |

1868.

| — | Spike Island. | Mountjoy Female. | Smithfield and Lusk. | Mountjoy Male. | Total, 1868. |
|---|---|---|---|---|---|
| No. of Convicts, | [illegible] | [illegible] | 74 | 154 | [illegible] |
| Average daily No. of Sick, | 12 | 21 | 3 | 3 | [illegible] |
| No. of Deaths, | 9 | 4 | – | 1 | 14 |
| Per-centage of Deaths on prison population, | 1·1 | 1·2 | – | ·6 | ·1 |

1869.

| — | Spike Island. | Mountjoy Female. | Smithfield* and Lusk. | Mountjoy Male. | Total, 1869. |
|---|---|---|---|---|---|
| No. of Convicts, | [illegible] | [illegible] | 61 | 114 | [illegible] |
| Average daily No. of Sick, | 13 | 22 | 5 | 5 | 40 |
| No. of Deaths, | 3 | 7 | – | 1 | 11 |
| Per-centage of Deaths on prison population, | ·4 | 1·7 | – | ·8 | ·8 |

* Smithfield Prison was closed and the Prisoners transferred to Lusk on [illegible] June, [illegible].

RETURN showing the PROPORTION of SICK and DEATHS to the Number of Convicts in the Irish Convict Prisons for the years 1870, 1871 1872, 1873, and 1874.

1870.

| — | Spike Island. | Mountjoy Female. | Lusk. | Mountjoy Male. | Total, 1870. |
|---|---|---|---|---|---|
| No. of Convicts, | 673 | [illegible] | 61 | 187 | [illegible] |
| Average daily No. of Sick, | 15 | 13 | ·6 | ·4 | [illegible] |
| No. of Deaths, | 2 | 6 | 1 | – | 9 |
| Percentage of Deaths on prison population | ·3 | 1·7 | 1·6 | – | ·7 |

1871.

| — | Spike Island. | Mountjoy Female. | Lusk. | Mountjoy Male. | Total, 1871. |
|---|---|---|---|---|---|
| No. of Convicts, | 694 | [illegible] | 61 | 138 | [illegible] |
| Average daily No. of Sick, | 11 | 22 | ·2 | 6 | [illegible] |
| No. of Deaths, | 4 | 5 | – | 1 | 10 |
| Percentage of Deaths on prison population, | ·5 | 1·4 | – | ·7 | ·8 |

1872.

| — | Spike Island. | Mountjoy Female. | Lusk. | Mountjoy Male. | Total, 1872. |
|---|---|---|---|---|---|
| No. of Convicts, | 694 | 330 | 47 | 131 | 1,173 |
| Average daily No. of Sick, | 13 | 15 | ·4 | 8 | [illegible] |
| No. of Deaths, | 8 | 5 | – | – | 13 |
| Percentage of Deaths on prison population, | 1·2 | 1·5 | – | – | 1·1 |

1873.

| — | Spike Island. | Mountjoy Female. | Lusk. | Mountjoy Male. | Total, 1873. |
|---|---|---|---|---|---|
| No. of Convicts, | 640 | [illegible] | 45 | 141 | [illegible] |
| Average daily No. of Sick, | 11 | 13 | ·2 | 6 | [illegible] |
| No. of Deaths, | 8 | 5 | – | 1 | 14 |
| Percentage of Deaths on prison population, | 1·3 | 1·6 | – | ·6 | 1·2 |

1874.

| — | Spike Island. | Mountjoy Female. | Lusk. | Mountjoy Male. | Total, 1874. |
|---|---|---|---|---|---|
| No. of Convicts, | [illegible] | 362 | 33 | 154 | [illegible] |
| Average daily No. of Sick, | 13 | 15 | ·1 | 4 | [illegible] |
| No. of Deaths, | 7 | 3 | – | 1 | 11 |
| Percentage of Deaths on prison population, | 1·0 | 1·0 | – | ·6 | ·9 |

**Return** showing the **Proportion** of **Sick** and **Deaths** to the Number of Convicts in the Irish Convict Prisons for the years 1875, 1876, 1677, 1878, and from 1st April, 1879, to 31st March, 1880.

1875.

| — | Spike Island. | Mountjoy Female. | Lusk. | Mountjoy Male. | Total, 1875. |
|---|---|---|---|---|---|
| No. of Convicts, | 670 | 262 | 49 | 156 | 1,149 |
| Average daily No. of Sick, | 14 | 15 | ·8 | 7 | 34·5 |
| No. of Deaths, | 7 | 3 | – | 1 | 11 |
| Percentage of Deaths on prison population, | 1 | 1·7 | – | ·6 | 1·1 |

1876.

| — | Spike Island. | Mountjoy Female. | Lusk. | Mountjoy Male. | Total, 1876. |
|---|---|---|---|---|---|
| No. of Convicts, | 641 | 279 | 42 | 150 | 1,182 |
| Average daily No. of Sick, | 11 | 18 | ·8 | 7 | 31·3 |
| No. of Deaths, | 6 | 3 | – | 1 | 10·0 |
| Percentage of Deaths on prison population, | ·9 | 1·0 | – | ·6 | 0·9 |

1877.

| — | Spike Island. | Mountjoy Female. | Lusk. | Mountjoy Male. | Total, 1877. |
|---|---|---|---|---|---|
| No. of Convicts, | 680 | 248 | 42 | 167 | 1,138 |
| Average daily No. of Sick, | 15 | 12 | ·4 | 8 | 36·4 |
| No. of Deaths, | 10 | 4 | – | 2 | 16 |
| Percentage of Deaths on prison population, | 1·4 | 1·6 | – | 1·2 | 1·4 |

1878.

| — | Spike Island. | Mountjoy Female. | Lusk. | Mountjoy Male. | Total, 1878. |
|---|---|---|---|---|---|
| No. of Convicts, | 563 | 259 | 42 | 181 | 1,055 |
| Average daily No. of Sick, | 14·5 | 6 | ·3 | 10·5 | 31·8 |
| No. of Deaths, | 5 | 2 | . | 3 | 11 |
| Percentage of Deaths on prison population, | 1 | ·69 | . | 1·6 | 1 |

From 1st April, 1879, to 31st March, 1880.

| — | Spike Island. | Mountjoy Female. | Lusk. | Mountjoy Male. | Total. |
|---|---|---|---|---|---|
| No. of Convicts, | 430 | 182 | 48 | 412 | 1,084 |
| Average daily No. of Sick, | 17·76 | 7·77 | 0·8 | 8·13 | 34·48 |
| No. of Deaths, | 7 | 2 | – | – | 9 |
| Percentage of Deaths on prison population, | 1·63 | 1·1 | – | – | 973 |

**RETURN showing the PROPORTION of SICK and DEATHS to the Number of Convicts in the Irish Convict Prisons from 1st April, 1880, to 31st March, 1881, from 1st April, 1881, to 31st March, 1882, and from 1st April, 1882, to 31st March, 1883.**

From 1st April, 1880, to 31st March, 1881.

| — | Spike Island. | Mountjoy Female. | Lusk. | Mountjoy Male. | Total. |
|---|---|---|---|---|---|
| No. of Convicts, | [illegible] | [illegible] | [illegible] | 416 | [illegible] |
| Average daily No. of Sick, | [illegible] | [illegible] | [illegible] | [illegible] | [illegible] |
| No. of Deaths, | 1 | 4 | – | – | 5 |
| Per-centage of Deaths on prison population, | [illegible] | [illegible] | – | – | [illegible] |

From 1st April, 1881, to 31st March, 1882.

| — | Spike Island. | Mountjoy Female. | Lusk. | Mountjoy Male. | Total. |
|---|---|---|---|---|---|
| No. of Convicts, | [illegible] | [illegible] | [illegible] | [illegible] | [illegible] |
| Average daily No. of Sick, | [illegible] | [illegible] | [illegible] | [illegible] | [illegible] |
| No. of Deaths, | 4 | 1 | – | 2 | 7 |
| Per-centage of Deaths on prison population, | 1 | [illegible] | – | [illegible] | [illegible] |

From 1st April, 1882, to 31st March, 1883.

| — | Spike Island. | Mountjoy Female. | Lusk. | Mountjoy Male. | Total. |
|---|---|---|---|---|---|
| No. of Convicts, | [illegible] | [illegible] | [illegible] | [illegible] | [illegible] |
| Average daily No. of Sick, | [illegible] | [illegible] | [illegible] | [illegible] | [illegible] |
| No. of Deaths, | 3 | 3 | – | 1 | [illegible] |
| Per-centage of Deaths on prison population, | [illegible] | [illegible] | – | [illegible] | [illegible] |

TABLE II.—NUMBER of PRISONERS in each of the CONVICT PRISONS on the FIRST

| Prisons. | 1st April, 1881. | | | 1st May, 1881. | | | 1st June, 1881. | | | 1st July, 1881. | | | 1st August, 1881. | | | 1st September, 1881. | | |
|---|---|---|---|---|---|---|---|---|---|---|---|---|---|---|---|---|---|---|
| | M. | F. | Tot. | M. | F. | Tot. | M. | F. | Tot. | M. | F. | Tot. | M. | F. | Tot. | M. | F. | Tot. |
| Cork (Male), . . | 55 | – | [illegible] | 57 | – | 57 | 39 | – | 39 | 86 | – | 86 | 36 | – | 36 | 31 | – | 31 |
| Maryborough, . | 40 | – | 40 | 58 | – | 58 | 49 | – | 49 | 51 | – | 51 | 48 | – | 48 | 49 | – | 49 |
| Mountjoy (Male), . | 151 | – | 151 | 146 | – | 146 | 148 | – | 148 | 154 | – | 154 | 176 | – | 176 | 179 | – | 179 |
| Mountjoy (Female), | – | 129 | 129 | – | 138 | 134 | – | 132 | 132 | – | 144 | 144 | – | 134 | 134 | – | 119 | 119 |
| Spike Island, . | 396 | – | 396 | 401 | – | 401 | 390 | – | 390 | 377 | – | 377 | 366 | – | 366 | 364 | – | 364 |
| Lusk, . . . | 30 | – | 30 | 36 | – | 36 | 40 | – | 40 | 31 | – | 31 | 22 | – | 22 | 29 | – | 29 |
| Total, . . | 679 | 129 | [illegible] | 683 | 134 | 807 | 643 | 132 | 785 | 649 | 144 | 794 | 649 | 134 | 783 | 617 | 119 | 736 |

| Prisons. | 1st April, 1882. | | | 1st May, 1882. | | | 1st June, 1882. | | | 1st July, 1882. | | | 1st August, 1882. | | | 1st September, 1882. | | |
|---|---|---|---|---|---|---|---|---|---|---|---|---|---|---|---|---|---|---|
| | M. | F. | Tot. | M. | F. | Tot. | M. | F. | Tot. | M. | F. | Tot. | M. | F. | Tot. | M. | F. | Tot. |
| Cork (Male), . . | 21 | – | 21 | 15 | – | 15 | 16 | – | 16 | 16 | – | 16 | 16 | – | 16 | 12 | – | 12 |
| Maryborough, . | 17 | – | 17 | 13 | – | 13 | 15 | – | 15 | 16 | – | 16 | 11 | – | 11 | 11 | – | 11 |
| Mountjoy (Male), . | 242 | – | 242 | 244 | – | 244 | 215 | – | 215 | 246 | – | 246 | 246 | – | 246 | 274 | – | 274 |
| Mountjoy (Female), | – | 108 | 108 | – | 104 | 104 | – | 108 | 108 | – | 109 | 109 | – | 110 | 110 | – | 110 | 110 |
| Spike Island, . | 478 | – | 478 | [illegible] | – | [illegible] | 461 | – | 461 | 404 | – | 404 | 492 | – | 492 | 460 | – | 460 |
| Lusk, . . . | 79 | – | 79 | 28 | – | 28 | 26 | – | 26 | 27 | – | 27 | 23 | – | 23 | 26 | – | 26 |
| Total, . . | [illegible] | 108 | 787 | 691 | 104 | 795 | 697 | 108 | 805 | 703 | 109 | 812 | 706 | 110 | 816 | 724 | 110 | 834 |

TABLE III.—RETURN of PRISON OFFENCES and PUNISHMENTS in

| Prisons. | Total Number of Prisoners' Offences during the Year. | Corporal Punishments. | Number of Prisoners in Solitary Confinement. | Prison Punishments. Punishment Cells. | Prison Punishments. Dietary Punishment. | Total number of Prisoners Punished. |
|---|---|---|---|---|---|---|
| Mountjoy Male Convict Prison, . . . | 878 | – | 8 | 177 | 177 | 164 |
| Mountjoy Female Convict Prison, . . . | 145 | – | 31 | 43 | 14 | 90 |
| Spike Island Convict Prison,* . . . | 792 | 3 | 48 | 116 | 473 | 379 |
| Lusk Convict Prison, . | 76 | – | – | – | – | 141 |
| Totals 1882–83, . . | 1,424 | 6 | 95 | 978 | 663 | 478 |
| Totals 1881–82, . . | 1,301 | 9 | 81 | 816 | 794 | 587 |

* See Memo. on page 131.

**Day in each Month of the Years ended 31st March, 1882 and 1883.**

| 1st October, 1881. | | | 1st November, 1881. | | | 1st December, 1881. | | | 1st January, 1882. | | | 1st February, 1882. | | | 1st March, 1882. | | | Prisons. |
|---|---|---|---|---|---|---|---|---|---|---|---|---|---|---|---|---|---|---|
| M. | F. | Tot. | M. | F. | Tot. | M. | F. | Tot. | M. | F. | Tot. | M. | F. | Tot. | M. | F. | Tot. | |
| 61 | – | [illegible] | [illegible] | – | 62 | 94 | – | 94 | [illegible] | – | [illegible] | [illegible] | – | 61 | 18 | – | 18 | Cork (Male). |
| 67 | – | 67 | [illegible] | – | 40 | 28 | – | [illegible] | [illegible] | – | 14 | 14 | – | 14 | 10 | – | 10 | Maryborough. |
| 173 | – | 173 | 178 | – | 178 | 185 | – | 185 | [illegible] | – | [illegible] | 210 | – | 210 | [illegible] | – | [illegible] | Mountjoy (Male). |
| – | 116 | 116 | – | 109 | 109 | – | 105 | 105 | – | 110 | 110 | – | 111 | 111 | – | 109 | 109 | Mountjoy (Female). |
| 544 | – | 544 | 470 | – | 470 | 600 | – | [illegible] | 473 | – | 473 | [illegible] | – | [illegible] | 544 | – | [illegible] | Spike Island. |
| 57 | – | [illegible] | 52 | – | 52 | 57 | – | 57 | 41 | – | 41 | [illegible] | – | [illegible] | 66 | – | 66 | Lusk. |
| [illegible] | 116 | [illegible] | 647 | 109 | [illegible] | 647 | 109 | 756 | [illegible] | 110 | [illegible] | [illegible] | 111 | [illegible] | [illegible] | 109 | [illegible] | Total. |

| 1st October, 1882. | | | 1st November, 1882. | | | 1st December, 1882. | | | 1st January, 1883. | | | 1st February, 1883. | | | 1st March, 1883. | | | Prisons. |
|---|---|---|---|---|---|---|---|---|---|---|---|---|---|---|---|---|---|---|
| M. | F. | Tot. | M. | F. | Tot. | M. | F. | Tot. | M. | F. | Tot. | M. | F. | Tot. | M. | F. | Tot. | |
| 11 | – | 11 | 14 | – | 14 | 17 | – | 17 | 12 | – | 12 | 14 | – | 34 | 64 | – | 64 | Cork (Male). |
| 24 | – | 24 | 21 | – | 21 | 24 | – | [illegible] | 19 | – | 19 | 18 | – | 18 | 16 | – | 16 | Maryborough. |
| [illegible] | – | 572 | 711 | – | 711 | 670 | – | [illegible] | [illegible] | – | 646 | 641 | – | 641 | 158 | – | 158 | Mountjoy (Male). |
| – | 116 | 116 | – | 104 | 104 | – | 104 | 104 | – | 106 | [illegible] | – | 104 | 104 | – | [illegible] | [illegible] | Mountjoy (Female). |
| 448 | – | 448 | 456 | – | 456 | 458 | – | [illegible] | 424 | – | [illegible] | 401 | – | 401 | 440 | – | 440 | Spike Island. |
| [illegible] | – | [illegible] | 27 | – | 27 | 21 | – | 21 | 27 | – | 27 | [illegible] | – | [illegible] | [illegible] | – | [illegible] | Lusk. |
| [illegible] | 116 | 842 | 760 | 104 | 864 | 734 | 104 | 841 | [illegible] | 106 | [illegible] | [illegible] | 104 | 907 | [illegible] | [illegible] | [illegible] | Total. |

**Convict Prisons from 1st April, 1882, to 31st March, 1883.**

| Prison Offences. | | | | | | Prison. |
|---|---|---|---|---|---|---|
| Violence. | Escapes and Attempts at Escape. | Idleness. | Other breaches of Regulations. | Total Offences. | Deprivation of Marks. | |
| 2 | 3 | 5 | 253 | 265 | 84 | Mountjoy Male Convict Prison. |
| 69 | – | – | 87 | 147 | 19 | Mountjoy Female Convict Prison. |
| 22 | 1 | 35 | 844 | 875 | 467 | Spike Island Convict Prison.* |
| [illegible] | 1 | – | 14 | 15 | 1 | Lusk Convict Prison. |
| 104 | 4 | 44 | 1,200 | 1,402 | 565 | Totals, 1882–83. |
| 160 | 3 | 42 | 864 | 1,215 | 497 | Totals, 1881–82. |

* Removed to Mountjoy 2, and in 12 cases convicts were punished by deduction from their gratuities.

I

**Spike Island Convict Prison,**
**28th May, 1883.**

Memo.

The returns in connexion with the Annual Report for the year ended 31st March, 1883, called for by Memo. of the 27th ultimo, are forwarded herewith.

With reference to the return of punishments on Form No. 1, I beg to explain that the total number of punishments is 318 less than the number of offences, the difference being made up of 233 cases that were dealt with by stoppage of marks or suspension of classification only, 68 by admonitions, 15 by the forfeiture of a portion of their gratuity, and 2 by the civil power.

Of the 328 individual prisoners shown as punished, many were punished several times during the year.

All dietary punishments at Spike Island, except stoppage of suppers, of which there were 40 cases during the year, have been carried out in the punishment cells; the 116 cases entered under heading, "Punishment Cells," comprise 108 who were placed in dark refractory cells at Spike Island Prison, 7 at Cork, and 1 at Maryboro' Prisons.

There were only 224 cases of deprivation of marks where no other punishment was ordered, and the remainder of the 437 cases of deprivation of marks shown were in addition to the dietary punishment.

Sixty-four of the 975 offences were committed at Cork and Maryboro' Prisons.

P. Hay, Governor.

To the Chairman, General Prisons Board,
Dublin Castle.

---

# C.—REGISTRATION OF CRIMINALS.

## I.—Return of the Number of Criminals sentenced to Police Supervision during each of the following years:—

| Year. | Males. | Females. | Total. | Year. | Males. | Females. | Total. |
|---|---|---|---|---|---|---|---|
| *1870, | – | – | – | 1878, | 41 | 8 | 49 |
| 1871, | 4 | 2 | 6 | 1879, | 43 | 9 | 52 |
| 1872, | 66 | 32 | 98 | 1880, | 32 | 7 | 39 |
| 1873, | 46 | 26 | 72 | 1881, | 19 | 5 | 24 |
| 1874, | 50 | 15 | 65 | 1882, | 21 | 10 | 31 |
| 1875, | 34 | 19 | 53 | | | | |
| 1876, | 30 | 7 | 37 | Total, | 416 | 148 | 563 |
| 1877, | 29 | 8 | 37 | | | | |

* No record kept.

| | Males. | Females. | Total. |
|---|---|---|---|
| Number sentenced during year ended 31st March, 1883, | 27 | 4 | 31 |

## II.—Return of Criminals discharged from Prison in each of the following years, and subject to Police Supervision:—

| Year. | Males. | Females. | Total. | Year. | Males. | Females. | Total. |
|---|---|---|---|---|---|---|---|
| 1870, | 4 | 6 | 10 | 1878, | 38 | 19 | 57 |
| 1871, | 54 | 36 | 90 | 1879, | 43 | 10 | 53 |
| 1872, | 63 | 33 | 96 | 1880, | 39 | 14 | 53 |
| 1873, | 40 | 20 | 60 | 1881, | 32 | 11 | 43 |
| 1874, | 34 | 14 | 48 | 1882, | 34 | 9 | 43 |
| 1875, | 34 | 13 | 47 | | | | |
| 1876, | 61 | 29 | 90 | Total, | 511 | 232 | 743 |
| 1877, | 48 | 25 | 73 | | | | |

| | Males. | Females. | Total. |
|---|---|---|---|
| Number discharged during year ended 31st March, 1883, | 24 | 4 | 28 |

III.—Return of Licence Holders discharged from Prison during each of the following years:—

| Year. | Males. | Females. | Total. | Year. | Males. | Females. | Total. |
|---|---|---|---|---|---|---|---|
| 1870, - | 141 | 64 | 205 | 1878, - | 149 | 62 | 211 |
| 1871, - | 161 | 72 | 233 | 1879, - | 188 | 45 | 233 |
| 1872, - | 137 | 58 | 195 | 1880, - | 111 | 44 | 155 |
| 1873, - | 124 | 56 | 180 | 1881, - | 109 | 60 | 169 |
| 1874, - | 106 | 68 | 174 | 1882, - | 114 | 40 | 154 |
| 1875, - | 133 | 64 | 197 | | | | |
| 1876, - | 104 | 50 | 154 | Total, | 1,704 | 746 | 2,450 |
| 1877, - | 117 | 60 | 177 | | | | |

| | Males. | Females. | Total. |
|---|---|---|---|
| Number discharged during year ended 31st March, 1883, | 98 | 25 | 123 |

IV.—Return of Convicts discharged from Prison on completion or commutation of their sentences during each of the following years:—

| Year. | Males. | Females. | Total. | Year. | Males. | Females. | Total. |
|---|---|---|---|---|---|---|---|
| 1870, - | 28 | 20 | 48 | 1878, - | 54 | 15 | 69 |
| 1871, - | 25 | 24 | 49 | 1879, - | 53 | 19 | 72 |
| 1872, - | 35 | 25 | 60 | 1880, - | 48 | 6 | 54 |
| 1873, - | 37 | 23 | 60 | 1881, - | 28 | 6 | 34 |
| 1874, - | 42 | 13 | 55 | 1882, - | 48 | 9 | 57 |
| 1875, - | 27 | 14 | 41 | | | | |
| 1876, - | 29 | 12 | 41 | Total, | 491 | 208 | 699 |
| 1877, - | 48 | 18 | 66 | | | | |

| | Males. | Females. | Total. |
|---|---|---|---|
| Number discharged during year ended 31st March, 1883, | 23 | 5 | 28 |

V.—Return of Licence Holders discharged during each of the following years, subject to Police Supervision on expiration of Licence:—

| Year. | Males. | Females. | Total. | Year. | Males. | Females. | Total. |
|---|---|---|---|---|---|---|---|
| 1870, - | – | – | – | 1878, - | 14 | 9 | 23 |
| 1871, - | – | – | – | 1879, - | 13 | 6 | 19 |
| 1872, - | – | – | – | 1880, - | 14 | 5 | 19 |
| 1873, - | – | – | – | 1881, - | 9 | 6 | 15 |
| 1874, - | 2 | 1 | 3 | 1882, - | 12 | 1 | 13 |
| 1875, - | 6 | 3 | 9 | | | | |
| 1876, - | 33 | 18 | 51 | Total, | 127 | 58 | 185 |
| 1877, - | 24 | 12 | 36 | | | | |

| | Males. | Females. | Total. |
|---|---|---|---|
| Number discharged during year ended 31st March, 1883, | 11 | 8 | 19 |

VI.—Return of Convicts discharged on expiration of sentence during each of the following years, and subject to Police Supervision:—

| Year. | Males. | Females. | Total. | Year. | Males. | Females. | Total. |
|---|---|---|---|---|---|---|---|
| 1870, - | – | – | – | 1878, - | 3 | – | 3 |
| 1871, - | – | – | – | 1879, - | 5 | 1 | 6 |
| 1872, - | – | – | – | 1880, - | 5 | - | 5 |
| 1873, - | – | – | – | 1881, - | 6 | 2 | 8 |
| 1874, - | – | – | – | 1882, - | 6 | 4 | 10 |
| 1875, - | – | – | – | | | | |
| 1876, - | 9 | – | 9 | Total, | 33 | 11 | 44 |
| 1877, - | 7 | 4 | 11 | | | | |

| | Males. | Females. | Total. |
|---|---|---|---|
| Number discharged during year ended 31st March, 1883, | 5 | – | 5 |

VII.—Return showing the number of queries as to Prisoners in Custody awaiting Trial, received from Prisons and Police during each of the following years, and showing the per-centage known:—

| Year. | Queries received from | | Per-centage known. | |
|---|---|---|---|---|
| | Prisons. | Police. | Prisons. | Police. |
| 1870a, | — | — | — | — |
| 1871b, | 47 | 27 | 31·9 | 15· |
| 1872, | 99 | 43 | 35·96 | 25· |
| 1873, | 151 | 24 | 37·98 | 48· |
| 1874, | 183 | 42 | 40·6 | 33·09 |
| 1875, | 164 | 33 | 32·54 | 15·03 |
| 1876, | 130 | 25 | 28·15 | 8· |
| 1877, | 92 | 24 | 19·56 | 29· |
| 1878, | 73 | 28 | 26· | 25· |
| 1879, | 57 | 35 | 21· | 8·8 |
| 1880, | 158 | 75 | 54·9 | 1·07 |
| From 1/4/80 to 31st March, '81, | 148 | 52 | 60·8 | ·6 |
| From 1/4/81 to 31st March, '82, | 140 | 18 | 73·9 | 7·7 |
| From 1/4/82 to 31st March, '83, | 99 | 16 | 81·8 | 6·6 |

a. No record kept. b. Commencing August 1871.

VIII.—Return showing the number of habitual criminals registered in:—

| Year | No. | Year. | No. |
|---|---|---|---|
| 1870, | 907 | 1878, | 979 |
| 1871, | 1,058 | 1879, | 305 |
| 1872, | 840 | 1880, | 294 |
| 1873, | 1,118 | From 1st April, 1880, to 31st March, 1881, | 229 |
| 1874, | 1,062 | Year ended 31/3/82, | 294 |
| 1875, | 936 | " 31/3/83, | 189 |
| 1876, | 884 | | |
| 1877, | 609 | | |

# D. EXPENDITURE—CONVICT AND LOCAL PRISONS

(Inclusive of Bridewells).

---

## RETURN

SHOWING

## THE EXPENDITURE UNDER EACH HEAD OF SERVICE,

In the Year ended 31st March, 1883.

# D.—EXPENDITURE—CONVICT AND LOCAL

Return showing the Expenditure under each Head

| Heads of Service. | Total Expenses. £ s. d. | Mountjoy, Male. £ s. d. | Mountjoy, Female. £ s. d. | Lusk. £ s. d. |
|---|---|---|---|---|
| Daily Average, inclusive of Minor Prisons, and exclusive of Bridewells. | — | [illegible] | [illegible] | [illegible] |
| **Cost of Staff.** | | | | |
| Pay and allowances of officers, including uniforms, &c. | [illegible] 0 6 | [illegible] 10 10 | 4,109 9 4 | [illegible] |
| **Maintenance of Prisoners.** | | | | |
| Victualling for prisoners, | 20,791 9 9 | 3,971 9 6 | 1,040 18 2 | [illegible] |
| Medicines, surgical instruments, &c., | [illegible] | 64 12 0 | 96 3 8 | 11 16 6 |
| Soap, scouring and cleaning articles, | 1,059 7 5 | 142 16 2 | 138 2 7 | 9 7 10 |
| Clothing for prisoners, | 7,186 10 4 | 429 18 7 | [illegible] | [illegible] |
| Fuel, light, and water, | [illegible] | 1,496 4 9 | 1,225 0 9 | 74 10 6 |
| Total expenses of Maintenance, | [illegible] | 6,312 15 2 | [illegible] | [illegible] |
| **Other Expenses.** | | | | |
| Bedding for prisoners, | 1,716 3 4 | 64 10 2 | [illegible] | 16 7 11 |
| Gratuities to prisoners, | 1,907 16 4 | [illegible] | [illegible] | [illegible] |
| Buildings, including furniture, repairs, alterations, &c. | [illegible] | [illegible] | [illegible] | [illegible] |
| Kitchen utensils, crockery, &c., | [illegible] | 27 16 5 | 13 1 9 | — |
| Rent, | [illegible] | — | — | 1 14 1 |
| Incidental expenses, | [illegible] | [illegible] | [illegible] | [illegible] |
| Total of Other Expenses, | [illegible] | [illegible] | [illegible] | [illegible] |
| Gross Total Expenses, | [illegible] | [illegible] | [illegible] | [illegible] |

| Heads of Service. | Clonmel. £ s. d. | Cork, Male. £ s. d. | Cork, Female. £ s. d. | Downpatrick. £ s. d. |
|---|---|---|---|---|
| Daily Average, inclusive of Minor Prisons, and exclusive of Bridewells. | 64 | [illegible] | [illegible] | [illegible] |
| **Cost of Staff.** | | | | |
| Pay and allowances of officers, including uniforms, &c. | [illegible] 1 6 | [illegible] 12 9 | [illegible] | [illegible] 10 10 |
| **Maintenance of Prisoners.** | | | | |
| Victualling for prisoners, | [illegible] | [illegible] | [illegible] | 434 18 4 |
| Medicines, surgical instruments, &c., | [illegible] | 36 1 8 | [illegible] | [illegible] |
| Soap, scouring and cleaning articles, | [illegible] | [illegible] | [illegible] | [illegible] |
| Clothing for prisoners, | [illegible] | [illegible] | [illegible] | [illegible] |
| Fuel, light, and water, | [illegible] | [illegible] | [illegible] | [illegible] |
| Total expenses of Maintenance, | 1,387 10 10 | [illegible] | [illegible] | [illegible] |
| **Other Expenses.** | | | | |
| Bedding for prisoners, | 1 7 0 | [illegible] | [illegible] | [illegible] |
| Gratuities to prisoners, | [illegible] | [illegible] | [illegible] | [illegible] |
| Buildings, including furniture, repairs, alterations, &c. | [illegible] | [illegible] | [illegible] | [illegible] |
| Kitchen utensils, crockery, &c., | [illegible] | [illegible] | [illegible] | [illegible] |
| Rent, | [illegible] | — | [illegible] | [illegible] |
| Incidental expenses, | [illegible] | [illegible] | [illegible] | [illegible] |
| Total of Other Expenses, | [illegible] | [illegible] | [illegible] | [illegible] |
| Gross Total Expenses, | [illegible] 11 3 | [illegible] | [illegible] | [illegible] 9 10 |

## PRISONS (inclusive of Bridewells).

**of Service, in the year ended 31st March, 1883.**

| Spike Island. | Armagh. | Belfast. | Castlebar. | Heads of Service. |
|---|---|---|---|---|
| [illegible] | [illegible] | [illegible] | [illegible] | Daily Average, inclusive of Minor Prisons, and exclusive of Bridewells. |
| £ s. d. | £ s. d. | £ s. d. | £ s. d. | Cost of Staff. |
| [illegible] | [illegible] | [illegible] | [illegible] | Pay and allowances of officers, including uniforms, &c. |
| | | | | Maintenance of Prisoners. |
| [illegible] | [illegible] | [illegible] | [illegible] | Victualling for prisoners. |
| [illegible] | [illegible] | [illegible] | [illegible] | Medicines, surgical instruments, &c. |
| [illegible] | [illegible] | [illegible] | [illegible] | Soap, scouring and cleaning articles. |
| [illegible] | [illegible] | [illegible] | [illegible] | Clothing for prisoners. |
| [illegible] | [illegible] | [illegible] | [illegible] | Fuel, light, and water. |
| [illegible] | [illegible] | 4,106 16 3 | [illegible] | Total expenses of Maintenance. |
| | | | | Other Expenses. |
| [illegible] | [illegible] | [illegible] | [illegible] | Bedding for prisoners. |
| [illegible] | [illegible] | [illegible] | [illegible] | Gratuities to prisoners. |
| [illegible] | [illegible] | [illegible] | [illegible] | Buildings, including furniture, repairs, alterations, &c. |
| [illegible] | [illegible] | [illegible] | [illegible] | Kitchen utensils, crockery, &c. |
| — | — | [illegible] | — | Rent. |
| [illegible] | [illegible] | [illegible] | [illegible] | Incidental expenses. |
| [illegible] | [illegible] | [illegible] | [illegible] | Total of Other Expenses. |
| [illegible] | [illegible] | [illegible] | [illegible] | Gross Total Expenses. |

| Drogheda. | Dundalk. | Galway. | Grangegorman. | Heads of Service. |
|---|---|---|---|---|
| [illegible] | [illegible] | [illegible] | [illegible] | Daily Average, inclusive of Minor Prisons and exclusive of Bridewells. |
| £ s. d. | £ s. d. | £ s. d. | £ s. d. | Cost of Staff. |
| [illegible] | [illegible] | [illegible] | [illegible] | Pay and allowances of officers, including uniforms, &c. |
| | | | | Maintenance of Prisoners. |
| [illegible] | [illegible] | [illegible] | [illegible] | Victualling for prisoners. |
| — | [illegible] | [illegible] | [illegible] | Medicines, surgical instruments, &c. |
| [illegible] | [illegible] | [illegible] | [illegible] | Soap, scouring and cleaning articles. |
| [illegible] | [illegible] | [illegible] | [illegible] | Clothing for prisoners. |
| [illegible] | [illegible] | [illegible] | [illegible] | Fuel, light, and water. |
| [illegible] | [illegible] | [illegible] | [illegible] | Total expenses of Maintenance. |
| | | | | Other Expenses. |
| [illegible] | [illegible] | [illegible] | [illegible] | Bedding for prisoners. |
| [illegible] | [illegible] | [illegible] | [illegible] | Gratuities to prisoners. |
| [illegible] | [illegible] | [illegible] | [illegible] | Buildings, including furniture, repairs, alterations, &c. |
| — | [illegible] | [illegible] | [illegible] | Kitchen utensils, crockery, &c. |
| — | [illegible] | — | — | Rent. |
| [illegible] | [illegible] | [illegible] | [illegible] | Incidental expenses. |
| [illegible] | [illegible] | [illegible] | [illegible] | Total of Other Expenses. |
| [illegible] | [illegible] | [illegible] | [illegible] | Gross Total Expenses. |

CONVICT AND LOCAL PRISONS

RETURN showing the Expenditure under each Head

| HEADS OF SERVICE. | Kilkenny. | Kilmainham. | Limerick, Male. | Limerick, Female. |
|---|---|---|---|---|
| Daily Average, inclusive of Minor Prisons, and exclusive of Bridewells. | [illegible] | [illegible] | [illegible] | [illegible] |
| COST OF STAFF. | £ s. d. | £ s. d. | £ s. d. | £ s. d. |
| Pay and allowances of officers, including uniforms, &c. | [illegible] | [illegible] | [illegible] | [illegible] |
| MAINTENANCE OF PRISONERS. | | | | |
| Victualling for prisoners, | [illegible] | [illegible] | [illegible] | [illegible] |
| Medicines, surgical instruments, &c., | [illegible] | [illegible] | [illegible] | [illegible] |
| Soap, scouring and cleaning articles, | [illegible] | [illegible] | [illegible] | [illegible] |
| Clothing for prisoners, | [illegible] | [illegible] | [illegible] | [illegible] |
| Fuel, light, and water, | [illegible] | [illegible] | [illegible] | [illegible] |
| Total expenses of Maintenance, | [illegible] | [illegible] | [illegible] | [illegible] |
| OTHER EXPENSES. | | | | |
| Bedding for prisoners, | [illegible] | [illegible] | [illegible] | [illegible] |
| Gratuities to prisoners, | [illegible] | [illegible] | [illegible] | [illegible] |
| Buildings, including furniture, repairs, alterations, &c., | [illegible] | [illegible] | [illegible] | [illegible] |
| Kitchen utensils, crockery, &c., | [illegible] | [illegible] | [illegible] | [illegible] |
| Rent, | — | — | — | — |
| Incidental expenses, | [illegible] | [illegible] | [illegible] | [illegible] |
| Total of Other Expenses, | [illegible] | [illegible] | [illegible] | [illegible] |
| Gross Total Expenses, | [illegible] | [illegible] | [illegible] | [illegible] |

| HEADS OF SERVICE. | Omagh. | Richmond. | Sligo. | Tralee. |
|---|---|---|---|---|
| Daily Average, inclusive of Minor Prisons, and exclusive of Bridewells. | [illegible] | [illegible] | [illegible] | [illegible] |
| COST OF STAFF. | £ s. d. | £ s. d. | £ s. d. | £ s. d. |
| Pay and allowances of officers, including uniforms, &c. | [illegible] | [illegible] | [illegible] | [illegible] |
| MAINTENANCE OF PRISONERS. | | | | |
| Victualling for prisoners, | [illegible] | [illegible] | [illegible] | [illegible] |
| Medicines, surgical instruments, &c., | [illegible] | [illegible] | [illegible] | [illegible] |
| Soap, scouring and cleaning articles, | [illegible] | [illegible] | [illegible] | [illegible] |
| Clothing for prisoners, | [illegible] | [illegible] | [illegible] | [illegible] |
| Fuel, light, and water, | [illegible] | [illegible] | [illegible] | [illegible] |
| Total expenses of Maintenance, | [illegible] | [illegible] | [illegible] | [illegible] |
| OTHER EXPENSES. | | | | |
| Bedding for prisoners, | [illegible] | [illegible] | [illegible] | [illegible] |
| Gratuities to prisoners, | [illegible] | [illegible] | [illegible] | [illegible] |
| Buildings, including furniture, repairs, alterations, &c., | [illegible] | [illegible] | [illegible] | [illegible] |
| Kitchen utensils, crockery, &c., | [illegible] | [illegible] | [illegible] | [illegible] |
| Rent, | — | [illegible] | [illegible] | [illegible] |
| Incidental expenses, | [illegible] | [illegible] | [illegible] | [illegible] |
| Total of Other Expenses, | [illegible] | [illegible] | [illegible] | [illegible] |
| Gross Total Expenses, | [illegible] | [illegible] | [illegible] | [illegible] |

(inclusive of Bridewells)—*continued*.

of Service, in the year ended 31st March, [illegible]—*continued*.

| Londonderry. | Maryborough. | Mullingar. | Naas. | Nenagh. | Heads of Service. |
|---|---|---|---|---|---|
| [illegible] | [illegible] | [illegible] | [illegible] | 44 | Daily Average, inclusive of Minor Prisons, and exclusive of Bridewells. |
| £ s. d. | £ s. d. | £ s. d. | £ s. d. | £ s. d. | Cost of Staff. |
| [illegible] | [illegible] | [illegible] | [illegible] | [illegible] | Pay and allowances of officers including uniforms, &c. |
| | | | | | Maintenance of Prisoners. |
| [illegible] | [illegible] | [illegible] | [illegible] | [illegible] | Victualling for prisoners. |
| [illegible] | [illegible] | [illegible] | [illegible] | [illegible] | Medicines, surgical instruments, &c. |
| [illegible] | [illegible] | [illegible] | [illegible] | [illegible] | Soap, scouring and cleaning articles. |
| [illegible] | [illegible] | [illegible] | [illegible] | [illegible] | Clothing for prisoners. |
| [illegible] | [illegible] | [illegible] | [illegible] | [illegible] | Fuel, light, and water. |
| [illegible] | [illegible] | [illegible] | [illegible] | [illegible] | Total expenses of Maintenance. |
| | | | | | Other Expenses. |
| [illegible] | [illegible] | [illegible] | [illegible] | [illegible] | Bedding for prisoners. |
| [illegible] | [illegible] | [illegible] | [illegible] | [illegible] | Gratuities to prisoners. |
| [illegible] | [illegible] | [illegible] | [illegible] | [illegible] | Buildings, including furniture, repairs, alterations, &c. |
| [illegible] | [illegible] | [illegible] | [illegible] | [illegible] | Kitchen utensils, crockery, &c. |
| — | — | [illegible] | — | — | Rent. |
| [illegible] | [illegible] | [illegible] | [illegible] | [illegible] | Incidental expenses. |
| [illegible] | [illegible] | [illegible] | [illegible] | [illegible] | Total of Other Expenses. |
| [illegible] | [illegible] | [illegible] | [illegible] | [illegible] | Gross Total Expenses. |

| Tullamore. | Waterford. | Wexford. | Total Expenses. | | Heads of Service. |
|---|---|---|---|---|---|
| [illegible] | [illegible] | [illegible] | — | | Daily Average, inclusive of Minor Prisons, and exclusive of Bridewells. |
| £ s. d. | £ s. d. | £ s. d. | £ s. d. | | Cost of Staff. |
| [illegible] | [illegible] | [illegible] | [illegible] | | Pay and allowances of officers including uniforms, &c. |
| | | | | | Maintenance of Prisoners. |
| [illegible] | [illegible] | [illegible] | [illegible] | | Victualling for prisoners. |
| [illegible] | [illegible] | [illegible] | [illegible] | | Medicines, surgical instruments, &c. |
| [illegible] | [illegible] | [illegible] | [illegible] | | Soap, scouring and cleaning articles. |
| [illegible] | [illegible] | [illegible] | [illegible] | | Clothing for prisoners. |
| [illegible] | [illegible] | [illegible] | [illegible] | | Fuel, light, and water. |
| [illegible] | [illegible] | [illegible] | [illegible] | | Total expenses of Maintenance. |
| | | | | | Other Expenses. |
| [illegible] | [illegible] | [illegible] | [illegible] | | Bedding for prisoners. |
| [illegible] | [illegible] | [illegible] | [illegible] | | Gratuities to prisoners. |
| [illegible] | [illegible] | [illegible] | [illegible] | | Buildings, including furniture, repairs, alterations, &c. |
| [illegible] | [illegible] | [illegible] | [illegible] | | Kitchen utensils, crockery, &c. |
| — | — | [illegible] | [illegible] | | Rent. |
| [illegible] | [illegible] | [illegible] | [illegible] | | Incidental expenses. |
| [illegible] | [illegible] | [illegible] | [illegible] | | Total of Other Expenses. |
| [illegible] | [illegible] | 3,703 14 8 | 126,380 18 [illegible] | | Gross Total Expenses. |

## (E. BRIDEWELLS.)

RETURN showing the name and situation of the BRIDEWELL referred to, par. 6, page 6, discontinued since the date of last report, viz:—

| Bridewell. | County. |
| --- | --- |
| Baltinglass, . | Wicklow. |

www.ingramcontent.com/pod-product-compliance
Lightning Source LLC
Chambersburg PA
CBHW030606270326
41927CB00007B/1063
*9783741105814*